formatio
TRADITION. EXPERIENCE.
TRANSFORMATION.

Formatio books from InterVarsity Press follow the rich tradition of the church in the journey of spiritual formation. These books are not merely about being informed, but about being transformed by Christ and conformed to his image. Formatio stands in InterVarsity Press's evangelical publishing tradition by integrating God's Word with spiritual practice and by prompting readers to move from inward change to outward witness. InterVarsity Press uses the chambered nautilus for Formatio, a symbol of spiritual formation because of its continual spiral journey outward as it moves from its center. We believe that each of us is made with a deep desire to be in God's presence. Formatio books help us to fulfill our deepest desires and to become our true selves in light of God's grace.

SPIRITUAL DISCIPLINES
Handbook

Practices That Transform Us

Adele Ahlberg Calhoun

 IVP Books

An imprint of InterVarsity Press
Downers Grove, Illinois

InterVarsity Press
P.O. Box 1400, Downers Grove, IL 60515-1426
World Wide Web: www.ivpress.com
E-mail: email@ivpress.com

InterVarsity Press® is the book-publishing division of InterVarsity Christian Fellowship/USA®, a movement of students and faculty active on campus at hundreds of universities, colleges and schools of nursing in the United States of America, and a member movement of the International Fellowship of Evangelical Students. For information about local and regional activities, write Public Relations Dept., InterVarsity Christian Fellowship/USA, 6400 Schroeder Rd., P.O. Box 7895, Madison, WI 53707-7895, or visit the IVCF website at <www.intervarsity.org>.

All Scripture quotations, unless otherwise indicated, are taken from the Holy Bible, New International Version®. NIV®. Copyright ©1973, 1978, 1984 by International Bible Society. Used by permission of Zondervan Publishing House. All rights reserved.

Design: Cindy Kiple

Images: mustafa deliormanli/iStockphoto

ISBN 978-0-8308-3330-6

Printed in the United States of America ∞

Library of Congress Cataloging-in-Publication Data

Calhoun, Adele Ahlberg, 1949-
  Spiritual disciplines handbook: practices that transform us /
  Adele
Ahlberg Calhoun.
    p. cm.
  Includes bibliographical references.
  ISBN 0-8308-3330-7 (pbk.: alk. paper)
  1. Spiritual life—Christianity. I. Title.
BV4501.3.C34 2005
248.4—dc22
                                                                          2005018540

| P | 30 | 29 | 28 | 27 | 26 | 25 | 24 | 23 | 22 | 21 | 20 | 19 | 18 | 17 | 16 | 15 | 14 | 13 | 12 | 11 |
| Y | 28 | 27 | 26 | 25 | 24 | 23 | 22 | 21 | 20 | 19 | 18 | 17 | 16 | 15 | 14 | 13 | 12 | 11 | 10 | |

For fellow pilgrims at

Christ Church of Oak Brook,

Park St. Church, Boston, and

IVCF/IFES.

Your desires for God have graced my journey.

CONTENTS

ACKNOWLEDGMENTS

THE *SPIRITUAL DISCIPLINES HANDBOOK* ORIGINATED FROM requests from my colleagues at Christ Church of Oak Brook. They wanted resources that rooted our congregation in a transformational journey with God. No one asked for a book. There was simply the shared desire to introduce people to the myriad ways they could make space in their lives for God. We wanted our church family to experience what it was like to partner with the Holy Spirit for change and renewal.

Andy Morgan, the singles pastor, was the first one to ask me for input. He wanted material that could guide single adults toward appropriate self-care. Vickie Bare, director of children's ministries, wanted to talk about spiritual practices for children. Doug Calhoun, the missions pastor, asked for disciplines to help missionaries restore their souls. Dave Mahar, the high school pastor, was looking for spiritual practices that connected with high school students. Bob Geelhoed, the care and counseling pastor, encouraged the use of the growing catalog of disciplines in the "Growing Your Soul" curriculum. Both our senior pastor, Dan Meyer, and our executive pastor, Greg Ogden, invited me to introduce our elders and staff to various spiritual disciplines. Then they gave me time in staff and elder meetings to guide people into these practices. How could this book not be for them? They are often my instigators and inspiration.

Eventually Doug and Marilyn Stewart, on staff with IVCF, took my growing compilation of spiritual disciplines to Russia for use with the International Fellowship of Evangelical Students (IFES). When they returned, they suggested other disciplines for the growing file. I am indebted to these friends and their desires, encouragement, insights and love.

Dave and Marcia Courtney and Greg and Paul Rocque offered their wonderful homes to me for writing. Ruth Haley-Barton, Rich Plass and Mary Jo Valenziano, urged, prodded and encouraged. Shirley Morlock and Jim and Ruth Nyquist plowed through the manuscript as it evolved. Glenda Simpkins-Hoffman offered creative input. Kathleen MacDougal and Rama Ziegenhals kept the word *book* in front of me—for years! Joe Sherman, Christine Anderson and Cindy Bunch carried me across the publication hurdle. Thank you for believing in me when I didn't believe in myself.

A cadre of spiritual friends cared for my soul throughout the process. Lovelace Howard and Gallaudet Howard are beloved sounding boards. Louise Midwood, Kathy Keller, Jane Frazier, Cindy Widmer and Gayle Somers remain my teachers through reunions and a "Round Robin Letter" now in its fourth decade. I am also deeply accompanied by my covenant group: Karen Mains, Marilyn Stewart, Linda Richardson, Sybil Towner and Jane Rubietta. These friends have shaped my soul.

I would be remiss not to mention the spiritual tutors that I know only through books: Dorothy Bass, Eugene Peterson, Gerald May, M. Basil Pennington, Dallas Willard, Phyllis Tickle, Fredrick Buechner, Richard Foster, Henri Nouwen, Richard Rohr, Jonathan Edwards, Francis de Sales, Teresa of Ávila, John of the Cross, Ignatius Loyola, St. Benedict, Julian of Norwich and many more. Their ideas, voices and examples have shaped my own words and experience of the disciplines.

My parents, Phil and Coralee Ahlberg, were my first examples of people who faithfully practiced spiritual disciplines. They launched me into memory verses, prayer and "offering." My husband, Doug, serves and loves me to the end. In him and our children, Nathaniel and Annaliese, I have better love than I ever deserve. Thank you parents and family for never giving up on me. You are images of Christ to me.

Spiritual Disciplines and Desires

INTRODUCTION
DISCOVERING YOUR DESIRE

WEEK AFTER WEEK good church people come to me with their R-rated lives and a question: "Does God's presence in me really change anything?" A woman who reads the Bible every day asks, "Why don't I get something out of all that reading? Isn't it supposed to help me when my husband is verbally abusive?" An overtired, busy bank officer asks, "Is spiritual dryness a permanent state?" A distressed pastor uncomfortably sits in my office and asks, "What does it mean when I'm too busy to pray?" A married couple asks why God seemed closer to them before they were married. The banker, the woman, the pastor and the couple have something in common. In the midst of busy, scattered, exhausted and hurting lives they want to experience a great love with God. Desire and desperation gnaw at their hungry souls, and they want to know if God will show up for them.

In Matthew 11:28-30 Jesus said:

Are you tired? Worn out? Burned out on religion? Come to me. Get away with me and you'll recover your life. I'll show you how to take a real rest.

Walk with me and work with me—watch how I do it. Learn the unforced rhythms of grace. I won't lay anything heavy or ill-fitting on you. Keep company with me and you'll learn to live freely and lightly. (*The Message*)

Living "freely and lightly" can sound too good to be true. How can hectic and demanding schedules yield to the aching desire for "unforced rhythms of grace"? What good is a desire to "recover your life" if you're plain old "burned out"?

I believe the desire for a different sort of life doesn't appear out of thin air. The longing for something more, no matter how weak or crackling with heat, is evidence that God is already at work in your life. You wouldn't want more of God if the Holy Spirit wasn't first seeking you. It is the Trinity's action within that fans the small flame of desire motivating us to "keep company" with Jesus. In fact, the very desire or desperation you feel can be God's way of readying you to walk and work with Jesus. Take heart, transformation happens as you keep company with Jesus.

What Do You Want Jesus to Do for You?

Wanting to work with and watch Jesus is where transformation begins. Willpower and discipline *alone* can never fix your soul. Striving, pushing and trying harder will not recover your life. Unforced rhythms of grace depend on something more than self-mastery and self-effort. The simple truth is that *wanting* to keep company with Jesus has a staying power that "shoulds" and "oughts" seldom have. Jesus wants us to recognize that hidden in our desperations and desires is an appetite for the Lord and Giver of life. In fact, he says, "You're blessed when you've worked up a good appetite for God. He's food and drink in the best meal you'll ever eat" (Matthew 5:6 *The Message*).

The very first thing Jesus asked his soon-to-be disciples was, "What do you want?" (John 1:37). Over and over again he asked about desires:

- "What is it you want?" (Matthew 20:21)

- "What do you want me to do for you?" (Matthew 20:32; Mark 10:36, 51)

- "Do you want to get well?" (John 5:6)

Jesus knew you wouldn't get well if you didn't *want* the responsibility that came with wellness. He also knew that the mother of James and John was clueless about the meaning of her request to have her sons be power brokers in Jesus' kingdom (Matthew 20:21). So he pressed her to consider what her desire might mean. Jesus never attempts to shut down people's longings; nor does he ask people to transcend their longings as some religions do. He knew human desire to be an incurable black hole of opportunity. Accompany him and watch him welcome people who want something more:

- "A man with leprosy . . . begged [Jesus], . . . 'If you are willing, you can make me clean.' " (Mark 1:40)

- "They pleaded with [Jesus] to leave their region." (Matthew 8:34)

- "Save us! We're going to drown!" (Matthew 8:25)

- "Grant that one of these two sons of mine may sit at your right and the other at your left." (Matthew 20:21)

- "Sir, give me this water." (John 4:15)

- "If you can do anything, take pity on us and help us." (Mark 9:22)

- "The man who had been demon-possessed begged to go with [Jesus]." (Mark 5:18)

- "Lord, teach us to pray." (Luke 11:1)

Jesus doesn't grant requests like a genie in a bottle. He works with people, allowing their desires to draw him into the core conversations of life. For Jesus, requests for water, healing, rest, vindication, approval, status and so on all engage soul hungers. Misguided, self-destructive, true or addictive desperations and desires opened doors to relationship.

Learn from Jesus as he keeps company with people who *want something*. Watch him attend to the hole in their heart that is bigger than the galaxy. Many of his deepest interactions with people get at two things: (1) the true nature of people's desires, and (2) a spiritual practice that helps them make space for God in their lives (in the verses below, the spiritual discipline is in quotation marks).

- Martha desperately wants Mary to help her. Jesus tells Martha to "detach" from her drivenness to serve and attend to the first thing—to him (Luke 10:41-42).

- The man cured of demon possession wants to go with Jesus, but Jesus calls him to be a "witness," knowing that telling his story to those who know him can change their lives (Mark 5:19).

- The rich young ruler wants eternal life, but he doesn't want it enough to give his earthly wealth away. Jesus calls him to "confess" and reorder his priorities (Mark 10:21).

I love the fact that the Lord's Prayer comes to us through a disciple's desire to connect with God like Jesus did. "Lord, teach us to pray" (Luke 11:1). Jesus gave the disciple a spiritual practice to *learn* and *do*. He offered him a prayer to *say*. There was no seminar on prayer. No steps and techniques for talking to God. Through praying this prayer the disciples had access to the same relationship with the heavenly Father that Jesus did.

Centuries of Connection Between Discipline and Desire

From its beginning the church linked the desire for more of God to intentional practices, relationships and experiences that gave people space in their lives to "keep company" with Jesus. These intentional practices, relationships and experiences we know as *spiritual disciplines*. The basic rhythm of disciplines (or rule) for the first believers is found in Acts 2:42: "They devoted themselves to the apostles' teaching [a practice] and to the fellowship [relationships], to the breaking of bread [an experience] and to prayer [another practice]."

The desire to know and love God fueled these disciplines. But as the early church community ran into new situations of want, conflict, temptation and persecution, they wanted and needed help to persevere in keeping company with Jesus. The book of Acts recounts a variety of ways the first-century believers made space for God as they faced difficulties:

- Acts 3—the discipline of compassion
- Acts 4—the disciplines of witness, intercession and detachment
- Acts 7—the discipline of service
- Acts 3:1; 10:9—the discipline of fixed-hour prayer
- Acts 14:23—the discipline of fasting
- Acts 15—the discipline of discernment

It can be freeing as well as overwhelming to realize how many disciplines thread their way through the church era. As the gospel spread throughout the Roman world, the church continued to respond to people's desires to keep company with Jesus. The *Didache,* an early Christian text, gave instruction to believers on how to grow in love of God and neighbor. It addressed disciplines like stewardship, chastity, fasting, prayer, humility and the Lord's Supper. In the fourth and fifth centuries, as the church was relieved of its persecution, the desert fathers found that the politicized and nominal nature of Christianity sabotaged their first love. Longing to recover the passionate flame of love for God that characterized the early church, they moved into the desert where they could more intentionally partner with Jesus for transformation. Their longing to be conformed to the image of Christ gave rise to spiritual disciplines of silence, solitude, contemplation, spiritual direction and detachment. The desert fathers' passion to love and keep company with Jesus reverberated through the secular life of Rome. Believers who shared a desire to go deep with God established communities characterized by spiritual rhythms that made space in their lives for God. These monastic communities forged their lives around disciplines of fixed-hour prayer, memorization, devotional reading, service, chastity, simplicity, hospitality, meditation and service. During this period of church growth, public worship also developed into fixed liturgies that guarded the church from heresy. These liturgies and their derivatives are still in use in the Catholic and Orthodox traditions today.

In the sixteenth century the coinciding advent of the printing press, world-class sailing ships and the Reformation fanned the flames of change. The Bible was translated from Latin into native tongues and made available to ordinary people. God's written Word could literally go to the world's end. Ministries focusing on mission outreach and service were launched by both Catholics and Protestants. Bible study, witness, stewardship, discernment and intercessory prayer became the property of common people, not just the educated elite.

The modern era ushered industrialization, individualism, psychology, ecology and global awareness into the mainstream of Western life. People began to keep company with Jesus through journaling, self-care, care of the earth, conversational prayer, accountability partners, small groups, mentoring and inner-healing prayer.

The technological age, with its peculiar temptations and desires, is opening paths into disciplines like slowing, centering prayer and unplugging. Furthermore, classical disciplines like solitude, silence, rest, spiritual direction and retreat are resurging as people desperately seek a quiet, still center in the midst of the whirlwind.

Throughout the centuries the disciplines of prayer, confession, worship, stewardship, fellowship, service, attending to Scripture and the Lord's Supper have remained constant channels and disciplines of grace. These time-resilient disciplines give the church in every age and culture ways to keep company with Jesus. In Christ's presence, temptations, weaknesses, sin, and life's desires and desperations are addressed. It is not spiritual disciplines per se that transform us into the likeness of Christ. Without the work of God's Spirit within, practices guarantee nothing. Paul says, "Such regulations [disciplines] indeed have an appearance of wisdom, with their self-imposed worship, their false humility and their harsh treatment of the body, but they lack any value in restraining sensual indulgence" (Colossians 2:23). Disciplines done for the wrong reasons actually sabotage transformation and numb us toward God and the truth. When we use spiritual practices to gain secondary things like spiritual cachet, success, approval and respect, we rob the discipline of its God-given grace. Jesus said of the most spiritually disciplined people of his day:

> These people honor me with their
>   lips,
>   but their hearts are far from me.
> They worship me in vain;
>   their teachings are but rules
>   taught by men. (Matthew 15:8-9)

Spiritual practices don't give us "spiritual brownie points" or help us "work the system" for a passing grade from God. They simply put us in a place where we can begin to notice God and respond to his word to us.

Spiritual disciplines give the Holy Spirit space to brood over our souls. Just as the Spirit hovered over the face of the deep at the dawn of creation, so he hovers over us today, birthing the ever-fresh Christ-life within. The Christ-in-me identity is not bound to a generic one-size-fits-all program for union with God. The Holy Spirit knows the spiritual practices, relationships and experiences that best suit our unique communion with God. He knows how to help us move into the "unforced rhythms of grace" that Jesus offers to teach us.

Spiritual transformation, "recovering your life," comes from partnering with the Trinity for change. That doesn't mean we give the Holy Spirit an agenda or a demand. We simply *desire*. We bring our ache for change, our longing for belonging, our desperation to make a difference. Then we keep company with Jesus by making space for him through a spiritual discipline. Our part is to offer ourselves lovingly and obediently to God. God then works within us doing what he alone can do. Our desires don't obligate the holy One. God is free to come to us in spiritual disciplines as he wills, not as we demand. But unless we open ourselves to him through spiritual practices, we will miss his coming altogether.

Keeping company with Jesus in the space between wanting to change and not being able to change through effort alone can be a difficult thing to do. Desiring God and not demanding an outcome keeps us in the risky place of waiting and longing. The truth is that we do not know how God intends to conform us to the image of his Son. God's Spirit of truth may use our spiritual practice to reveal false self-conceptions and idols of our heart. Becoming aware of what is true and false about us is essential for spiritual growth, and it is not always comfortable. So when we find ourselves in the space between desire and demand, when we are waiting on God and nothing seems to be happening, we must remember this space is an opportunity. In the unfixables of our lives we are invited to keep company with Jesus and take a risk that God's intentions toward us are good. Day after day this is what Jesus did. It is called trust. He calls us: "Keep company with me and you'll learn to live freely and lightly" (Matthew 11:30 *The Message*).

Spiritual Disciplines Open Us to God

I believe the root of all desire stems from our innate need to open our lives to God in worship. Consequently, I have chosen to catalog spiritual disciplines in accordance with the acronym WORSHIP. But there are many other ways of getting your hands around the disciplines. Richard Foster divides the disciplines into inward, outward and corporate. *Inward* disciplines are practiced in the privacy of our intimate walk with Jesus. *Outward* disciplines affect how we interface with the world. And *corporate* disciplines are practiced with others. Dallas Willard distinguishes between disciplines of engagement and disciplines of abstinence. Disciplines of *engagement* connect us to the needs of others and the call to be God's heart and hands in this world. They address sins of commission. Disciplines of *abstinence* detach us from hurry, clutter and busyness, and open us to being with God alone. They remind us that we are human *beings,* not human *doings,* and that God is more concerned with who we become than what we accomplish. They address sins of omission.

Worship is not something we work up or go to on Sunday morning. Worship is *every* discipline's end game! We miss the point and endanger our souls when we think of spiritual disciplines as ends in themselves. Spiritual practices exist to open us into God. They are never the "be all and end all" of discipleship. The "be all and end all" is a loving trust of and obedience to the God who is within us yet beyond us and our very best efforts.

In worship we live into the reality that the first and best thing in life is nothing less than a transforming relationship with the God who made us, named us and called into being. Worship ignites and attaches us to this truest and best-of-all desire—the desire to let God have his way with us. There is nothing more valuable, nothing more desirable, nothing more worthwhile and nothing more wondrous than the divine life of the holy Three. From the beginning we were designed to be part of their divine community. We are not soul freelancers, but beings created to dance in the arms of the Trinity. And our worship is always a response to the Trinity's unchanging ardor and desire for us. Spiritual disciplines that do not help us partner with the Trinity in worship are "empty worthless acts and a perfect waste of time."

Disciplines are intentional ways we open space in our lives for the worship of God. They are not harsh but grace-filled ways of responding to the presence of Christ with our bodies. Worship happens in our bodies, not just our heads. Paul writes in Romans 12:1, "Offer your bodies as living sacrifices, holy and pleasing to God—this is your spiritual act of worship."

Offering our bodies to God lands us smack in the middle of our weakness and limits. We don't have unlimited energy, time and personal resources. We are finite. We need to be realistic about what our body can do and sustain. Burning the candle at both ends can burn out the soul as well as the body. Spiritual disciplines are ways we give our bodies to unhurried rhythms of grace. They are ways we unhurry our souls before God. It is important to remember that we are not meant to do all the practices at once.

Following Desire to a Discipline

Each letter of the word *worship* points us toward a particular way of creating space for God in our lives. Within each letter you can find particular spiritual disciplines that stem from your God-given desires. Listen to your desires and desperations. Your desires may reflect

- your needs
- an area of struggle
- desperation
- barrenness in routines or relationships
- concern with lack of motivation and what is not working in your life

Ask yourself, *How do I want to or need to be with God?* Circle the letter in WORSHIP that most catches your attention.

Worship God

Open myself to God

Relinquish the false self and idols
   of my heart

Share my life with others

Hear the word of God

Incarnate Christ's love for the world

Pray to God

(If you are not particularly intuitive or find self-reflection on your desires difficult, consider using the Spiritual Health Planner in appendix 1.)

Once you have chosen a particular letter, turn to the list of spiritual disciplines and desires at the front of the book (pp. 11-13) and slowly read through the desires in your chosen category. Which desire catches you? Make a mark beside the corresponding discipline. Remember, you are not choosing a spiritual discipline all on your own or in a vacuum. The Holy Spirit is at work in you stirring up your desire. Because *reading* about spiritual disciplines can be a great deal easier than *practicing* them, don't spend lots of time reading *every* discipline in the category you chose. Mastery of every discipline is not the goal. Surrendering to God is. Follow your desire to the Trinity. At times you may notice that you are off track and have lost your way. You may find you

- compare yourself to others
- think you are further along than you really are
- turn a spiritual discipline into a legalistic requirement
- substitute the means for the end

Do not berate yourself. The Holy Spirit is helping you recognize how you still try to fix your spiritual life by yourself. Be thankful for what you see, and gently return to God and begin again. The spiritual journey is made in small incremental steps. We rise and we fall and we rise again. Remember the *Spiritual Disciplines Handbook* won't make you disciplined, fix your spiritual life or force something to happen in your soul. A book can never make God appear on demand. But this book can give you a way of following your heart's desire into the arms of God. Let it help you keep company with Jesus through disciplines that give God room to work in your relationships, attitudes, appetites and nature. As you intentionally embrace disciplines that conform you to the image of Christ, you will find that you can learn to live like Jesus did—"freely and lightly." Ronald Rolheiser, in his book *The Shattered Lantern*, says, "Freedom is always experienced in relationship to some lord."

Remember, the discipline you are being called to needs to fit with your life now. It must work within the givens of your human limits. If after reading about your discipline it seems impossible, check out the appendix "Seasons, Stages and Ages of Transformation."

Practice in Community

My life has been shaped by men and women who loved me and handed me something of God in their very human lives. Their spiritual practices were woven into the fabric of their lives on the loom of relationships—both with God and with me. They had no halos. They told me the truth about their good, bad and ugly while passing on the lore of the spiritual terrain they had traversed. I believe this is the way spiritual disciplines are to be learned. We are to learn them in relationships.

For the sake of brevity, this handbook often leaves the stories and relationships surrounding spiritual disciplines for another to tell. For me all these disciplines come with faces and names and times and places. It is my prayer that these thumbnail sketches of spiritual practices will open you to the breathtaking and inexhaustible world of relationship—relationship with God, others and even yourself. Let these disciplines draw you deeper into your life and the people you live and work with. Let them reveal the human, authentic, God-given truth of you that we all long to see.

How to Use the Disciplines Catalog— a Journey, Not a Fix

For those of you with an antipathy to reading a book cover to cover—relax. This is *not* a book you read from beginning to end. In fact, it's probably a bad idea to try. The *Spiritual Disciplines Handbook* is like a compass that gives you your bearings. It provides you with ways of responding to Jesus, the pole star of the soul. Once you figure out how to navigate the material, you can find your way forward from any point on the spiritual journey.

Many of the disciplines found in this book can be practiced alone or in community. Feel free to experiment with the discipline in both contexts. Some of the disciplines could easily be in more than one category. For the sake of simplicity they appear only once. Other disciplines, like community, small groups, retreat, intercession and contemplative prayer, are container disciplines for a number of other disciplines that appear in this book. If you are looking for a particular discipline, be sure to check the index.

Which letter of WORSHIP best matches your longings or hungers or desperations?

- Set aside fifteen or twenty minutes to orient yourself to the disciplines in this letter.
- Scan the desires preceding the spiritual disciplines. Which ones resonate with your longing?
- Note the fruit of the discipline at the bottom of the chart. Which of these transformative changes resonate with your desire to become more like Jesus?
- Read the short description of the disciplines that intrigue you, and choose your practice based on what best suits your life situation now.

1. Set aside twenty minutes for the practice of your chosen discipline. (Some disciplines cannot be done in a twenty-minute time slot, but twenty minutes is a good starting point for many of them.)

2. Pray a short prayer of dedication, such as, "Here I am, Lord. I want to be with you. Open me up." Express your desire to be with God.

   - Unhurriedly read the Scripture preceding your discipline. Let it settle into your heart. You may want to copy it out and place it somewhere your eyes normally land in the course of a day.

   - Turn to the desire at the top of the chart. Thank the Lord for giving you the fuel of desire. Offer your desire and your body to Jesus. Acknowledge that while the desire does not entitle you or obligate God, you are open to take the path desire has opened before you.

3. Follow the guidelines for the practice. Respond to any invitation you sense from the Holy Spirit. Don't hurry. You can pick up where you left off on another day.

- The reflection questions offer you ways of searching your heart in the presence of Christ. The questions take your spiritual pulse and enable you to explore resistance you may feel, past experiences—positive and negative—that might affect your practice of the discipline or areas of confusion that might bog you down. You may find some of the questions make you feel uncomfortable; remember Jesus' words to his disciples in John 16:12: "I still have many things to tell you, but you can't handle them now. But when the Friend comes, the Spirit of Truth, he will take you by the hand and guide you into all the truth there is" *(The Message)*. The more intentionally open we are to the truth about ourselves, the more authentic our dialogue with the Trinity can be.

You are not wasting time by answering the reflection questions. John Calvin wrote in *The Institutes:* "Without knowledge of self, there is no knowledge of God. Nearly all the wisdom we possess, that is to say, true sound wisdom, consists of two parts: the knowledge of God and of ourselves." Our partnership with the Holy Spirit is the linchpin of the transformation process.

You do not need to take the questions in order or do more than one at a time. Take your time with them, listening deeply to the Spirit and to what your life wants to tell you. If you process your thoughts well on paper, journal your response. If you think best when you walk, then go for a walk. You may find that when you return to the same question at a later time, the Holy Spirit has taken you to a deeper place of self-awareness so the dialogue with God can deepen even more.

- The spiritual exercises provide hands-on ways to begin practicing the discipline. Read through the exercises, choosing one that is possible for you at this time. Don't try to do a different exercise every day. You can stay with one exercise for as long as you want. When you are ready to begin a spiritual exercise:

4. Set aside the last five minutes to respond to God in prayer. Tell God what it was like for you to practice the spiritual discipline. Express your thoughts and feelings freely. Gratitude, anger, frustration, impatience—bring it all to God. Ask the Holy Spirit to seal in your memory what you need to remember.

5. Take one word or thought with you into the rest of your day. Returning to this word over time develops soul reflexes of attention to God. The practice of noticing God throughout our day shapes the way we live and interact with others.

6. Offer yourself to God and place yourself in his hands for the remainder of your day.

The *Spiritual Disciplines Handbook* invites you to journey with Jesus into the God-given desires within you, to "learn the unforced rhythms of grace." It is my prayer that Jesus will give you a way of keeping company with him that opens you wide to God.

Part One

WORSHIP

HUMAN BEINGS ARE MADE FOR WORSHIP. Everyone worships someone or something. In *The Everlasting Man,* G. K. Chesterton wrote, "The crux and crisis is that man found it natural to worship; even natural to worship unnatural things. . . . If man cannot pray, he is gagged; if he cannot kneel, he is in irons." Human beings cannot help but assign ultimate value and worth to someone or something. Of course, that doesn't mean everyone worships God. One's ultimate devotion can rest in money, success, a person, a garden, a creed, a cause and so forth. Ultimately what we are devoted to will shape our lives.

Many of us are devoted to the same things our culture worships: houses, money, retirement plans, vacations, comforts, success. In and of themselves none of these things is bad. But when we value these things more than we value God, we end up worshiping secondary things. Secondary things can never satisfy core longings. Only a love relationship with our Creator can do that.

In worship we fall into the arms of God and say "Have your way with me." The early church fathers sometimes spoke of a dancing Trinity. The Father, Son and Holy Spirit moved together in a rhythm of self-giving love. Worship is a response to God's invitation to join the dance. It is a way we tap into what is true about us—we do desire God. As Ruth Haley Barton writes in *Invitation to Solitude & Silence,* "Your desire for God and your capacity to connect with God as a human soul is the essence of who you are."

Spiritual disciplines are one way we join the dance and learn basic rhythms and steps that help us respond to God. Disciplines of worship put us in a place to be receptive and responsive to the Holy Spirit's movements and invitations.

Though all disciplines lead to worship, for the sake of cataloging the disciplines, only classical worship practices have been included under the letter *W.* The classical disciplines of worship focus our attention on the beauty of the Trinity—the source of all that is good, true and beautiful.

"May the Son of God who is already formed in you grow in you—so that for you he will become immeasurable, and that in you he will become laughter, exultation, the fullness of joy which no one can take from you."—Isaac of Stella

CELEBRATION

DESIRE	to take joyful, passionate pleasure in God and the radically glorious nature of God's people, Word, world and purposes
DEFINITION	Celebration is a way of engaging in actions that orient the spirit toward worship, praise and thanksgiving. Delighting in all the attentions and never-changing presence of the Trinity fuels celebration.

SCRIPTURE	"The LORD your God is with you,
	    he is mighty to save.
	He will take great delight in you,
	    he will quiet you with his love,
	    he will rejoice over you with singing." (Zephaniah 3:17)
	
	"I will praise the LORD who counsels me. . . .
	Therefore my heart is glad and my tongue rejoices;
	    my body also will rest secure. . . .
	You have made known to me the path of life;
	    you will fill me with joy in your presence,
	    with eternal pleasures at your right hand." (Psalm 16:7, 9, 11)
	
	"Applause, everyone. Bravo, bravissimo! Shout God-songs at the top of your lungs!" (Psalm 47:1 *The Message*)
	
	"I praise you because I am fearfully and wonderfully made;
	    your works are wonderful,
	    I know that full well." (Psalm 139:14)

PRACTICE INCLUDES	Identifying and pursuing those things that bring the heart deep gladness and reveling in them before the Lord. This may include time spent with others, sharing meals, working, serving, worshiping, laughing, listening to music, dancing and so on.
GOD-GIVEN FRUIT	• keeping company with Jesus no matter what happens • living from a mentality of abundance rather than of scarcity • participating in the celebration and love of the Trinity • rejoicing always in the God who rejoices over you (Zephaniah 3:17) • enjoying every good and perfect gift as coming from God • living out of the joy of your salvation • cultivating a spirit of gladness • taking yourself less seriously • freedom from the addiction to criticism or negativity • having holiday traditions that guide your celebration

CELEBRATION

GOD CELEBRATES. HE INVENTED DELIGHT, JOY AND CELEBRATION. And one way we enter into the divine life of the Trinity is through celebration. Whether solemn or exhilarating, formal or spontaneous, celebration can enlarge our capacity to enjoy and serve God. Celebrating God does not depend on perfect circumstances or happy feelings. Even in prison Paul and Silas found something to sing about (Acts 16). And Jeremiah, the weeping prophet, wrote:

> My soul is downcast within me.
> Yet this I call to mind
>   and therefore I have hope:
> Because of the LORD's great love we are not consumed,
>   for his compassions never fail.
> They are new every morning. (Lamentations 3:20-24)

Jeremiah found reason to delight and hope in God even in a lament.

The world is filled with reasons to be downcast. But deeper than sorrow thrums the unbroken pulse of God's joy, a joy that will yet have its eternal day. To set our hearts on this joy reminds us that we can choose how we respond to any particular moment. We can search for God in all circumstances, or not. We can seek the pulse of hope and celebration because it is God's reality. Heaven is celebrating. Right now the cherubim, seraphim, angels, archangels, prophets, apostles, martyrs and all the company of saints overflow with joy in the presence of their Creator. Every small experience of Jesus with us is a taste of the joy that is to come. We are not alone—and that in itself is reason to celebrate

To abandon ourselves to celebration can feel like a risky thing. What if we are misunderstood or seem to take hard things too lightly? King David was so "undignified" in his celebration of the Lord that his wife rebuked him for his public impropriety! But David replied, "I will celebrate before the LORD. I will become even more undignified than this, and I will be humiliated in my own eyes" (2 Samuel 6:21-22). Set your eyes on God as you celebrate, and forget how you look. God delights in all kinds of worship.

REFLECTION QUESTIONS

1. Where are you most prone to celebrate God? Alone? With others? In worship? In music? In nature?

   What does this tell you about how God made you and how you most naturally meet with him?

2. How is your celebration enhanced or curtailed by your ability to remember the past, live in the moment or anticipate the future?

3. When you see others celebrating God in a way that is new or foreign to you, what goes on in your mind and heart?

4. If there is a heaviness about you, an overly serious side or an entrenched critical spirit, how might celebrating God affect these traits and move you into new areas of transformation?

5. Who do you know who really celebrates life and God?

6. What attracts you to them?

SPIRITUAL EXERCISES

1. Identify the place you most readily connect with God. Is it in nature? listening to Christian music? participating in corporate worship? solitude? Go to that place. What do you want to tell God about the joy you receive there?

2. Intentionally place yourself in the presence of God. Recall all of God's gifts, provisions, guidance and love toward you. • To celebrate God's grace to you, write a song of celebration, make a collage that represents your joy, write a poem of praise, play music and dance before the Lord, or memorize a verse of praise and repeat it all through the coming days.

3. Familiarize yourself with the church calendar. (If you don't know about the church year, do a Web search for "church calendar.") • Consider ways you can go all-out in your celebration of Lent, Easter, Pentecost, Advent, Christmas, Epiphany and All Saints Day this year. Plan a way of celebrating God alone or with friends.

4. Attend to the people who give you joy. Ask God how you might celebrate them in a way that encourages them.

5. Plan to celebrate someone's birthday, Mother's Day or Father's Day in a way that reminds the person of how precious he or she is to you and to God.

6. Consider how God loves you. Read Zephaniah 3:17. Then be still and listen. How is God celebrating you? • Celebrate the God who celebrates you. Intentionally ask for the gift of appreciating yourself the way God does.

Resources on Celebration

Celebration of Discipline, chapter 13, by Richard Foster

"But we who would be born again indeed, must wake our souls unnumbered times a day."
—George MacDonald

GRATITUDE

DESIRE	to be sensitive to the Holy Spirit's prompting to live with a grateful heart, cognizant of God's work in my life and my abundant resources
DEFINITION	Gratitude is a loving and thankful response toward God for his presence with us and within this world. Though "blessings" can move us into gratitude, it is not at the root of a thankful heart. Delight in God and his good will is the heartbeat of thankfulness.

SCRIPTURE	"Give thanks to the LORD, for he is good;
	      His love endures forever.
	Give thanks to the God of gods.
	      His love endures forever.
	Give thanks to the Lord of lords:
	      His love endures forever." (Psalm 136:1-2)
	
	"Be joyful always; pray continually; give thanks in all circumstances, for this is God's will for you in Christ Jesus." (1 Thessalonians 5:16-18)
	
	"Do not be anxious about anything, but in everything, by prayer and petition, with thanksgiving, present your requests to God." (Philippians 4:6)

PRACTICE INCLUDES	• prayers and songs that focus on God's generosity to us • gratefully giving and sharing all I am and have as a sign of your thankfulness to God • expressing gratitude to others; the habit of saying "thank you," "I am so grateful," "you are so kind" and so forth • gratefully noticing God's presence and gifts throughout the day • practicing an *abundance* mentality; counting the blessings of life • keeping a gratitude journal of the myriad gifts God has brought you
GOD-GIVEN FRUIT	• keeping company with Jesus no matter what happens • being aware of the abundance of gifts, benefits, mercies and grace that have been poured into your life • curbing critical tendencies by upstaging them with thanksgiving • seeing what you have as quickly as you see what you don't have • treasuring and valuing people by thanking them often and clearly for who they are to you or to someone else • daily thanking the Lord for his presence in your life • noticing your lack of gratitude and repenting of the idol that has your heart at that moment • receiving everything you have as a gift rather than as an entitlement

GRATITUDE

I HAVE A FRIEND WHO IS BENT ON TEACHING her grandchildren about gratitude. When one of them begins to complain or cry about some disappointment, she says, "Sweetheart, I know you don't like what is happening, but you have the choice of making this a happy day or a sad day. What kind of day do you want to have? Do you remember all we have to be glad about in this day?"

Thankfulness is a thread that can bind together all the patchwork squares of our lives. Difficult times, happy days, seasons of sickness, hours of bliss—all can be sewn together into something lovely with the thread of thankfulness. Jesus was especially good at doing this. Once he was in a tough situation with a lot of hungry people on his hands, and all he had were five loaves of bread and two fish. He could have complained that God shouldn't expect him to feed five thousand people with so little. But Jesus didn't write off the loaves and fish as nothing. He noticed what was given and "gave thanks" for it (Mark 8:6). And in these less-than-perfect circumstances, God supplied all that was needed. We, like Jesus, have choices about how to respond to what life dishes up. We each have the power to interpret the facts of our lives. We make the choices that turn us into bitter or grateful people. Gratitude is rooted in the reality that "bidden or unbidden, God is present." Carl Jung discovered (and popularized) this statement among the Latin writings of Erasmus: *vocatus atque non vocatus, deus aderit.*

Thanksgiving is possible not because everything goes perfectly but because God is present. The Spirit of God is within us—nearer to us than our own breath. It is a discipline to choose to stitch our days together with the thread of gratitude. But the decision to do so is guaranteed to stitch us closer to God. Attend to the truth that "bidden or unbidden, God is present."

REFLECTION QUESTIONS

1. When you feel at the bottom of the food chain and dead last in terms of priority, how do you move toward gratitude?

2. When have you found that in retrospect you could have been thankful for something that you were not grateful for at the time it was happening?

   How can this perspective inform your life now?

3. How has a grateful person affected your own vision of what matters in life?

   How has someone who lives out of bitterness affected your life?

4. How does your disposition influence your attitude toward gratitude?

5. How are you addicted to criticism, analysis and negativity?

   How might thankfulness be an antidote to a critical spirit?

SPIRITUAL EXERCISES

1. Begin a gratitude journal by keeping a record of the "abundances" God has given you. Next to each abundance write what it means to you to have a God who interacts and intervenes in your life. • Notice what you have been given that you did not deserve. What do you want to say to God about these things?

2. End every day by saying thank you to God for at least one thing. Then tell God what that one thing meant for you.

3. Write a letter of thanks to someone who has touched your life in the past year, the past month, the past week.

4. Get a current hardship firmly in mind. How do you feel about this hardship? Tell the truth to God. • Where is there evidence of God's presence in this hardship? Is there anything you can be thankful for? • If you cannot find God in your hardship, spend some time with Jesus in the Garden of Gethsemane. What does he want to tell you?

5. What sorts of things tend to encourage you in thankfulness? Praise songs? Worship? Time spent with friends? Giving and receiving presents? • Plan ways of incorporating the things that encourage thankfulness into your life on a regular basis.

6. Hold a thank-you party. Invite the people you want to honor with a thank you.

7. Create a thank you scrapbook. Beside photos and pictures, write your prayers of thanksgiving.

8. Notice your tendency to make comparisons that result in feelings of dissatisfaction or entitlement. Practice abstaining from comparative statements about what you don't have. Instead give thanks for what you do have.

Resources on Gratitude

Life Signs or *Here and Now* by Henri Nouwen

"When Jesus holds up the cup and offers what is in it as the fluid of forgiveness, he is not talking to people with a short list of minor sins. He is talking to people who will turn him in, who will scatter to the four winds at the first sign of trouble, and who will swear they never knew him. He is talking to people who should have been his best friends on earth who turn out not to have a loyal bone in their bodies, and he is forgiving them ahead of time, as surely as if he had said, 'I know who you are. I know you will not be innocent of the blood of this cup, but I will not let that come between us. . . . Let my life become your life, through the blood of this covenant.'"—Barbara Brown Taylor

HOLY COMMUNION

DESIRE	to be nourished by Christ, tasting the sweet depths of redemption
DEFINITION	The Lord's Supper celebrates God's redemptive plan through the sacrificial death of Jesus. Through this meal of bread and wine (or grape juice) we join ourselves to Christ and feed on him in our hearts through faith.
SCRIPTURE	"While they were eating, Jesus took bread, gave thanks and broke it, and gave it to his disciples, saying, 'Take it; this is my body.' Then he took the cup, gave thanks and offered it to them, and they all drank from it. 'This is my blood of the covenant, which is poured out for many,' he said to them." (Mark 14:22-24) "For whenever you eat this bread and drink this cup, you proclaim the Lord's death until he comes." (1 Corinthians 11:26) "Every day they continued to meet together in the temple courts. They broke bread in their homes and ate together with glad and sincere hearts, praising God and enjoying the favor of all the people." (Acts 2:46-47) "Because there is one loaf, we, who are many, are one body, for we all partake of the one loaf." (1 Corinthians 10:17)
PRACTICE INCLUDES	partaking of Christ's body and blood in the sacrament of communion
GOD-GIVEN FRUIT	• keeping company with Jesus no matter what happens • having nourishment for the journey • developing a deeper love for Jesus • a growing awareness of your own spiritual poverty • more fully appreciating Jesus'; sacrificial love to rescue you • appreciating the diversity of other believers who take of the Lord's Supper with you • having a passion for unity of the church worldwide

HOLY COMMUNION

ONE OF THE VERY FIRST PRACTICES IN THE EARLY CHURCH was the observance of Communion, also known as the Lord's Supper or celebration of the Eucharist. Jesus himself instituted this practice with his disciples just hours before his death. This Supper ties the blood of the Old Testament sacrifices to God's radical rescue of humankind through his Son. Kathleen Norris writes in *Amazing Grace,* "The incarnation (and I might add communion) remains a scandal to anyone who wants religion to be a purely spiritual matter, an anesthetized, bloodless bliss." It reminds us that our faith is not ethereal and bodiless. The radical nature of our sin problem resolves itself in innocent blood. In Exodus 24:7-8 we read: "[Moses] took the Book of the Covenant and read it to the people. . . . Moses then took the blood, sprinkled it on the people and said, 'This is the blood of the covenant that the LORD has made with you in accordance with all these words.'" Building on the old covenant, Jesus ushers in the new covenant.

> While they were eating, Jesus took bread, gave thanks and broke it, and gave it to his disciples saying, 'Take it; this is my body.'
>
> "Then he took the cup, gave thanks and offered it to them, and they drank from it.
>
> " 'This is my blood of the covenant, which is poured out for many,' he said to them." (Mark 14:22-24)

Jesus becomes the innocent lamb that takes away the sin of the world. Sacrificing his own life, he opens a doorway from death to life, from rebellion to friendship, from separation to communion and from senseless suffering to redemptive suffering.

The significance of the Lord's Supper is revealed in its sacramental nature. A sacrament is an outward and visible sign of an inward and invisible reality. Holy Communion invites us into deeper unity and communion with Jesus and his body. The bread broken and the wine poured out signify the cost of the Communion meal. Christ's blood and body were sacrificed for *us!* And his sacrifice becomes a pattern for our own journey. The "feast" of Christ's table nourishes us and strengthens us with heavenly food. This new manna is the way we get from here to home. In receiving this nourishment we anticipate another feast—the marriage supper of the Lamb—the table of eternal union and communion.

In many ways the Lord's Supper opens us wide to a divine mystery. This mystery is sometimes dubbed the "paschal mystery" of redemption: Christ has died; Christ is risen; Christ will come again. Explaining this mystery may be beyond us, but that does not mean we cannot participate in it. In Communion, Christ is here for us. We eat of his body and are part of his body—the one loaf. Though we may feel alone in our journey, we are part of the train of apostles, prophets, martyrs, saints and all servants of God. The meal reminds us that we belong and are not alone. Because of Jesus, all will be well.

Years ago Tim Keller used this illustration from *The Lord of the Rings* to convey the immense meaning of the Lord's table. Enemies and dread weapons pummel the walls of the city of Gondor. As the city gates begin to give way, death, doom and the bitterness of defeat take hold. The evil dark lord grimly claims the city for himself. But in that moment of bleak despair the Riders of Rohan come charging, their horns blowing. J. R. R. Tolkien writes in *The Lord of the Rings: The Return of the King*, "Pippin rose to his feet, . . . and he stood listening to the horns, and it seemed to him that they would break his heart with joy. And never in after years could he hear a horn blown in the distance without tears starting in his eyes."

The Lord's Supper reminds us that when the dark lord looms before us shrieking "all is lost," the Lord of light stepped forth and said, "This is my body broken for you." When we partake, we taste what redemption cost God in order to call us home. Indeed it is hard to see the bread and the wine without "tears starting in [our] eyes."

REFLECTION QUESTIONS

1. What is participating in the Lord's Supper like for you?

2. What do you hope to receive at the Lord's table?

3. Have you ever participated in Communion at a church that celebrated it differently than was your custom? What was that like for you?

SPIRITUAL EXERCISES

1. Prepare yourself for Communion ahead of time. Read John 13:1-17. Imagine you are there at the table with Jesus. What are your feelings and thoughts? How does it feel to have Jesus wash your feet? How does it feel to drink the cup knowing your own betrayals? Confess your sins and then attend Communion with what is in your heart to say to God.

2. If you are in a tradition that bakes the bread for Communion and dresses the table for this meal, offer to make the bread or set the table. As you do this, contemplate the import of what this all means.

3. If you are in a tradition that "adores the host," spend time in the Lord's presence thanking him for his body given for us.

Resources on Holy Communion

That We May Perfectly Love Thee by Robert Benson

"It is my conviction that our heavenly Father says the same to us every day: 'My dear child, you must always remember who you are.' "—John Stott

RULE FOR LIFE

DESIRE	to live a sane and holy rhythm that reflects a deep love for God and respect for how he has made me
DEFINITION	A rule for life offers unique and regular rhythms that free and open each person to the will and presence of Christ. The spiritual practices of a rule provide a way to partner with the Holy Spirit for personal transformation.
SCRIPTURE	"This commandment that I'm commanding you today isn't too much for you, it's not out of your reach. . . . Look at what I've done for you today: I've placed in front of you Life and Good Death and Evil. And I command you today: Love GOD, your God. Walk in his ways. Keep his commandments, regulations, and rules so that you will live, really live, live exuberantly, blessed by GOD, your God, in the land you are about to enter and possess. . . . Choose life so that you and your children will live. And love GOD, your God, listening obediently to him, firmly embracing him. Oh yes, he is life itself." (Deuteronomy 30:11, 15, 16, 19-20 *The Message*) "The one who calls you is faithful and he will do it." (1 Thessalonians 5:24) "I have come that they may have life, and have it to the full." (John 10:10)
PRACTICE INCLUDES	• nurturing disciplines that draw you more deeply into loving God • creating rhythms that honor your desires and limits • periodically assessing the spiritual journey not by comparison to others but through your unique rule for personal growth • developing a spiritual growth pathway that perfectly suits your stage and personality • developing regular, repeated relationships, experiences and practices that make space for God in the busyness of life
GOD-GIVEN FRUIT	• partnering with the Holy Spirit for deep-down change • living out of rhythms that cooperate with the Holy Spirit's work in your life • keeping the chaotic "whatever" life at bay • intentionally and practically loving God with all your mind, heart, soul and strength • choosing personal disciplines in response to hearing from God and with the awareness of your heart's deep desires • resting and freedom to not do it all • having a God-accessible and obedience-centered life

RULE FOR LIFE

WE ALL HAVE RULES LIKE "DO YOUR BEST." "Never give up." "Never say never." "Just do it." These mottos tether us to certain behaviors and attitudes so we can, in the words of another rule, "be all we can be." They help us live toward what we most want. Developing a "rule for life" is a way of being intentional about the personal rhythms and guidelines that shape our days. One of the early Christian rules for life is found in Acts 2:42. Here we find that believers "devoted themselves to the apostles' teaching and to the fellowship, to the breaking of bread and to prayer." This rule shaped their lives and hearts in the circumstances they were in. It acknowledged the impossibility of becoming like Christ through effort alone. The rule offered disciplines that made space to attend to the supernatural presence of the Trinity at work in and among them. The rule of the early church described distinct practices that were different than the cultural norms. Over the years Christians have developed rules and rhythms for living that center their lives in loving Christ rather than the world. The Rule of Saint Benedict is an example of an ancient rule still in practice today.

A rule for life is a simple statement of the regular rhythms we choose in order to present our bodies to God as our "spiritual act of worship" (Romans 12:1). Each rule, or rhythm, is a way we partner with God for the transformation only he can bring. Rules keep our lives from devolving into unintended chaos. They aren't a burdensome list of do's and don'ts, enumerating everything you might do in a day. Life-giving rules are a brief and realistic scaffold of disciplines that support your heart's desire to grow in loving God and others.

A rule honors your limits and God-given longings. It mitigates against grandiosity and must be written for who you are, not for who you aren't. It addresses your world, your sphere of influence, your fears of loss of productivity, your relationships. It takes into account where you need to stretch and change as well as where you are tired and need balance.

Don't be afraid to experiment with a rule; it can easily be changed and revised, but should not be subject to whims. Allow yourself to settle into the rule so it has time to shape your life. Ultimately a rule will help you love God more. If it becomes a legalistic way of earning points with God, it should be scrapped.

Before making a rule, take stock of your desires, natural rhythms, limits and times of closest connection to God. The following questions can provide you with insights about what is most important to you in a rule. (If the word *rule* makes you anxious, write a "rhythm for life.")

Writing a Rule

1. When and where do you feel closest to God? How do you enter most deeply into an awareness of his love for you?

   Pay attention to the experiences, practices and relationships that draw you toward God. Are there particular practices that open you to God?

   Are there practices that seem to stymie you?

2. What is most important to you?

   What gives you a sense of security and self-worth?

   What would people who know you best say it's like to live and work with you?

   Where do your relationships need attention?

   Who do you want to become?

   What receives the most attention in your life? Your spouse? Job? Family? Friends? Hobbies? (These are not bad things. But when we love them more than God, we have an idol in our heart. See "Detachment.")

   If you had six months to live, how would you spend your time?

   If you could write your own eulogy, what would you want to say?

3. What do you currently do to realize your goals and longings? Work? Study? Pray? Network? Socialize? Diet? Work out?

   Which of these things hinder and help your spiritual journey?

4. What practices suit your daily, monthly and yearly rhythms and cycles?

   What limitations are built into your life at this moment?

   What longings remain steady throughout?

   What responsibilities and rhythms change with various seasons?

5. Where do you want to change? Where do you feel powerless to change? Ask the Holy Spirit to help you do through grace what you cannot do through effort alone.

6. Choose several disciplines that arise from your desire for God's transforming work and that suit the limits and realities of your life. Begin your practice.

Sample Rules for Life

- Dedicate every day (in the morning) for the glory of God.
- Confess my sins before I go to bed.

- Worship the Lord alone and with others.
- Practice the presence of God.
- Don't hold grudges—forgive others.
- Eat sensibly.
- Pray for others.
- See my spiritual director once a month.
- Give all wandering thoughts to my Savior.

A Rule from Psalm 16

"I said to the LORD, 'You are my Lord;
    apart from you I have no good thing.'"

- Set my heart on God.

"As for the saints who are in the land,
    they are the glorious ones in whom is all my delight."

- Journey with friends.
- Delight in the body of Christ.
- Reach out.

"The sorrows of those will increase
    who run after other gods."

- Confess

"LORD, you have assigned me my portion and my cup;
    you have made my lot secure.
The boundary lines have fallen for me in pleasant places;
    surely I have a delightful inheritance."

- Give thanks.

"I will praise the LORD, who counsels me;
    even at night my heart instructs me."

- Worship and praise.
- Listen, pay attention, be teachable.

"I have set the LORD always before me.
    Because he is at my right hand,
    I will not be shaken."

- Persevere and hope.
- Speak courageously.

"Therefore my heart is glad and my tongue rejoices;
    my body also will rest secure."

- Take myself less seriously.
- Receive my body as it ages.

"you will fill me with joy in your presence,
   with eternal pleasures at your right hand."

- Live in the presence of God.

REFLECTION QUESTIONS

1. What unspoken rules govern your life right now?

2. How do you determine what you will and won't do?

3. Does the idea of a rule for life appeal to you? Why or why not?

4. How has being disciplined affected your life?

5. How does a rule for life differ from a mission statement?

SPIRITUAL EXERCISES

1. Write a rule for life using the questions in "Writing a Rule." Take your time. Answer a question a day until you feel you have the information you need to write a life-giving rule.

2. Read the Rule of St. Benedict. What does this ancient rule show you about the Christian life? • What parts of this rule might encourage you today?

3. Look at the disciplines that consistently thread their way through Jesus' life. How do they shape what he did or didn't do? • Which of these disciplines do you consistently practice?

4. Consider where you are longing to change yet find changing difficult to impossible. Talk to God about this area in your life. Acknowledge your powerlessness to change through your own efforts. Ask God to give you a way of making space for him in the middle of this difficult place. • Consider which spiritual practice can provide you with a rhythmic awareness of God's work in and through you to accomplish his good purpose. Consistently practice your discipline. When you fail, gently come to God and begin again.

5. A rule for life can act like a plumb line, allowing you a still point from which you can gauge the intentionality of your spiritual journey. On a regular basis look at your life in light of your rule. What do you see? • Where is God drawing you? • What is giving you life? • Where is your life out of control and not centered in Christ?

Resources on a Rule for Life

Living with Contradiction by Esther de Wall
The Rule of St. Benedict
Soul Feast by Marjorie Thompson

"Sabbath is not dependent upon our readiness to stop. We do not stop when we are finished. We do not stop when we complete our phone calls, finish our project, get through this stack of messages, or get out this report that is due tomorrow. We stop because it is time to stop."—Wayne Muller

SABBATH

DESIRE	to set apart one day a week for rest and worship of God
DEFINITION	Sabbath is God's gift of repetitive and regular rest. It is given for our delight and communion with God. Time for *being* in the midst of a life of *doing* particularly characterizes the sabbath.
SCRIPTURE	"Therefore, since the promise of entering his rest still stands, let us be careful that none of you be found to have fallen short of it. . . . There remains, then, a Sabbath-rest for the people of God; for anyone who enters God's rest also rests from his own work, just as God did from his. Let us, therefore, make every effort to enter that rest." (Hebrews 4:1, 9-11) "The Sabbath was made for man, not man for the Sabbath." (Mark 2:27) "Remember the Sabbath day by keeping it holy. Six days you shall labor and do all your work, but the seventh day is a Sabbath to the LORD your God." (Exodus 20:8-10)
PRACTICE INCLUDES	• setting aside time for intimacy with God and others you love • resting in God one day per week • practicing restful activities: walks, picnics, a Sunday afternoon nap, a phone visit with someone you love, tea or coffee with a friend, family time, games with your kids, love-making • letting go of things that stress you out for twenty-four hours • letting the difficult conversations happen another day • not developing a to-do list for Sunday • refraining from competition that moves you into a bad place
GOD-GIVEN FRUIT	• keeping company with Jesus through the sabbath • freedom from the addiction to busyness, rush and hurry • acknowledging your human limits and living within them • honoring the way God created you by living a healthy and intentionally rested life • living a weekly rhythm of rest followed by six days of work • delighting in God, family, the seasons, meals and all good gifts of creation • trusting God for all that you're not doing and taking care of on Sunday

SABBATH

THE FOURTH COMMANDMENT READS: "Remember the Sabbath day by keeping it holy. Six days you shall labor and do all your work, but the seventh day is a Sabbath to the LORD your God. On it you shall not do any work" (Exodus 20:8-10). The Jewish understanding of sabbath embraced a special twenty-four hour rest time that was different from every other day. Other days of the week were given over to work, but the sabbath reminded people that they were finite. They could not constantly be on the go. There were limits to their energy. And to honor these limitations was to honor the infinite God, who himself worked and rested.

Jewish sabbath began in the evening when the family set aside all the to-dos of the work week. As the lamps were lit, everyone settled into the evening calm of *Shabbat*. Candles, prayers, blessings, food, the empty chair at the table—it all represented delight and refreshment in the presence of God and each other. When bedtime came, the family rested in God's covenant protection. They woke on sabbath morning to a world they didn't make and a friendship with God they didn't earn. Over time, this one intentional day for delight and refreshment turned into a sobering legalistic exercise. Enjoying God and others was replaced by scrupulously keeping sabbath rules. The day God had given as a respite from work became simply another kind of work.

Jesus took specific aim at this misunderstanding of the sabbath. As Lord of the sabbath (see Matthew 12:1-14; Luke 6:1-10), he freely interpreted the sabbath command, claiming that God gave it to people as a restorative and recuperative gift. God did not intend for life to be all effort, so he punctuated each week with twenty-four hours of sabbath rest, during which people could remember what life is about and who it is for.

Sadly, everything about us works against slowing down. Our compulsion to produce and not waste time invades the space God gave for us to rest. Children's athletics, national sporting events, round-the-clock accessibility to work, e-mail and stores also fill up the sabbath day, so we never stop. When you get indignant over how seemingly incompatible sabbath is with the tiring and relentless demands already facing you, consider what your tiredness means. Animals don't think about how tired they are. And they don't have a sabbath *they* set aside for rest. It's humans who recognize the difference between work and rest. The fact that we make distinctions between being tired and rested is an indication that we need to do both. Made in the image of God, we are like God, who on the seventh day "rested" from all his labor.

Sabbath is God's way of saying, "Stop. Notice your limits. Don't burn out." It is a day he gives us to remember who and what work is for as well as what matters most. Sunday generously hands us hours to look into the eyes of those we love. We have time for loving and being loved. Rhythmically, the sabbath reminds us that we belong to the worldwide family of God. We are citizens of another kingdom—a kingdom not ruled by the clock and the tyranny of the urgent. God's sabbath reality calls us to trust that the Creator can manage all that concerns us in this world as we settle into his rest.

REFLECTION QUESTIONS

1. What difficulties or compulsions surround your resting on the sabbath?

2. How does taking a sabbath enhance your enjoyment and worship of God?

3. What makes a sabbath day nourishing and replenishing to you?

4. What happens to you when you go without regular rhythms that allow you to rest in God?

SPIRITUAL EXERCISES

1. Plan a twenty-four-hour sabbath you can enter with anticipation. The night before your sabbath, remind your body how long it has to luxuriate and rest in God. • Consider the things that would nourish you: worship, music, a nap, making love, walking, reading, playing with children, afternoon tea. Plan them spaciously into the day.

2. Gather your family together to discuss how to arrange your sabbath for refreshment, renewal and relationships. Ask "How do you intentionally leave the school- and work-week behind? • Let everyone tell one thing they love to do on Sunday. • Share what makes Sundays difficult for you. • If getting to church is a hurried time that brings distress to the family, spend some time talking together about how to take the pressure off "getting out the door on time." Should you consider going to church at another time? Would the family enjoy having Dad fix breakfast? Would they rather just drink juice and share a family brunch? What can be done the night before to make it easier to get going in the morning? • How can you approach sabbaths in ways that do not force, rush or demand?

3. Begin your sabbath gently on Saturday evening. Light a candle. • Invite the presence of Christ to guide you through your sabbath. • Eat with friends and family. • Go to bed early, speaking peace to one another. • Pray for Christ to give you deep, refreshing sleep. Rest in his arms. Commit your dreams to the Lord.

4. Prepare a "sabbath box or basket." Choose a basket or cover a grocery-size box with gift paper. Each Saturday evening, gather as a family to put all the things you don't need to

take with you into Sunday. Drop cell phones, credit cards and pagers into the box. Put work projects and homework in the box. • Tell one another what you are looking forward to as you enter Sunday. • Pray together to receive the gift of sabbath.

5. The night before your sabbath day, enter into sleep as a spiritual act of worship. Consciously let go of your compulsion to be indispensable. Drop all that brings you anxiety into the arms of your heavenly Father. Lay your head on the pillow imagining that you are putting your head into the lap of God. Commit your body and dreams to him. Relax in God and rest.

6. Awake gently to your sabbath day. If it is possible, don't set an alarm. Let your body wake naturally. As you come to consciousness, take several deep breaths and open your body wide to God for the new day. Stretch out and feel the full length of yourself. Thank God that you are fearfully and wonderfully made. Thank him for the gift of the day before you. • Is God speaking to you in any way? Listen and respond. • Get up slowly and attend to your desire to encounter God today.

Resources on Sabbath

Sabbath by Wayne Muller
Sabbath Keeping by Lynne M. Baab

"If worship does nothing else for us, it helps us discover the things that are important. Real worship will transform your life."—Warren Wiersbe

WORSHIP

DESIRE	to honor and adore the Trinity as the supreme treasure of life
DEFINITION	Worship happens whenever we intentionally cherish God and value him above all else in life. Worship reveals what is important to us.

SCRIPTURE	"You are worthy, our Lord and God,
	    to receive glory and honor and power,
	for you created all things,
	    and by your will they were created
	    and have their being." (Revelation 4:11)
	
	"Worship the Lord your God, and serve him only." (Matthew 4:10)
	
	"God is Spirit, and his worshipers must worship in spirit and in truth." (John 4:24)
	
	"Therefore, since we are receiving a kingdom that cannot be shaken, let us be thankful, and so worship God acceptably with reverence and awe, for our 'God is a consuming fire.' " (Hebrews 12:28-29)

PRACTICE INCLUDES	• focusing on and responding to God with your whole being • offering my body as a "spiritual act of worship" (Romans 12:1) • responding to God's truth with loving obedience • regularly engaging with a worshiping community • seeking first the kingdom of God, keeping secondary things second
GOD-GIVEN FRUIT	• keeping company with Jesus no matter what happens • fulfilling your God-given longing to adore and praise your Creator • meeting God and bringing him pleasure • filling your mind and heart with the wonder and mystery of God • joining the company of saints in heaven and on earth who continually magnify the Lord • delighting in the Lord and living out of gratitude • doing your part in growing your relationship with God • growing in faith, hope and love by basking in the presence of God • focusing on God so you taste more of his goodness and worthiness • loving God and enjoying him forever

WORSHIP

WORSHIP IS A WORD MOST OFTEN ASSOCIATED WITH RELIGION. But worship can be found in the lives of secularists, agnostics and even atheists. The simple truth is that everybody looks to something or someone to give their lives meaning. Worship reveals the somethings or someones we value most. What we love and adore and focus on forms us into the people we become. Some of us highly value our independence. Others pour our time and energy into totems of power, approval, success, control or happiness. We may not consider our obsession with these things acts of worship, but they are. They are what we look to, to get us up in the morning and keep us going throughout the day.

True worship does not equal going to church on Sunday. This is not a particularly new thought. Jesus knew people could attend the synagogue while focusing on the closing of their business deal on Monday or the new house addition on Tuesday. He put it simply: "These people honor me with their lips, / but their hearts are far from me" (Matthew 15:8). Worship can be offered in the power of the self rather than in response to the Spirit.

True worship of God happens when we put God first in our lives. When what God says matters more than what others say, and when loving God matters more than being loved. Discipline, willpower, giftedness and going to church can be good things. But they do not guarantee transformation. Transformation comes through valuing God above all else. Jesus knew people could do the same things he did: they could heal and perform miracles and preach—but that did not mean that they loved and worshiped God.

His words are devastatingly clear: "Many will say to me on that day, 'Lord, Lord, did we not prophesy in your name, and in your name drive out demons and perform many miracles?' Then I will tell them plainly. 'I never knew you' " (Matthew 7:22-23).

The heart of worship is to seek to know and love God in our own unique way. Each one of us fulfills some part of the divine image. Each one of us loves and glorifies God in a particular way that no one else can. It should not surprise us then that worship styles and tastes differ: traditional, contemporary, liturgical, folk, emerging. One style of worship is not better than another. The quality of worship emerges from the heart and its focus.

Worship can touch our deepest feelings. But that is not the litmus test for worship. Feelings can come and go. But the joyous Trinity remains forever worthy. In light of the Trinity's beauty and loveliness everything else on the horizon of our attention takes its proper secondary place. Above and before all other good things remains the Pearl of great price, the King of all kings, and the Lord of all lords.

REFLECTION QUESTIONS

1. How did a particular style of worship—charismatic, traditional, contemporary, liturgical—shape you and your image of God?

2. How does a particular form or style of worship shape you now?

3. Who is God to you?

   What name for God—Shepherd, Lord, Father, Day Spring, Bread of Life—best describes your relationship with him right now?

   What does this name mean to you?

   See the "Names for Worshiping God" appendix for a catalog of names for God.

4. How does worshiping alone and worshiping with others affect you?

5. What about God moves you to worship?

SPIRITUAL EXERCISES

1. Consider the many names God uses to reveal himself to us (see the names for worshiping God found in appendix 5). Which of these names identifies where God is in your life now? • Talk to God about what this revelation of who he is means to you. Use this name when you pray.

2. Since God reveals himself to us in worship, visit a worship service with a different tradition or style than you are used to. Attend an ethnic service or a children's service if you wish. Ask God to open you up to seeing him in new ways. What do you sense about the worshipers? Do you see anything new about God in their worship?

3. Think of the times you have been deeply moved in worship. What was happening in your life at that time? • What was going on in worship? • Put yourself in places where you most easily connect with God in worship.

4. Write a letter or song to God expressing your love and honor of him.

5. Come before God with an open and listening ear. Write the question, "What do I value most?" at the top of a sheet of paper. Answer the question. • Then answer this question from the viewpoint of your kids, your spouse, your colleagues, family members, church friends and God. What do you see about yourself through their eyes? • How might what you worship need to change?

Resources on Worship

Streams of Living Water by Richard Foster

The Dynamics of Spiritual Formation, chapter 6, by Mel Lawrenz

Part Two

OPEN MYSELF TO GOD

NOTICING WHEN SOMEONE SHOWS UP FOR US is an important part of developing a relationship. But the truth is we can become so preoccupied with all we have to do that we look right through people and neglect even those we love. Being open and present for others doesn't happen automatically. It requires intention and desire. If we cannot develop human relationships on the fly, we cannot expect to develop the divine friendship without intent and desire.

Intentionally learning to notice when God shows up is a huge part of the spiritual journey. After all, we cannot open ourselves to someone we do not notice. The *O* spiritual disciplines help us pay attention to our lives and God's activity within them. They *open* us to truths about ourselves. And inevitably one truth leads to another and another. The more we tell God the truth about ourselves, the more authentic our relationship with the Trinity can be.

The "opening" disciplines specifically address how to make space in a crowded life to notice the movements of the Spirit of God. They can take us into deep places of knowing how we are accepted, received and lovingly known by God. And it is receiving this love that moves us to worship.

"The greatest of all illusions is the illusion of familiarity."—G. K. Chesterton

CONTEMPLATION

DESIRE	to wake up to the presence of God in all things
DEFINITION	"Contemplation is about waking up. To be contemplative is to experience an event fully, in all its aspects." (Ronald Rolheiser in *The Shattered Lantern*)
SCRIPTURE	"So we fix our eyes not on what is seen, but on what is unseen. For what is seen is temporary, but what is unseen is eternal." (2 Corinthians 4:18) "Now the Lord is the Spirit, and where the Spirit of the Lord is, there is freedom. And we, who with unveiled faces all reflect the Lord's glory, are being transformed into his likeness with ever-increasing glory, which comes from the Lord, who is the Spirit." (2 Corinthians 3:17-18) "God did this so that men would seek him and perhaps reach out for him and find him, though he is not far from each one of us. 'For in him we live and move and have our being.' As some of your own poets have said. 'We are his offspring.' " (Acts 17:27-28)
PRACTICE INCLUDES	• practicing the presence of God • breath prayer, simple prayer, prayer of the heart • taking time to truly see and gaze on life, others, arts and so forth • refusing the compulsion to go everywhere, see everything and try out all that is novel • reflecting on experiences so as to benefit from their happening • sensitivity and obedience to God's revelation • savoring the symbolic nature of life and faith • noticing how symbols can give meaning to particular actions
GOD-GIVEN FRUIT	• keeping company with Jesus all the time • freedom from a preoccupation with self that keeps you from focusing on others • living the tensions of life reflectively rather than avoiding them • relishing your humanness and the beauty of each of your brothers and sisters • seeing there is more to life than efficiency and productivity • being patient with life • being, not just doing • developing an awareness of the richness of the interior life • knowing through faith, hope and love, not just the mind

CONTEMPLATION

WE ARE HASTY PEOPLE BENT ON EXPERIENCING as much of life as we can. The faster we move, the more we can see, do and produce. The more we network, the more options will be ours. The more options, the more living we can do. For many of us the very notion of slowing down or saying no to an option is repugnant. We crowd our schedules and run late, but at least we are getting our money's worth. No wonder contemplation has fallen on hard times. In a world where people anchor their identity on the shifting seas of performance and accomplishments, contemplation seems inefficient and too unproductive for the daily grind.

But it is contemplation, not just having experiences, that truly opens us wide to life. Experiences can be lost to us in the mad rush to simply accumulate more. Contemplation invites us to enter in to the moment with a heart alive to whatever might happen. It is not just thinking about or analyzing an event or person. Contemplation asks us to see with faith, hope and love. It asks us to seek God and the "meanings" threaded through our days and years, so that our experience of being embedded in the triune life of God deepens and grows.

A contemplative person recognizes that every experience offers more than meets the eye. They know that "bidden or unbidden, God is present." Consequently contemplatives are open to seeing the unseen world. They sift the days for symbols and scan the sunsets for meaning. They enter into the being of life, alert to transcendencies in ordinary things. They believe God may be found and reverenced if one is prepared to notice how marvelously mysterious and personal life in this world is. So contemplatives invite us into the moment and tell us to *be*.

A. W. Tozer writes in *The Roots of Righteousness*, "Historically the West has tended to throw its chief emphasis upon doing and the East upon being. . . . Were human nature perfect there would be no discrepancy between being and doing. The unfallen man would simply live from within, without giving it a thought. His actions would be the true expression of their inner being." But being is not rewarded in our society today. Doing is what counts.

Doing is important. But eventually we come to the end of doing. Tasks get done sooner or later. Experiences end for better or for worse. But we never come to the end of a "being." Being is a mystery that originated in the God who says, "I AM WHO I AM." Knowing God or another human being completely will always be beyond what we can know. But through contemplation, intimacy with God and others can grow. Gazing on God, our neighbor or the created order with faith, hope and love can increase our awareness and experience of both. Contemplation can lead us out of ourselves and into realities of which we only skimmed the surface before.

REFLECTION QUESTIONS

1. How do you respond to the word *contemplation*?

2. What sort of things do you contemplate? What happens to you when you contemplate?

3. How do you contemplate your spiritual journey and relationship with God?

SPIRITUAL EXERCISES

1. Contemplate Jesus. Intentionally place yourself in the presence of God. Become quiet. • Express to God your intention to rest in his love. Use your imagination: you may want to picture yourself leaning on Jesus' breast as John did or sitting at Jesus' feet as Mary did or kneeling before Jesus as other desperate people before you have. Be with Jesus. (When thoughts and distractions interrupt, gently return to Jesus. Begin again and again.) • What is it like to receive God's gift of new beginnings?

2. Palms down, palms up.

   • Sit comfortably with both feet on the floor and your hands on your lap. Breathe deeply and relax. Intentionally place yourself in the presence of Jesus.

   • Turn your palms down and begin to drop your cares, worries, agendas and expectations into Jesus' hands. Let go of all that is heavy or burdensome. Relax. Breathe deeply.

   • When you have given your cares to Jesus, turn your palms up on your knees. Open your hands to receive God's presence, word and love. Listen.

   • When you feel prompted to end, tell the Lord what it is like for you to simply be with him.

3. Take a contemplative walk with Jesus. Express your intention to be alone with God. • Enjoy moving your body. Smell the air. Take in the sights. Appreciate God's good handiwork within and without. • Love God for his gifts and goodness to you.

4. Contemplate people. Set aside time to really look into the eyes of those you love. Listen with your heart. See them through the eyes of God. • Be with them over a meal. • If you like to journal, write down what you think you know as well as what is mysterious to you about them.

5. Contemplate your experience. Commit yourself to remaining present to an experience. Pay attention to any feelings that rise within you. You may feel heat in your body.

You may notice impatience, embarrassment or a need to hide or defend. • Attend to others and what is happening for or in them. • When you leave the experience, spend some unhurried time reflecting on what you noticed. Where did you respond out of past wounds? • What did this experience symbolize for you? What gave it meaning?

Resources on Contemplation

The Cloud of Unknowing edited by William Johnson
The Shattered Lantern by Ronald Rolheiser
Becoming Christ by Brian C. Taylor

"The examen makes us aware of moments that at first we might easily pass by as insignificant, moments that ultimately can give direction for our lives."—Dennis Linn

EXAMEN

DESIRE	to notice both God and my God-given desires throughout the day
DEFINITION	The examen is a practice for discerning the voice and activity of God within the flow of the day. It is a vehicle that creates deeper awareness of God-given desires in one's life.
SCRIPTURE	"For this reason, since the day we heard about you, we have not stopped praying for you and asking God to fill you with the knowledge of his will through all spiritual wisdom and understanding." (Colossians 1:9) "And this is my prayer: that your love may abound more and more in knowledge and depth of insight, so that you may be able to discern what is best and may be pure and blameless until the day of Christ, filled with the fruit of righteousness that comes through Jesus Christ—to the glory and praise of God." (Philippians 1:9-10)
PRACTICE INCLUDES	a regular time of coming into the presence of God to ask two questions (possible ways of asking the questions are below) • For what moment today am I most grateful? For what moment today am I least grateful? • When did I give and receive the most love today? When did I give and receive the least love today? • What was the most life-giving part of my day? What was the most life-thwarting part of my day? • When today did I have the deepest sense of connection with God, others and myself? When today did I have the least sense of connection? • Where was I aware of living out of the fruit of the Spirit? Where was there an absence of the fruit of the Spirit? • Where did I experience "desolation"? Where did I find "consolation"?
GOD-GIVEN FRUIT	• keeping company with Jesus throughout all the highs and lows of the day • recognizing God's presence in your experiences • developing more discernment and receptivity to God's voice • freedom from "acting the guru"; pointing others toward listening to God, not to me • fostering gratitude • being aware of your growing edges • being aware of God-given desires • being aware of invitations to prayer that God presents to you throughout the day

Examen

THROUGHOUT THE CENTURIES PRAYERFUL PEOPLE have found direction for their lives through the practice of the examen (also known as the "examination of consciousness"). The examen provides a way of noticing where God shows up in our day. It is a practice that attends to what we might otherwise miss in the press of duties and busyness. The questions of the examen open our attention to how God's internal movement is present in our external comings and goings. They lead us to listen deeply to the data of our lives. These questions help us pay attention to our mental state, our body responses and our emotional baggage. Our insomnia, nervous stomach, difficult interaction and headache can all take their place as a possible way of more deeply leaning into God. The examen helps us recognize the things that bring us death and life. Once these things are known, they become part of our ongoing interaction with God in prayer.

The examen can open us to both the difficult and beautiful in our lives, relationships and profession. The examen is also a useful way of reflecting alone or with others on what God is saying to us through a meeting, a class, a meal, a service project, a relationship or a conflict.

Examen questions include

- For what moment today am I most grateful? For what moment today am I least grateful?

- When did I give and receive the most love today? When did I give and receive the least love today?

- What was the most life-giving part of my day? What was the most life-thwarting part of my day?

- When today did I have the deepest sense of connection with God, others and myself? When today did I have the least sense of connection?

- Where was I aware of living out of the fruit of the Spirit? Where was there an absence of the fruit of the Spirit?

The examen is a wonderful tool for discerning the places you feel most alive, most grateful, most present to the fruit of the Spirit as well as the times and places where you do not. Those with melancholic tendencies may find that while the day's low points stand out clearly, they need the examen to help them recognize the life-giving moments the Spirit brings during the day. Those naturally inclined to optimism need the examen to help them name the difficult things in life. The examen invites attention to both low and high points, recognizing both of these as an invitation to prayer.

Perspective and direction for the future happen through listening to where and how God shows up in your day and then interacting with God in prayer. Awareness of the Spirit's enlivening and enlightening presence puts you in touch with the kind of person God created you to be. When you begin to recognize who God created you to be, you have the raw material for discerning God's unique call and design for your life.

REFLECTION QUESTIONS

1. How do you tend to recognize God's presence in your day?

   How do you respond to God's presence?

2. How does the presence of the fruit of the Spirit in your life reveal God's presence and his will?

3. What has God been doing in your life in the past six months?

   What themes are emerging, and how will you attend to them?

SPIRITUAL EXERCISES

1. Gather together the threads of your daily encounters and activities. Attending to them one at a time, ask yourself some of the examen questions:

   • Where did I give or receive love in this activity or interaction? How did I withhold love in this activity or interaction?

   • What activity gave me the greatest high? Which one made me feel low?

   Reflect on where God was in the highs and lows of the day. How is God inviting you to pray about these things before you nestle into his arms and fall asleep?

2. Make a list of feeling words. For example: *accepted, anxious, apathetic, confused, defeated, disgusted, ecstatic, enraged, paranoid, weepy, undecided.* Then begin to ask yourself the examen questions. Let these words help you articulate what drains or saps you and what gives you life. Let this knowing inform your choices.

3. Light a candle and become still in the presence of Christ. • Place your hand on your heart and ask the Holy Spirit to bring to mind the moment of the day you are most grateful for. When were you most able to give and receive love? • Talk to God about what it was like for you to be in that moment. What made it important to you? • Breathe in your gratitude to God. Journal your gratitude to God. • What have you learned about yourself in this?

4. Find a quiet moment to reflect on your day or week. Open your palms and ask the Holy

Spirit to show you the moment for which you are least grateful. What made that moment difficult? • Be with your feelings; don't try to change them or make them acceptable. Offer them up to God. Talk to him about them. • Where was God in this moment? You may want to thank God that he is always ready to be with you and talk to you.

5. Look back over the past year. List the things that brought you life and the times you were able to truly give and receive love. • Make another list of the life-thwarting moments. • What do you discover about yourself? How can this self-awareness help you choose a healthier, God-directed life?

6. Teach your children the practice of finding God in their daily life. You can teach the examen by playing "I spy God." At the dinner table invite your children to tell you where they have spied God in their day.

Resources for Examen

Sleeping with Bread by Dennis Linn, Sheila Fabricant Linn and Matthew Linn
The God Hunt by Karen Mains

"The meaning of earthly existence is not, as we have grown used to thinking, in prosperity, but in the development of the soul."—Alexander Solzhenitsyn

JOURNALING

DESIRE	to be alert to my life through writing and reflecting on God's presence and activity in, around and through me
DEFINITION	Journaling is a tool for reflecting on God's presence, guidance and nurture in daily comings and goings. Journals can be kept regularly or during time of transitions.

SCRIPTURE	"I will praise the LORD, who counsels me;
	    even at night my heart instructs me." (Psalm 16:7)
	
	"Show me your ways, O LORD,
	    teach me your paths." (Psalm 25:4)
	
	"What's God going to say to my questions? I'm braced for the worst. I'll climb to the lookout tower and scan the horizon.
	    I'll wait to see what God says,
	    how he'll answer my complaint." (Habakkuk 2:1 *The Message*)
	
	"Do not let this Book of the Law depart from your mouth; meditate on it day and night, so that you may be careful to do everything written in it." (Joshua 1:8)
	
	"Open my eyes that I may see
	    wonderful things in your law." (Psalm 119:18)

PRACTICE INCLUDES	• keeping a written record of God's ways in your life; journals can include a collection of clippings, drawings, collage, articles, poems, quotes and so forth • journaling daily or weekly or during significant events and transitions • making journals and scrapbooks for children or others • recording external or internal journeys—or both • telling your "exodus" story in a journal • recording prayers, prayer requests, answers to prayers and responses to God in all of this
GOD-GIVEN FRUIT	• keeping company with Jesus through reflective journaling • listening to God and praying your life • slowing down and reflecting on where God shows up in ordinary routines • remembering God's faithfulness throughout your journey • leaving a legacy for others • awareness of God's way of turning all things for the good of those who love him (Romans 8:28) • awareness of phases and stages of your personal pilgrimage

JOURNALING

IN A CONSUMER SOCIETY IT'S EASY TO accumulate experiences, believing the more we have the better! Yet experiences don't necessarily bring wisdom, nor do they automatically transform us. We need to listen and reflect on our experiences in the presence of the Holy Spirit to learn from them. Journaling is a way of paying attention to our lives—a way of knitting the vast ball of our experiences into something with shape that attests to the state of our soul. Fredrick Buechner reminds us in *Listening to Your Life* that "there is no chance thing through which God cannot speak." On the pages of a journal, in the privacy of a moment, we can take tentative steps into truth and scour our feelings, hurts, ideas and struggles before God. Over time repetitious themes, sins, compulsions, hopes and concerns emerge. We begin to recognize our besetting sins, limitations and desires. During times of transition, travel, loss, joy, illness and decision making, journaling can provide a way of processing the hopes, fears, longings, angers and prayers of our heart. It can be the place we sound off before God so we don't sound off in an inappropriate way to others.

The ongoing nature of a journal catalogs the journey of a soul into God. It reveals how we hammer out our identity as a Christ-follower through the ups and downs of daily routines as well as in times of crisis. There is no right way to journal. You don't need to journal every day or even every week. Find the rhythm of journaling that suits your phase and stage of life. If writing isn't your thing, make a journal of photos or drawings or articles. Assign key words or thoughts or themes to the entries. If you don't write well, remember that you don't need to write beautifully or use complete sentences. Journaling is a way for you to be with God and your thoughts, not an exercise in language arts. Tell the truth to God and yourself as best you can. Review what you write on a regular basis. As you do, you will begin to recognize recurring life themes, desires, frustrations and patterns of interaction. These insights become matters for dialogue with God.

REFLECTION QUESTIONS

1. If you live your life at full tilt, when and how do you reflect on your life and your experiences?

2. How does writing help you focus or know what you think?

3. If writing is not a medium you enjoy, what other ways might you process and reflect on your experiences in the presence of God?

4. What is it like for you to read someone else's published journal?

5. How does the thought of someone reading your journal strike you?

SPIRITUAL EXERCISES

1. As you read magazines and newspapers, cut out articles or photos that touch your heart. Paste them in your journal. Use these clippings to help you pray and join in God's care for the world.

2. Develop a journal for quotes, poetry and Scripture that have touched you. Reflect on these words and their significance to you.

3. If you enjoy art, create a collage journal. Express your thoughts and feelings to God through pictures, textures and colors.

4. Keep a prayer journal: record requests, prayers, answered prayers.

5. Make a journal for a child, a parent or a friend, recording some significant event and your prayers for them.

6. Use your journal as a place for your unedited thoughts, feelings and reactions. • Out of this overflow ask the Holy Spirit to form a godly response in you. Write the response you hear from God. • Ask for grace to live out of this graced place.

7. It can be helpful to divide your journal into particular sections that reflect

   • your journey with God
   • events of the day
   • prayers for the world
   • prayers for those you love
   • desires of your heart

Resources on Journaling

An Ordinary Day with Jesus by John Ortberg and Ruth Barton
Spiritual Disciplines for the Christian Life by Donald S. Whitney

"Several times during the day, . . . ask yourself for a moment if you have your soul in your hands or if some passion or fit of anxiety has robbed you of it. . . . Quietly bring your soul back to the presence of God, subjecting all your affections and desires to the obedience and direction of his divine will."
—St. Francis de Sales

PRACTICING THE PRESENCE

DESIRE	to develop a continual openness and awareness of Christ's presence living in me
DEFINITION	Practicing the presence is an invitation to see and experience every moment as a gift of God. It is to live alive to union with the Trinity.
SCRIPTURE	"Your new life, which is your real life—even though invisible to spectators—is with Christ in God. He is your life. When Christ (your real life, remember) shows up again on this earth, you'll show up, too—the real you, the glorious you. Meanwhile, be content with obscurity, like Christ." (Colossians 3:3-4 *The Message*) "The word is very near you; it is in your mouth and in your heart so you may obey it." (Deuteronomy 30:14) "You have your heads in your Bibles constantly because you think you'll find eternal life there. But you miss the forest for the trees. These Scriptures are all about me! And here I am, standing right before you, and you aren't willing to receive from me the life you say you want." (John 5:39-40 *The Message*)
PRACTICE INCLUDES	• developing a rhythm of living that brings God to mind throughout the day • intentionally recollecting yourself before God as you engage in the activities and duties of life • seeking to see others through the eyes of God • stopping throughout the day to listen to God • carrying or placing symbols in your office and home that remind you of Christ's presence • using breath prayer, centering prayer
GOD-GIVEN FRUIT	• keeping company with Jesus all day long • having a deeper union with Christ • living a new way of *being* by letting go of your need to manipulate, compete and control • living as though the present moment has no competition • receiving each moment as sacred • abiding in Christ so that you see him in those who drain, irritate and anger • seeing yourself through God's eyes rather than the eyes of others • finding Christ as your joy, sorrow, emptiness and fullness • remaining open and teachable at all moments • growing in awareness of your constant need of God

PRACTICING THE PRESENCE

WE ALL LIVE OUR LIVES IN THE PRESENCE OF GOD. In fact, we cannot *not* live our lives in the presence of God. In *Letters to Malcolm: Chiefly on Prayer,* C. S. Lewis wrote, "We may ignore, but we can nowhere evade, the presence of God. The world is crowded with Him. He walks everywhere incognito." Yet we become so preoccupied with the to-do list and so overwhelmed by the pace of life that we forget to look for God sightings in our day.

In her book *The God Hunt,* Karen Mains suggests that practicing the presence is like going on a "God hunt." It is a way we keep our soul awake to God. And God can jump out at us any time at all and say, "Boo. Here I am." The question is—are we paying attention?

The discipline of practicing the presence is often attached to the seventeenth-century French monk Brother Lawrence. He longed to maintain an ongoing conversation with God no matter what he was doing. In *The Practice of the Presence of God* he said:

> I make it my business to rest in His [Christ's] holy presence which I keep myself in
> by a habitual, silent, and secret conversation with God. This often causes in me joys
> and raptures inwardly, and sometimes also outwardly, so great that I am forced to
> use means to moderate them, and prevent their appearance to others.

Practicing the presence is a way of living into a deeper awareness of God's activity in our lives. Through many small pauses we begin a habit of turning our heart toward God. Through these acts of attention we express our intention to live in union with Christ. Before we pick up the phone we might say, "Lord I am here. Help me listen." As concerns cross our desk we might hold up a hand and turn the concern over to God before we move on. Breath prayer and the Jesus prayer are other ways of staying present to God in the moment. However, it is important to remember that practicing the presence is more about personal relationship than strategy. Practicing the presence of Christ is simply a way we love him and stay connected to him throughout the day.

REFLECTION QUESTIONS

1. Where do your thoughts go when they aren't focused on work or diverted by amusement?

   What do these thoughts reveal about your concerns and priorities?

2. How aware are you of the possibility of meeting God during your work day?

3. What is it like for you when God shows up at an unexpected moment?

4. How easy is it for God to get your attention?

   When are you best able to hear God's still, small voice?

4. What would it look like for you to intentionally seek deeper intimacy with God?

SPIRITUAL EXERCISES

1. Dedicate some task you are doing to the Lord. Talk to him about the task before you begin and again when you are done. • Do you become any more aware of God in the process? How?

2. Offer all of yourself to God for the day ahead. • Throughout the day ask yourself if you are still living your intention to be in God's presence. • Do not be discouraged when you stray from your intention to live in his presence; simply begin again. God loves for you to turn your heart back to him.

3. When a song comes to mind during the day, pay attention to it. Could this song be a word of God to you? If it is, tell God what it means to you to have him come near you in this way.

4. Practice the presence in interruptions. The intention to live in the presence of Christ is a way of saying, "I am here." Throughout your day—perhaps every time you are interrupted—tell God "I am here." Remind yourself that you are in the presence of Jesus, who had time for people who questioned and interrupted. Remember that some of Jesus' most gracious miracles occurred when he was interrupted. • What is it like for you to offer yourself to be present to God during interruptions?

5. Spend some time talking to someone who has lived their life attending to the fixed hours of prayer. What can you discover from them about living in a rhythm of prayer that draws you into the presence of Jesus?

6. Decide to stop several times throughout your day to pay attention to God and practice his presence. Set a clock to remind you. Spend five minutes reading Scripture, praying or just being with Jesus. • What is this like for you?

7. Develop some prayers that help you stay awake to God. For instance, find a verse or prayer that is your waking prayer, your in-the-shower prayer, your dressing prayer, your cooking prayer, your driving prayer and so on. Let these prayers lead you into deeper encounters with the God who is there.

Resources on Practicing the Presence

The God Hunt by Karen Mains
Invitation to Presence by Wendy Miller
Living Presence by Tilden Edwards
Practicing the Presence by Brother Lawrence

"People in a hurry never have time for recovery. Their minds have little time to meditate and pray so that problems can be put in perspective. In short, people in our age are showing signs of physiological disintegration because we are living at a pace that is too fast for our bodies."—Archibald Hart

REST

DESIRE	to honor God and my human limitations through restful rhythms
DEFINITION	Entering into rest depends on honoring our God-given limits. By paying attention to the physical, mental and spiritual needs of the body, we learn when and how to rest.

SCRIPTURE	"My soul finds rest in God alone." (Psalm 62:1)
	
	"Let the beloved of the LORD rest secure in him,
	    for he shields him all day long,
	    and the one the LORD loves rests between his shoulders."
	    (Deuteronomy 33:12)
	
	"Be at rest once more, O my soul,
	    for the LORD has been good to you." (Psalm 116:7)

PRACTICE INCLUDES	• setting aside unhurried time to rest and be refreshed rather than work • restful activities: curling up by the fireplace, walking on the beach, taking a catnap, calling your parents, talking to your kids, making love to your spouse, going on a picnic • setting margins in the day for moments of recollection and rest • taking vacations and days off • refraining from activities that drain: doing taxes, cleaning closets and so on • develop an intentional rhythm of rest and work in your life
GOD-GIVEN FRUIT	• keeping company with Jesus by curbing your addictions to busy-ness, rush and hurry • freedom from the compulsion to take your identity from what you do • honoring the way God created you by living a healthy and intentionally rested life • resting every day, every week, every month and every year of your life • taking regular retreats for silence and time alone with God • take time to delight in God, family, the seasons, meals and all good gifts of creation

REST

OUR CULTURE ACCEPTS THAT SLEEP DEPRIVATION and running on empty are norms. Living full throttle is expected. The ticking of the second hand defines our pace. And God's rhythms of rest and work give way to a nearly permanent state of exhaustion and impending burnout. You don't need to look far to see how workaholism is compromising our health as well as our relationships. Lack of adequate rest can ruin our families, damage our souls, even kill us.

When we burn the candle at both ends we

- lose sight of what we enjoy in our work
- find even the things we enjoy doing become a chore
- fail to give people the gift of our attention and presence
- impair our ability to hear God's voice and discern his movement in our lives
- become obsessive about the to-do list
- lose touch with the human limits that are meant to keep us in touch with God

Clearly, we were not made to work 24/7. We have limits. There is a finiteness to our time and energy. And to live as though there isn't is destructive as well as delusional. It can be hard to tell the truth about our human capacity and limits because few of us want to accept the losses that come with this truth. We can't say yes to everything. We can't go everywhere and see everyone. We can't have it all. We aren't indispensable. We are finite beings who need rest. And that is not a bad thing. It is a Godlike thing.

God created us in his image. He is a God who works and then rests. When we rest we honor the way God made us. Rest can be a spiritual act—a truly human act of submission to and dependence on God who watches over all things as we rest.

What is your alternative to work? Is it rest, or is it a different kind of work: work around the house or in the yard? Is doing finances, cleaning a closet or working out your alternative to work? Can you ever stop producing and let down? Honestly, where does rest fit in? Rest is a radical thing in our day and age. It reminds us that we are human beings, not human doings. We are meant to live sane lives that partake of a deep and playful holy leisure. There is enough time in each day for all that God requires of us. And part of what he requires is rest. So settle in and breathe deeply of his gift of rest.

REFLECTION QUESTIONS

1. What exhausts you or keeps you working past your limits?

2. When and where do you most deeply rest?

   Who helps you rest?

3. What is it like for you to set aside time to play?

   How regular and inviolable is that time?

SPIRITUAL EXERCISES

1. Write down what a perfect day of rest and recreation would look like to you. • Is it within the realm of possibility? Plan when you can take this day or a version of it. Schedule it on your calendar.

2. Intentionally place yourself in the presence of God, then do something you delight in: go for a walk, take a nap, talk to a friend, have a cup of coffee, play a game. Enjoy yourself in God. Receive the gift of rest. • Tell God what happens in you as you try to rest.

3. Consider whether or not your tiredness is about body or soul. • What kind of rest would refresh your body: exercise, a nap, going to bed early? • What kind of rest would refresh your soul: retreat, sleep, music, reading, centering prayer? • Choose two times this week when you will intentionally enter into rest for body and soul.

4. Think about your childhood experience of play. What was it like for you? • How does your past experience affect your ability to play today? • What is fun for you right now? Plan some time for play and fun into your week.

Resources on Rest

Adrenalin and Stress by Archibald Hart
Receiving the Day by Dorothy Bass

"Spiritual disciplines are means to prevent everything in your life from being filled up. It means somewhere you're not occupied and you're certainly not preoccupied. It means to create that space in which something can happen that you hadn't planned on or counted on."—Henri Nouwen

RETREAT

DESIRE	to make space in my life for God alone
DEFINITION	Retreats are specific and regular times apart for quietly listening to God and delighting in his company. Retreats remove us from the daily battle into times of refreshing, retooling, renewing and unwinding.

SCRIPTURE	"Then, because so many people were coming and going that they did not even have a chance to eat, he said to them, 'Come with me by yourselves to a quiet place and get some rest.' " (Mark 6:31)
	
	"Be still, and know that I am God." (Psalm 46:10)
	
	"Be silent before the Sovereign LORD,
	    for the day of the LORD is near." (Zephaniah 1:7)
	
	  "He makes me lie down in green pastures,
	he leads me beside quiet waters,
	  he restores my soul." (Psalm 23:2-3)

PRACTICE INCLUDES	• having short times apart as well as extended times away with God • detaching from productivity and doing in order to be in the presence of God and attend to his voice alone • having longer retreats of two to forty days • spending time in a hermitage • spending one day a month at a retreat site for time with God • having seasonal retreats for rest and renewal • withdrawing from life in order to see where your soul is in danger, to seek God's help in reengaging in the battle
GOD-GIVEN FRUIT	• in the company of Jesus, being able to quiet the noise inside and out • making space in your hectic schedule for the Lover of your soul • developing the ability to hear the still, small voice of God • freedom from the need to be seen and to produce • resting in God • gaining perspective on God's work and ways in your soul • ability to *be,* not just *do*

Retreat

In Ephesians 6:12 Paul describes the spiritual life as a struggle "not against flesh and blood, but against the rulers, against the authorities, against the powers of this dark world and against the spiritual forces of evil in the heavenly realms." The early church and desert fathers paid close attention to the dangerous battle for the soul. John Cassian writes at the end of the fourth century in his *Conferences* 6:

> But you must know that our battles are not all fought in the same order, because, as we mentioned that the attacks are not always made on us in the same way, each one of us ought also to begin the battle with due regard to the character of the attack which is especially made on him so that one man will have to fight his first battle against the fault which stands third on the list, another against that which is fourth or fifth.

Historically one way Christians persevered in the battle was to regularly retreat from the front lines of attack and spend solitary time with God. Times of retreat brought perspective to the mind while strengthening and nourishing the soul. Without retreat, followers of Jesus tired and became ineffective in the struggle. They needed to be alone with God and apart from others if they wanted to reengage the battle on different ground.

The tradition of retreating was still in good stead in the fifteenth century. At that time Europe had thirteen hundred Franciscan hermitages. But as the modern era has gained speed the habit of retreating has fallen out of the practice of many believers.

Rather than going on retreats that slow us down to listen and focus on God alone, we go on "retreats" filled with lectures, late nights, constant activity and interaction with all kinds of people. This sort of retreating is not a bad thing. It is simply not a retreat from the busyness and distractions of life. It is not time set apart with God alone.

Retreating, in the traditional sense, is not about gaining more information. It is not getting away to get things done. It is not a way to catch up on our reading or e-mail. Retreats are ways we pull back from the battle and rest. We take naps and go to bed early. In the presence of the holy One we enter into the silence and solitude and rest in God.

Resting gives us the energy it takes to build our relationship with God one on one. When we are rested, we listen better. When we are rested, we notice desires as well as lies buried in our souls.

We may feel that nothing really big or noteworthy happened on our retreat. The benefits of retreating often are not seen until we engage the battle again. Go away and trust God with what happens in your soul.

Retreat centers can be found in all parts of the country. Some retreat centers offer spiritual direction to their guests. If you would like the guidance of a spiritual director, check out this possibility while you are on retreat.

REFLECTION QUESTIONS

1. What makes it difficult for you to get away with God?

2. Can you describe your desire to get away alone with God?

   What is your soul aching for?

3. When you go on retreat, what do you tend to do?

4. How does simply *being* with God sound to you?

5. How do *doing* and *being* fit together in your spiritual journey?

6. How might retreating with God address some dangers that surround your soul?

SPIRITUAL EXERCISES

1. Find a retreat center near you and spend a day away with God. (Check the Web or Yellow Pages. Call a Catholic church and ask where they go on retreat.) Take a Bible and no other reading material. Take a journal along if journaling appeals to you. Enter the quietness. Rest into God. Sleep. Attend to Scripture. Do not hurry. Listen.

2. If you don't want to go to a retreat center, plan a day outside or in some other quiet setting where you can spend time with the Lord. Take only your Bible with you. • When your day is over, bring some small memento (a rock, a twig, a photograph) of your time with God. Let your retreat object remind you of your time with God.

3. Once a month or once a season set aside a day for retreat. Reflect on how you have seen God's presence in your life since your last retreat. How has God been with you? • How have you grown to love him? • Has God nudged you into some particular discussion about this time?

4. Celebrate your birthday by making a retreat. Spend some quality time with the God who made you and called you into being alive right now. • What is it like for you to know your time here on earth was appointed? That you are here with a purpose and a mission? • Listen; what is God telling you about your life and your calling for the next year?

5. As you become comfortable with silent retreats, consider taking an extended silent retreat. Many retreat centers are set up to have guests for eight- to forty-day retreats.

Resources on Retreat

A Guide to Prayer for Ministers and Other Servants by Reuben P. Job and Norman Shawchuck
Quiet Places or *Still Waters* by Janc Rubietta
www.pastorsretreatnetwork.com

"Make ready for the Christ, whose smile—like lightning—sets free the song of everlasting glory that now sleeps, in your paper flesh—like dynamite."—Thomas Merton

"Genuine spiritual disciplines are disciplines that intrude into our lives at points where we are in bondage to something that garbles, debases, and distorts the word God speaks us forth to be." —M. Robert Mulholland

SELF-CARE

DESIRE	to value myself as my heavenly Father values me
DEFINITION	Self-care honors God through nurturing and protecting the body, mind and spirit with their limits and desires.

SCRIPTURE	"I thank you, High God—you're breathtaking!
	    Body and soul, I am marvelously made!
	    I worship in adoration—what a creation!" (Psalm 139:14
	    The Message)
	
	"You realize, don't you, that you are the temple of God, and God himself is present in you?" (1 Corinthians 3:16 *The Message*)
	
	" 'So love the Lord God with all your passion and prayer and intelligence and energy.' And . . . 'Love others as well as you love yourself.' There is no other commandment that ranks with these." (Mark 12:30-31 *The Message*)

PRACTICE INCLUDES	• living in a way that honors your body as a living temple for God's presence • exercising and eating sensibly • observing appropriate boundaries • resting and keeping the sabbath • giving and receiving love • thanking God for the way he has designed you • encouraging rather than neglecting yourself • recognizing and practicing my spiritual gifts • choosing healthy rather than unhealthy relationships
GOD-GIVEN FRUIT	• valuing yourself as Jesus values you • having a sane and proper view of yourself • practicing self-awareness rather than self-absorption • freedom from the "Messiah trap" and trying to save the world to the detriment of your health • living within limits without burnout • having a deep awareness of God's love for you • freedom from addictions that destroy your health and relationships • being comfortable in your own skin

SELF-CARE

GOD INHABITS OUR BODIES, DELIGHTING IN EVERY INCH OF US. Every eccentricity and peculiarity is received. Every longing and self-destructive habit is known. God knows us through and through and still wants to make his home inside of us. The fact that the Holy Spirit wants to abide in us is one way we know how infinitely precious and beloved we are. We are God's own prized possessions. Prized possessions are something you take care of.

Yet for some of us, taking care of our bodies seems sub-biblical. Somewhere or other we learned an acronym for *JOY* that went like this: *J*esus first, *O*thers second, *Y*ourself last. There is truth in this adage, but it can also morph into a twisted theology about human worthlessness. Human beings are never worthless. God gave his dearest and only Son to love human beings—beings he treasures and adores. One of the greatest gifts we have next to Jesus is our own selves. We are gifts of God. His Spirit lives in us. And we are to receive the divine love that takes residence in our bodies. We are to take it in and let it form us into a place of prayer.

God's love within us gives birth to more love: love of God, of others and of ourselves. Love is not a quantity we use up. It is a quality of God that grows within us, enlarging our hearts and our capacity to give and receive. Self-love is not about self-centeredness. It's about caring for the body the Holy Spirit inhabits. Self-care can be a spiritual act of worship. In Romans 12:1-2 Paul says that spiritual act of worship happens in our bodies. Spirituality doesn't happen somewhere in your head, outside the concreteness of your own body life. The spiritual life shows up in bodies that love God and our neighbor as *ourselves*. Parker Palmer writes in *Let Your Life Speak*, "Self-care is never a selfish act—it is simply good stewardship of the only gift I have, the gift I was put on earth to offer others."

When we pay attention to our bodies, they tell us truth about ourselves. By listening to them we can detect lethargy, escape strategies, energy levels, dependence on caffeine, addictions to food, compulsions to work, signs of burnout and so on. These messages are meant to be taken seriously. Self-care need not be a selfish act. Exercise, rest and nourishing food aren't meant to be luxuries but the staples of good self-care. Regular checkups, eating healthy food, spending time with friend: these habits honor the way God made us.

Respecting our bodies (including their limitations) is a way God communicates his council and will to us. Our tiredness reveals that we are not infinite beings. We need boundaries. We need rest. We need to say no as well as yes. We need to know that what we can do sometimes, we cannot do all the time.

I have found in my own journey that my body lets me know how compulsive I can be about work. My neck aches when I sit at the computer for hours on end without a break. My eyes blur as I stare at the screen. And my propensity to try to improve everything and do my best keeps me working far past sane and healthy limits. I've come to realize I can't do everything my best. I have to pick and choose what gets done best and what just gets done—so I can rest. At times I have to say "Good enough is good enough." There is nothing wrong with excellence and doing my best. But when the quest for excellence drives my body beyond its limits I have left the realm of appropriate self-care and am trying to prove something to someone—even if it's me.

The Trinity doesn't call us to overload our bodies and ignore physical symptoms of disease and distress. Rather we are called to recognize body information that can help us make good choices about how to spend our time, grow relationships and nurture our souls. (For more information on body stages and seasons see appendix 10.)

As we practice self-care we intentionally receive ourselves as God's own beloved. Receiving this love into our bodies births the ability to give love and forgiveness to ourselves and others.

REFLECTION QUESTIONS

1. God created you "very good." Thank God for making you you.

   If you have a hard time thanking God for yourself, what does this reveal about how you value being made in his image?

2. Talk to God about what it is like to receive yourself as he receives you.

3. How have you neglected caring for your health, your body, your relationships?

   How might Jesus be inviting you more deeply into some area of self-care?

4. What is experiencing burnout like for you?

   What do you do to recover?

   How has it changed the way you live?

5. How might receiving yourself as a gift from God affect your life?

6. How do you protect yourself from receiving love from God and others?

SPIRITUAL EXERCISES

1. Make a list of things you like about yourself. Thank God you for making you you.

2. Stand in front of a mirror and take a good look at your body. What does your body tell you about where you came from? What you have done in life? Your choices? • Tell God

how you react to what you see. • What places of your past still need to be received and integrated into who you are?

3. Care for yourself by planning a day you would enjoy. Choose where you want to be and who you want to be with. Celebrate the gift of the day and yourself.

4. Where in your body life do you need a new beginning? What practices and patterns that tie into food, sex, rest, work or relationships would you like to change? • How can you cooperate with God in an effort to honor your body as his temple? Who can help you in this? • When you come down hard on yourself, remember that you can begin again. Confess your harsh self-treatment and ask God for grace to receive who you are. The Christian message is about new beginnings.

5. Sit quietly in a comfortable position. Breathe slowly and notice any tightness in your body. What is your body saying to you right now? Listen to it. Don't scold it. • How would Jesus want you to care for yourself right now?

6. Keep a record of how much you sleep. Are you respecting your God-given need for rest and recreation? • As a discipline, ask God how long he wants you to sleep. Is it more or less? • Readjust your sleeping or resting patterns for a week. What is it like for you?

7. Cultivate ways of nurturing and caring for your body: bubble baths, massages, exercise, soft sheets or pillows, buying some flowers or reading an engrossing book. Spend time with your hobbies and people who bring you life. Pick up an interest you left behind. It's okay to settle into down time. Watch your favorite TV program, rent a movie, cheer on Monday night football. If you like sports, join a league, gather some friends for ultimate Frisbee, go to a road rally or the driving range.

8. If you are recovering from a divorce, the death of a loved one or a deep grief, attend a support group or a divorce recovery workshop.

9. If you suffer from seasonal affect disorder (SAD), get a UV lamp or visit a tanning salon. You will feel the warmth nurture you.

Resources on Self-Care

Alcoholics Anonymous, ALANON, divorce recovery workshops and so on.

"'Tis a gift to be simple. 'Tis a gift to be free."—Shaker song

SIMPLICITY

DESIRE	to uncomplicate and untangle my life so I can focus on what really matters
DEFINITION	Simplicity cultivates the great art of letting go. Simplicity aims at loosening inordinate attachment to owning and having. Simplicity brings freedom and with it generosity.
SCRIPTURE	"Simply let your 'Yes' be 'Yes,' and your 'No,' 'No.' " (Matthew 5:37) "Do not store up for yourselves treasures on earth, where moth and rust destroy, and where thieves break in and steal. But store up for yourselves treasures in heaven. . . . For where your treasure is, there your heart will be also." (Matthew 6:19-21) " 'One thing you lack,' [Jesus] said. 'Go, sell everything you have and give to the poor, and you will have treasure in heaven. Then come, follow me.' " (Mark 10:21) "Actually, I don't have a sense of needing anything personally. I've learned by now to be quite content whatever my circumstances. I'm just as happy with little as with much, with much as with little." (Philippians 4:11-12 *The Message*)
PRACTICE INCLUDES	• assessing the things and activities that keep life convoluted, complicated and confusing; working to simplify these things • setting priorities that flow from loving God above all else • downsizing possessions • cutting back on shopping and discretionary spending • eating simple foods • enjoying simple pleasures that require no expense • removing distractions and preoccupation with things
GOD-GIVEN FRUIT	• living an uncluttered life • becoming clearer, more distilled as a person • creating more space in your life for loving and serving God • using simple, honest speech without dissembling and double meanings • experiencing freedom from envy and entitlement • being able to let go • staking your identity in God's love, not accumulations and possessions

SIMPLICITY

AN OLD SHAKER SONG GOES " 'Tis a gift to be simple. 'Tis a gift to be free." We may agree with the sentiment, but there has never been a more complicated, cluttered, bureaucratic society than the one we live in today. In fact, the "good life" is often defined by how full, busy and complicated our lives are. Modern life is *not* simple. It is always about adding one more thing. But the more we add, the more can go wrong: one car, one set of problems; two cars, two sets. Adding the latest, the biggest and the best to our lives wreaks havoc in our souls as well as our environment.

Keeping it simple has fallen on hard times. And though we like the idea, we also like our choices. Jesus teaches us that freedom is not found in having and doing but in keeping God and his will first in our heart. "Do not store up for yourselves treasures on earth, where moth and rust destroy, and where thieves break in and steal. But store up for yourselves treasures in heaven. . . . For where your treasure is, there your heart will be also" (Matthew 6:19-21). Jesus wants us to know that we don't *need* all the things or experiences we think we do. What we really need is to keep first things first—Jesus and his kingdom. Life becomes much more simple when one thing matters most.

Throughout church history followers of Jesus have intentionally vowed to live simply. Following the example of the Lord, they have given up comfort and possessions and the clutter of life to leave larger spaces for loving God and neighbor.

Simplicity creates margins and spaces and openness in our lives. It honors the resources of our small planet. It offers us the leisure of tasting the present moment. Simplicity asks us to let go of the tangle of wants so we can receive the simple gifts of life that cannot be taken away. Sleeping, eating, walking, giving and receiving love, the benefits we take for granted, are amazing gifts. Simplicity invites us into these daily pleasures that can open us to God, who is present in them all.

Aging has always been about simplifying and letting go. Sooner or later we realize that we can't manage all the stuff and activity anymore. We have to let go. The practice of letting go and embracing simplicity is one way we prepare ourselves for what is to come. One day we all will have to let go of *everything*—even our own breath. It will be a day of utter simplicity—a day when the importance of stuff fades. Learning to live simply prepares us for our last breath while cultivating in us the freedom to truly live here and now.

REFLECTION QUESTIONS

1. In what ways are you susceptible to the entitlement mentality of our age?

2. How has the "more is better" mentality shaped you?

3. Do you envy those who have more things or more opportunities than you? Explain.

4. How much of your identity is wrapped up in what you own and where you go?

   Who are you without all these acquisitions and opportunities?

5. What is it like for you to give away things you still want and like?

6. When have you downsized? What was it like for you?

SPIRITUAL EXERCISES

1. Ask God to help you speak the simple truth. • Practice speaking simply—no double meanings or half-truths that put you in the best light. • Let this practice help you become aware of when you rationalize, deny, blame and spin.

2. Uncomplicate your life by choosing a few areas in which you wish to practice "letting go." Clean out the garage, basement, closet or attic. Go on a simple vacation. Eat more simply. • What is this like for you?

3. Intentionally limit your choices. Do you need six different kinds of breakfast cereal, hundreds of TV channels or four tennis rackets? What is it like to limit your choices? • Does it feel free, or do want and envy surface? • Talk to God about this.

4. If someone admires something of yours, give it away. Find out just how attached you are to your things. • What is that like for you?

5. If you can get where you need to go by walking rather than driving, try walking.

6. Make a catalog of all the gadgets you have in your home, from the dishwasher to the lawnmower. • Which gadgets have made you freer? • Which could you share? Which could you get rid of and not really miss?

7. Where have you complicated your life with God? • Consider what actually brings you into the presence of Christ. Spend time there.

8. Practice giving no excuses, no apologies, no spontaneous yeses. • When you are tempted to say yes, stop yourself and say, "Let me think about this for a moment. I'll call you back in ten minutes." Even ten minutes can afford you the time to consider whether you really want to say yes. • When you are tempted to apologize for something like a messy house, don't. An apology can give the impression that your house is always neat and clean. Perhaps people need to see that you do live with a certain amount of clutter and that it's OK. • When you want to make an excuse for something

like being late or eating on the run, let the excuse go. Accept yourself and the reality of your life. • No excuses, no apologies and no spontaneous yeses can actually be a step in discerning what you truly need to apologize for.

Resources on Simplicity

Simplicity by Richard Foster

"If you can't take time to do nothing, you're a slave to doing. Doing nothing is a radical, revolutionary act. It frees you from the universal slavery of our age: slavery to the clock. The clock measures doing but not being."—Peter Kreeft

SLOWING

DESIRE	to curb my addiction to busyness, hurry and workaholism; to learn to savor the moment
DEFINITION	Slowing is one way to overcome inner hurriedness and addiction to busyness. Through slowing, the sacrament of the present moment is tasted to the full.
SCRIPTURE	"Then, because so many people were coming and going that they did not even have a chance to eat, he said to them, 'Come with me by yourselves to a quiet place and get some rest.'" (Mark 6:31) "Be still, and know that I am God." (Psalm 46:10) "Teach us to number our days aright, 　　that we may gain a heart of wisdom." (Psalm 90:12)
PRACTICE INCLUDES	deliberate slowdown techniques that provide relief from frantic activity: • driving in the slow lane • getting enough rest • speaking more slowly • looking people in the eyes • chewing slowly • sitting longer at the table • planning buffer time between meetings
GOD-GIVEN FRUIT	• keeping company with Jesus as you live at a saner pace • freedom from an addiction to hurry or spiritual shortcuts • patience—waiting with grace • living the present moment to the full • trusting God's unhurried time schedule • freedom from an addiction to cell phones, e-mail, instant messaging and all that speeds you up • living the truth that love and hurry are fundamentally incompatible • receiving interruptions graciously • realizing the work of the Spirit is not an "instant" work

SLOWING

A FRIEND OF MINE TELLS OF HOW THE WORD OF GOD came to her one day through her four-year-old daughter. The mother was busy hurrying her daughter out the door when the little girl replied, "Mommy. Stop! Why are we always in a hurry when we never go anywhere important?" The little girl intuitively knew that hurry got in the way of what was important. Life is too precious to miss, and the faster we go the more likely we are to miss what really matters.

We can get so busy doing urgent things and so preoccupied with what comes next that we don't experience *now*. Afraid of being late, we rush from the past to the future. The present moment becomes a crack between what we did and what we have yet to do. It is virtually lost to us. We don't get to our futures any faster if we hurry. And we certainly don't become better people in haste. More likely than not, the faster we go the less we become.

Slowing is a way we counter our culture's mandate to tend to the bottom line, to move it or lose it, to constantly be on the go. It is a way we honor our limits and the fact that God is found in the present moment. Through slowing we intentionally develop margins in our lives that leave us open to the present moment. Slowing ourselves down doesn't happen automatically. We may need to incorporate some practices that make us conscious of our haste. Perhaps we drive in the slow lane for a week. Or we may try to eat more slowly. Buffering in five to ten minutes between appointments can also slow us down. Sometimes I choose to stand in the longer line at the checkout counter. When I do this, I become aware of the internal compulsion to hurry and how it can rob me of the now. As I slow down I see the young mom with her kids in tow and send up a prayer. Or I notice the old woman who can't get her change right and help out. Ask God to help you live in the now. The present moment is the only moment we ever have to live. It is here, and it will never come again.

Hurry particularly affects the way the church does ministry. Expediency and efficiency and desire for quick results can take precedence over the slow, painstaking nature of spiritual growth. Knowing something in the head does not mean it is activated in the heart and life. Growth takes time. Hurrying people along their discipleship journeys can set them up to pretend they are further along than they are. Jesus gave his disciples time and space to grow. He was patient with the process. Dallas Willard suggests that though Jesus saw his work in the lives of others as urgent, he pursued it patiently. *Urgent* and *patient* may not seem like words that go together. But in the Christian journey a sense for both are absolutely necessary.

REFLECTION QUESTIONS

1. Are you addicted to hurry, rush and adrenalin? Explain.

2. How do you feel about being stuck behind cars that go slowly?

   How do you react to a slow sales clerk?

   What is your response to children who dawdle?

3. What is it like for you to choose to do things slowly?

4. When do you rely on adrenalin or caffeine to get through a tough part of the day?

5. What is it like for you to eat slowly rather than snarfing down your food?

6. How have deadlines, timelines and bottom lines affected the pace of your life?

   What sort of power have you given to these imaginary lines?

   What options do you have?

SPIRITUAL EXERCISES

1. Before you begin a meeting, allow time for people to become present. Say something like, "I want to give you a moment of silence to leave behind what you are coming from. I want us to be present to each other in our discussion together. Take some deep breaths and relax. We will start in one minute." • If you are meeting with Christians, ask them to place in the Lord's hands the things they are hurrying from. Then have them offer their next engagement to the Lord. Slowly and intentionally invite the entire group to be totally present to the moment, to each other and to the Lord. • After you have deliberately attended to becoming present, it is time to begin.

2. People who are rushed often feel anxious about their lives. So when you wake up, before your head leaves the pillow, offer God three central concerns of the day. Ask him to care for these things as you go about your daily tasks. • When your worries creep in, return to the moment when you handed God your concerns.

3. Enter into prayer in a leisurely way. You may wish to use "palms down, palms up" (see the "Contemplation" exercises).

4. Intentionally drive in the slow lane. Intentionally choose the longest line at the bank or grocery store. Intentionally sit longer over your meal. Intentionally chew your food. Intentionally take a longer shower. Relish the time. Be in the presence of God. • What rises to the surface of your mind? • What does this tell you about yourself?

5. Insert margins of rest and relaxation into your day. Remembering that it is better to be unavailable than inattentive, build some buffer times into your life:

- shorter appointments
- no back-to-back appointments without a break
- take some deep breaths before you pick up the phone

Ask God to make you present to the moment. • When people ask, "So how are you?" refrain from a litany about how busy you are. This simply reinforces that a revved-up existence is what matters.

6. Counter gut reactions that arise from feeling threatened or insecure by breathing slowly and deeply. Breathe in Christ's presence. Breathe out your anxiety and fear. • Breathe deeply several times before you speak and respond.

7. Read slowly. Read for transformation rather than information. When a word stands out or lights up, stop. Let the word roll around in your heart. Do not read any more. Meditate on what you have read.

Resources on Slowing

Adrenalin and Stress by Archibald Hart
An Ordinary Day with Jesus, a video series by John Ortberg and Ruth Barton

"The Lord of the dance summons us to the floor, and it takes time and discipline to learn the steps, to cease tripping over our own feet and to experience the obedient freedom of following God's lead."
—Craig Dykstra

TEACHABILITY

DESIRE	to remain a lifelong learner who is continually open to the fresh wind of the Holy Spirit
DEFINITION	Teachability is a propensity and openness to learn from God no matter who the teacher or what the experience may be.
SCRIPTURE	"You are in error because you do not know the Scriptures or the power of God." (Matthew 22:29) "You diligently study the Scriptures because you think that by them you possess eternal life. These are the Scriptures that testify about me, yet you refuse to come to me to have life." (John 5:39) "For whatever is hidden is meant to be disclosed, and whatever is concealed is meant to be brought out into the open. If anyone has ears to hear, let him hear. 'Consider carefully what you hear.'" (Mark 4:22-24)
PRACTICE INCLUDES	• an appropriate openness to new ideas, opinions, styles, people • curbing the know-it-all attitude • asking questions that lead to deeper God awareness • listening more, talking less • refraining from snap judgments based on appearances
GOD-GIVEN FRUIT	• openness to the Holy Spirit's doing a new thing • being a more perceptive listener, a more eager learner • developing humility • becoming aware of hardness of heart and unwillingness to love and grow • realizing you don't know it all and that you don't have everything right; thc ability to say, "I'm sorry. I messed up." "Can you help me?" "What do you think?" "That's helpful to me." • being a lifelong learner • freedom from attachment to your opinions, your words, your authority; attachment to Jesus and his love and care for others • freedom to resist being the teacher in social settings

TEACHABILITY

KNOWLEDGE IS A POWERFUL THING. That's why we like to be in the know, to have inside information and not to be left out of the loop. The irony is that we can become skilled in information acquisition and become no wiser for it. Information doesn't necessarily transform or shape us. Learning something new doesn't mean we are teachable. We can always use information to simply reinforce our own opinions and biases.

Jesus constantly looked for teachable people—people who would look beyond appearances and not make snap judgments. He warmed to those who asked honest questions. And he was grieved and dumbfounded by the educated who were hardhearted, unteachable and dense. He said to them, "You diligently study the Scriptures because you think that by them you possess eternal life. These are the Scriptures that testify about me, yet you refuse to come to me to have life" (John 5:39).

Jesus was passionate about those with ears to hear. He was attracted to those who willingly admitted how much they didn't know. People who could lay aside their prejudices and entertain something new were often the recipients of Jesus transforming word. Jesus is still looking for teachable disciples. How teachable are we? Do we hide behind our knowledge and feel uncomfortable being the learner? Will we be the student again and again and again?

REFLECTION QUESTIONS

1. What new things have you learned about God and yourself in the last month?

2. What positions have you rethought and changed your mind about in the last few years?

   What does this say about you and your journey?

3. Who do you know that exemplifies a person with a teachable heart?

4. How do you respond when you hear an opinion you don't agree with?

SPIRITUAL EXERCISES

1. Study some of the paradoxes of Scripture. Or study some of the hard sayings of Jesus. For instance:

   - "He who is not with me is against me, and he who does not gather with me scatters." (Matthew 12:30)
   - "For whoever is not against us is for us." (Mark 9:40)

   How do you live with the paradoxes of faith? • What do you do when you can't fully explain something? Are you comfortable with mystery? Are you comfortable saying, "I don't know"?

2. When have you learned something from someone who wasn't an authority or an expert? What did you learn? • What was it like for you? • Write your "teacher" and express your appreciation.

3. Become aware of your compulsions to let others know what you think. Notice when you're composing what you will say next rather than listening to the one who is speaking. • When do you feel the urge to pontificate or otherwise hold forth? • Ask God to give you a teachable heart and a will to listen. • What do you learn about yourself? about others? about what God values?

4. Choose a spiritual discipline that addresses a desire for growth. What would it look like to become teachable in this discipline? Who might help you? • Keep a log of the new things you are learning and experiencing with God.

5. Who do you want to be ten, twenty, thirty years from now? What will you have to learn to become that person? • Are you teachable in these areas now?

6. Ask some of the people who know you best how you come across. Are you open and teachable? Do you tend to instruct people or set them right? How do people feel about disagreeing with you?

Resources on Teachability

To Know and Be Known, or *The Courage to Teach* by Parker Palmer

"Spaciousness is always a beginning, a possibility, a potential, a capacity for birth."—Gerald May

UNPLUGGING

DESIRE	to be fully present to and uninterrupted in my interactions with God and others
DEFINITION	Unplugging calls us to leave the virtual world of technology (computers, e-mail, Blackberries, cell phones, PDAs, iPods, etc.) in order become present to God and others
SCRIPTURE	"What does a man get for all the toil and anxious striving with which he labors under the sun? All his days his work is pain and grief; even at night his mind does not rest." (Ecclesiastes 2:22-23) "Be imitators of God, therefore, as dearly loved children and live a life of love, just as Christ loved us and gave himself up for us as a fragrant offering and sacrifice to God." (Ephesians 5:1-2) "When you have eaten and are satisfied, praise the LORD your God for the good land he has given you. Be careful that you do not forget the LORD your God." (Deuteronomy 8:10-11)
PRACTICE INCLUDES	• unplugging electronic devices that interrupt relationships • refraining from the use of e-mail • abstaining from video recreation • devoting time and attention to others without interruption • communicating face to face rather than virtually • refusing to put sensitive human interaction into electronic form • not checking e-mail on the weekend • have a no–e-mail workday
GOD-GIVEN FRUIT	• settling into *uninterrupted* quiet with Jesus • creating space for face-to-face encounters with people • freedom from the compulsive and demanding nature of technological communication and its toll on the soul • freedom from addictions—accidental or otherwise—to cell phones, the Internet, video games and so forth • giving the gift of presence

UNPLUGGING

IT IS NOT UNCOMMON FOR MY FIRST TWO DAYS after vacation to be a technological marathon. Phone calls and hundreds of e-mails demand attention, swamping all face-to-face communication. I hunker down and proceed to "interact" without ever looking into anyone's eyes or sorting out the cues of body language. As the "out of office" notice disappears from my e-mail, colleagues write, "Glad you are back!" Then they hit send. We are back in "touch." Two or three days after my return, my e-mail inbox reaches its more or less constant threshold—but I have barely had any face-to-face contact.

Once the electronic swamp is cleared away I settle into life as normal. Normal life includes hours of staring at a computer screen, where I answer e-mail and write sermons and talks. The Internet is constantly at my disposal to help my "interaction" with colleagues and parishioners. Normalcy includes having a cell phone, which makes me available and interruptible at meals, in the middle of conversations, in meetings. Normalcy also includes meetings where people type notes into computers and PDAs—all the while looking down rather than at the face of the presenter. Just as campusless education, checkless banking, floorless stock trading and travelless meetings characterize the culture, faceless communication characterizes more and more of my world as a pastor. On my last birthday a colleague sent me an e-mail birthday wish, but he never made it the ten steps between our two office doors. I am as guilty as the next guy when it comes to convenience, but somehow this sort of "interaction" feels a bit sinister to me. Have I in fact left the world of interpersonal communication and entered that brave new fragmented world of technospeak?

The more I think about this, the more I wonder if Richard Mouw isn't right when he suggests that there is no "inter" to the Net. The galaxy of information the World Wide Web has offered me has fragmented my world and relationships, and left me alone.

Unplugging recognizes that personal beings are created for personal interaction by a personal God. We need to be in the presence of each other. Digital connections aren't enough to keep us healthy. We need to be touched. We need nonverbal signals. We need uninterrupted spaces in our lives for the presence of God and the presence of others.

With the aid of technology we can attempt to juggle multiple worlds at the same time. But we can't keep juggling for twenty-four hours a day and not get worn out.

In a world where people use the Internet an average of 30 hours a week and keep the TV or radio on 7.9 hours a day, we need to get unplugged from virtual reality and address our addiction to technology and the toxins it brings into our lives. Unplug, and look into the eyes of another human face—see the beauty of God's creation!

REFLECTION QUESTIONS

1. How has technology influenced your relationships?

   Do friends and family complain about the amount of time you spend online?

   What is their real concern?

2. Are you online for both work and pleasure?

   What do you like about being online? What don't you like about it?

3. What sort of temptations does cyberspace hold for you?

   How do you address these temptations?

4. Where are you using technology to avoid face-to-face encounters?

5. Have you ever been "yelled at" via e-mail? What was that like for you?

SPIRITUAL EXERCISES

1. Technology assessment: Keep track of the amount of time you spend on the computer or talking on the phone each day. How much time does this amount to each week? • Keep track of the uninterrupted time you spend in the presence of family and friends each day and week. Compare the times. • Is God inviting you to reprioritize anything based on this awareness? • If you cut back using the computer one hour a week, how could you use this time to be in the presence of God or others?

2. Plan a no–e-mail day or week. Let people know you will not be answering your e-mail—but you will take phone calls and meet with people.

3. What is it like for you to receive a handwritten letter from a friend? • Write a non-electronic letter to a friend. What surfaces in you while you take the time to do this? • What is gained and what is lost in electronic communication? What do you think of the trade-offs?

4. Which relationships in your life need face time? • Plan face-to-face time with several people this week. Do not let this time be interrupted by anything electronic.

Resources on Unplugging

The Freedom of Simplicity by Richard Foster

The Shattered Lantern by Ronald Rolheiser

The Unknown God by Alister McGrath

Part Three

RELINQUISH
THE FALSE SELF

EACH OF US HAS A BEAUTIFUL TRUE SELF INSIDE OF US. It is God's gift to us. But many of us can hardly take this in. Somewhere life taught us that our true self wasn't welcome or safe or wanted. Consequently, we learned to hide our true self. In its place we constructed a false self. The false self strives to cobble together an identity from secondary things: reputation, success, status, family, jobs, health. But an identity based on these things is rooted in idols. And idols can be lost! Things that can be here today and gone tomorrow provide a precarious mooring for the soul. Our truest identity can never be something we accomplish, earn or prove on our own. It is a gift we receive from Jesus. It is not something we earn through performance; it is what we are given. Scripture tells us that we are

- chosen (John 15:16)
- beloved children of God (1 John 3:1)
- friends of Jesus (John 15:15)
- the temple of God (1 Corinthians 3:16)
- God's work of art (Ephesians 2:10)
- fearfully and wonderfully made (Psalm 139:14)

This is our truest self. We are not defective failures. We are treasured by the Lord of the universe. And this is why we can feel good about ourselves.

The *R* disciplines of "relinquishment" detach us from the idols that vie for our attention, and attach us to our true identity in Christ. When we recognize and name the idols that consume our energy, time and hearts, we can ask God for the grace to "let go," relinquishing our dependence on these things. Through practices of relinquishment we detach from striving and unmask the false self with its pretense, attachments, agendas and grandiosities. In the presence of Christ we lay down the weight of having to manage an image. Francis de Sales writes in his *Treatise on the Love of God,* "No one can perfectly love God unless he gives up his affections for perishable things. . . . Our free will is never so free as when it is a slave to God's will, just as it is never so servile as when it serves our own will." Detachment from the false self and idols of our heart can be a painful process. But God's Spirit of truth longs to help us detach from the lies that shape us. Furthermore, the Holy Spirit bears witness to the truth of our belovedness and our "Christ-in-me identity."[*] An identity rooted in Christ has a restful center. Surrendering to and maturing in this Christ-in-me identity is helped along by the *R* disciplines.

---

[*]"Christ-in-me identity" is a phrase I heard used first by Judith Hougan.

"There is no better mirror in which to see your need than the Ten Commandments. "—Martin Luther

CONFESSION AND SELF-EXAMINATION

DESIRE	to surrender my weaknesses and faults to the forgiving love of Christ and intentionally desire and embrace practices that lead to transformation
DEFINITION	Self-examination is a process whereby the Holy Spirit opens my heart to what is true about me. This is not the same thing as a neurotic shame-inducing inventory. Instead it is a way of opening myself to God within the safety of his love so I can authentically seek transformation. Confession embraces Christ's gift of forgiveness and restoration while setting us on the path to renewal and change.

SCRIPTURE	"Search me, O God, and know my heart;
	    test me and know my anxious thoughts.
	See if there is any offensive way in me,
	    and lead me in the way everlasting." (Psalm 139:23-24)
	
	"Blessed is he
	    whose transgressions are forgiven,
	    whose sins are covered.
	Blessed is the man
	    whose sin the LORD does not count against him
	    and in whose spirit is no deceit." (Psalm 32:1-2)
	
	"Therefore confess your sins to each other and pray for each other so that you may be healed." (James 5:16)

PRACTICE INCLUDES	• admitting to God the natural propensity to rationalize, deny, blame and self-obsess • examining the "sin network" in your life as evidenced in presumptuous sins, besetting weaknesses, self-centered habits and broken relationships • replacing sinful habits with healthy ones • seeking God's grace to change • confessing sins by examining your life in light of (1) the seven deadly sins, (2) the Ten Commandments, (3) prayers of confession found in prayer books or Scripture (Psalm 51), (4) a life confession, journaling confessions and confessions made to others
GOD-GIVEN FRUIT	• keeping company with Jesus as he helps you with how much or how little you change • being transformed into Christlikeness • thinking of yourself with sober judgment, awareness of your blind spots • gaining insight into your temptations and God's work in your life • having compassion toward others in their faults • seeing yourself as God's loved and forgiven child no matter what you have done • living in thankfulness for God's work in your life • savoring the gift of salvation

CONFESSION AND SELF-EXAMINATION

CONFESSION MAY BE GOOD FOR THE SOUL, but it can be very hard to do. We are invested in *looking like* good moral people. After all, appearing good is one way of dealing with the notion that something is wrong with us. We haven't murdered anyone or robbed a bank. Furthermore, when we do wrong we try to fix it and make it better. We can put a great deal of energy into maintaining the image that we are good moral people. But this very appearance of goodness can be a way we defend ourselves against our sin. For when we can't see our sin we have nothing to confess.

The truth is that we all sin. Sin is *anything* that breaks relationships. Jesus is totally realistic about broken relationships. He experienced them. He was put to death by them. Yet Jesus taught that the damage done through sin was not the last word on life. Sin could be confessed. Sin could be forgiven. And sinful people could be set free.

Much of Jesus' teachings and at least a third of his parables are about forgiveness. Over and over again he modeled what it looked like to bless when you are cursed and to forgive when people don't deserve to be forgiven. Furthermore, one of the central pleas of the Lord's Prayer focuses on confession and forgiveness: "Forgive us our sins as we forgive those who sin against us."

True repentance means we open the bad in our lives to God. We invite him to come right in and look at our sin with us. We don't hide by being good, moral people or in neurotic self-recriminations. We don't pretend to be other than we are. We don't disguise the truth by carting out all the disciplines we practice. We tell it like it is—without rationalization, denial or blame—to the only person in the universe who will unconditionally love us when we are bad. We hand over the pretense, image management, manipulation, control and self-obsession. In the presence of the holy One we give up on appearing good and fixing our sin. We lay down our ability to change by the power of the self. We turn to Jesus and seek forgiveness.

Jesus, the only Son of God, died a violent, unspeakable death so we could know what freedom from sin tastes like. Jesus laid his power down, suffered and became sin so that we would not be condemned. Every time we confess how we have missed the mark of

God's love and truth, we open ourselves up to the mending work of the cross. Jesus' wounds hold true life-changing power. This is the shocking reality that confession can open up to us. Through confession and forgiveness we live into the truth of being God's new creation! The old is gone. The new has come.

REFLECTION QUESTIONS

1. Does your confession tend to be along the lines of "Forgive my sins, dear Lord" rather than specifically naming your sins one by one before the face of God?

   What does the lack of specific confession do to self-awareness?

2. What experiences have affected your ability to give and receive forgiveness?

   Talk to God about what this means.

3. When have you tasted the joy of forgiveness?

   What was that like for you?

4. What is it like for you to confess your sins before a friend or confessor?

5. Which of your sins hurts those closest to you?

SPIRITUAL EXERCISES

1. Imagine you are in a safe place, surrounded by the love of God. • Ask God to help you see yourself as he sees you. Remember he sees you absolutely and with love. • Using the Ten Commandments as a guide, journal your sins. When you have finished, go through each commandment one at a time, asking God to forgive you and help you to change. • Then burn your list in a symbolic act of what it means to have God remove your sins from you.

2. Set aside some time for confession and self-examination. In the presence of God ask for light to pierce your defenses. • Then ask yourself, *Who have I injured recently through thoughtlessness, neglect, anger and so on?* • As the Holy Spirit brings people to mind, confess your feelings about these people to God. Ask God to forgive you and if need be to give you grace to forgive them. • Write an apology, make a phone call or confess out loud in an attempt to put the relationship back on track.

3. Make a life confession—alone or to a trusted friend or confessor. • Dividing your life into seven-year segments, reflect on the sins particular to each segment. • Confess your sins aloud. Receive the freedom that comes in knowing you stand completely in the clear before a holy God.

4. Ask some of your family and close friends to help you see your blind spots. Ask questions like, What do I do that hurts you? How could I better love you? What is it like to be with me? Do I show interest in others or talk mostly about myself? Let their answers guide you in a time of confession.

5. Enter into a covenant group or an accountability relationship where you cannot hide.

Tell the truth about who you are and ask your partners to pray for you and help you change.

6. Imagine the kind of person you would like to become in your old age. Then look at your life and assess whether or not the way you live now is preparing you to become this person. • Confess where you need to change. Ask God and the community of faith for help.

7. Turn to Psalm 32 or Psalm 51. Use the psalm as a way of bringing your own sins before God. • How does God meet you in these confessions of David?

8. How in touch do you feel with your own sin? • If you feel out of touch with your sin, honestly consider where some of the following sins show up in your life: envy, lust, greed, gluttony, deceit, lying, exaggerating, envy, anger, pretense, avoidance of responsibility. • What do you see about yourself? How do you want to talk to God about these things? • Confess where you have fallen short of God's expectations, and receive his forgiveness.

9. Begin to notice your strong emotions. When do you feel yourself getting hot, defensive, angry, withdrawn? What is motivating your emotion? What behavior stems from your emotion? • As you attend to this internal world, ask God to make you alert to what triggers strong emotional reactions. Confess any sin relating to these reactions. • Practice noticing your internal world, and begin to develop a habit of immediate confession.

10. If you are interested in identifying your besetting sin or compulsion, read a book on the Enneagram such as *The Enneagram: A Christian Perspective* by Richard Rohr and Andreas Ebert.

Resources on Confession

Celebration of Discipline, chapter 10, by Richard Foster

"All great spirituality is about letting go. "—Richard Rohr

DETACHMENT

DESIRE	to nurture the spirit of trust that is attached to God alone
DEFINITION	Detachment means replacing the attachment to (1) idolatrous relationships and (2) self-serving goals and agendas for success, money, power, ego, productivity and image with wholehearted attachment to and trust in God alone.
SCRIPTURE	"[Jesus] said, 'Anyone who intends to come with me has to let me lead. You're not in the driver's seat; *I* am. Don't run from suffering; embrace it. Follow me and I'll show you how. Self-help is no help at all. Self-sacrifice is the way, my way, to saving yourself, your true self.' " (Mark 8:34-35 *The Message*) "Speaking to the people, he went on, 'Take care! Protect yourself against the least bit of greed. Life is not defined by what you have, even when you have a lot.' " (Luke 12:15 *The Message*) "Indeed, I have been crucified with Christ. My ego is no longer central. It is no longer important that I appear righteous before you or have your good opinion, and I am no longer driven to impress God. Christ lives in me. The life you see me living is not 'mine,' but it is lived by faith in the Son of God, who loved me and gave himself for me." (Galatians 2:20 *The Message*)
PRACTICE INCLUDES	• naming and confessing attachments that take priority over God • allowing others to lead and win • letting go of image management (e.g., not buying clothes just to stay in fashion) • letting go of notions that your money and possessions belong to you and make you who you are; living on less rather than more • trusting outcomes to God rather than your own capabilities • honoring the freedom of others; refusing to manipulate and control in order to get what you want
GOD-GIVEN FRUIT	• keeping company with Jesus in the letting go • freedom from an identity attached to image, possessions, achievements and so on • quickness to repent and center your identity in Jesus • freedom of addiction to your children, your family, your house, your money, your job and so forth • less need for temporal security; more trust in God • freedom to live as God's beloved • living out of your true self in Christ • dying to self; losing your life to find it • realizing that following Jesus includes descent, loss and death, and to live in a way that finds God in the midst of these things • learning the lessons of letting go so that you will be prepared for the final letting go of death

DETACHMENT

THERE WAS NOTHING JESUS WAS MORE ATTACHED TO than his Father. God came before his mission, his disciples or his family. Because God was the center of Jesus' life, worldly values came second. Certainly Jesus was tempted by the ascent to power, the need to appear successful and shortcuts to achieving his kingdom. But Jesus refused to let the world's values shape his life. He intentionally laid aside an identity built on being relevant, revered and upwardly mobile. He died to these things and fixed his eyes on what was unseen (2 Corinthians 4:18). Jesus was detached from making a name for himself that brought human applause. He embraced his humanness and staked his ministry on being God's beloved Son whether or not any one responded.

Jesus knows all about the discipline of detachment. He made the harrowing descent that relinquished heavenly privileges for a life of human limitations. The second person of the holy Trinity, Jesus Christ, exchanged heaven for earth, power for weakness, glory for obedience and suffering, success in human eyes for faithfulness in the eyes of God, and life for death. God was Jesus' first and only unloseable thing. Everything else could be lost.

Jesus let go; he detached. When faced with temptation he refused to use his divine prerogatives and lived like us, not like some superhero. Jesus did his life the same way we do ours. He risked everything by trusting the invisible God and his goodness when it appeared that this would mean dying in disgrace.

Part of the liturgy for many churches includes the words "Christ has died. Christ is risen. Christ will come again." This threefold pattern, known as the paschal mystery, describes how true transformation is found on the far side of detachment, relinquishment and letting go. Through many mini-crucifixions the life of Christ is born again in us. Christ's pattern of letting go is our paradigm for life.

As followers of Jesus we are called to live as Jesus did. Jesus said, "Anyone who intends to come with me has to let me lead. You're not in the driver's seat; *I* am. Don't run from suffering; embrace it. Follow me and I'll show you how" (Mark 8:34 *The Message*). We are to relinquish worldly values and detach from anything that stands in the way of desiring and knowing God. We are to embrace Jesus' path—the path of descent and the way of wounding. Richard Rohr writes in *Everything Belongs,* "Jesus crucified and resurrected is the whole pattern revealed, named, effected and promised for our own lives." A look at the cross makes this astringently clear.

Yet we often refuse relinquishment and remain blind to our attachments. We fail to see how our children or our goals for them and ourselves become the most important thing in our lives, receiving the bulk of our time, money and resources. We ignore our fixed attachment to our identity and how it is represented in our drive for possessions, control, comforts and achievements. We avoid any mini-death of relinquishment we possibly can. Relinquishment extends into the core of our identities, securities and addictions and says, "For the love of Jesus I will let go." It is only through letting go of the control streak that true trust in Jesus is born. As Jesus' apprentices we are to detach from the accolades of the world and receive ourselves as God's beloved. Detachment finds its true home in attachment to Jesus only.

In my own life this sort of detachment has touched me in simple practical ways.

My mother once commented on how much she liked a tablecloth in a friend's home. The friend whipped it off the table and gave it to her on the spot. This experience has worked its way into my own life. From time to time I give away what is admired in my home just as a reminder of what sort of things really matter. Furthermore, I see parting with a few beautiful things as a small discipline considering all the "letting go" I have yet to face.

Over Christmas when thousands of folks were snowed in at O'Hare airport, a friend called to tell me her son's flight had been canceled for twenty-four hours and that there was not a rental car to be found. Detachment in this instance meant letting go of our car for four days so a stranded traveler could drive the 150 miles to his home.

Moving to Chicago was also a deep lesson in detachment. Leaving the sea, the friends, the job, the church, the roots to follow Jesus to a new land came with losses and eventually a renewed sense of where my attachment lies.

REFLECTION QUESTIONS

1. How do you handle failure and weakness, suffering and loss?

   What does this tell you about how you attach and adapt to the world's view of success, power and self-worth?

2. What are some specific ways in which mistakes and failures have worked for your good?

3. When has loss made God more real to you?

4. What about yourself are you most attached to?

5. Imagine a testimonial dinner in your honor. What would you like people to say about you?

SPIRITUAL EXERCISES

1. Take an attachment inventory. Write a list of the defense mechanisms you are attached to (sarcasm, temper tantrums, aloofness, clowning around). • Ask God to make you

aware of the times you instinctively move into your defensive response. Consider what seems to trigger your response. • What response would you like to cultivate instead? • Share your observations with a trusted friend, asking them to pray with you. Ask the Holy Spirit to help you change your attachment to these behavioral patterns.

2. Practice letting go by giving away something you are attached to (money, time, possessions). Notice the feelings that arise in you when you think of giving something away. • Spend time talking to God about how attached you are to your things.

3. Walk through your home or office, and in your mind give all you have to God. Tell him that you could live without the things you see. • What is this time of prayer like for you?

4. Recognize your attachment to labels. How do you use labels to judge people? How attached are you to your professional label? Where do professional labels get in the way of really knowing others? • How might you enter a conversation without using the question, What do you do? as an entrée to conversation. Spend some time coming up with questions that lead you to a deeper appreciation of the person.

5. Where in your life do you need Christ's spirit of detachment? Where do you need grace to pray "Not my will but yours be done"? • Talk to God about what it means to you to pray this sort of prayer. • How does praying this prayer make the reality of Jesus' life touch your own?

6. Ask God to give you an opportunity to become more detached from secondary things. Share your car, your home, your second home, your time, your expertise with someone this week.

Resources on Detachment

Everything Belongs by Richard Rohr

"St. Ignatius of Loyola notes that sin is unwillingness to trust that what God wants is our deepest happiness. Until I am absolutely convinced of this I will do everything I can to keep my hands on the controls of my life, because I think I know better than God what I need for my fulfillment."
—David Benner

DISCERNMENT

DESIRE	to delight in and recognize the voice and will of God
DEFINITION	Discernment opens us up to listen to and recognize the voice and patterns of God's direction in our lives.
SCRIPTURE	"Unless I go away, the Counselor will not come to you; but if I go, I will send him to you." (John 16:7) "So this is my prayer: that your love will flourish and that you will not only love much but well. Learn to love appropriately. You need to use your head and test your feelings so that your love is sincere and intelligent, not sentimental gush." (Philippians 1:9-10 *The Message*) "Test the spirits to see whether they are from God." (1 John 4:1) "If any of you lacks wisdom, he should ask God, who gives generously to all without finding fault, and it will be given to him." (James 1:5)
PRACTICE INCLUDES	• taking time to listen to God; not hurrying to make a decision • seeking to bring both head and heart into alignment with God's will • asking for help, counsel and guidance • going on a retreat to gain perspective and listen to God • attending to the desires God has placed deeply inside you • naming your addictions, predilections, prejudices, unbelief and so on in order to understand how these play into making decisions
GOD-GIVEN FRUIT	• listening in prayer for the nudgings of the Spirit • ability to wait for God rather than just deciding • freedom from rationalizing your choices • seeking the Guide rather than a map for your life • recognizing your motivations and the source of your deep gladness • being able to read both your mind and heart when making decisions • being attached to God's love and will alone

DISCERNMENT

HAVE YOU EVER TRIED TO HELP A CHRISTIAN FRIEND make a decision? It can be a confusing process. Some Christians believe God's will can be found in the most difficult and sacrificial of two options. Others believe the will of God is whatever choice brings the most money, perks, success and personal gain at any particular moment. Some people believe that *not* wanting to do something is a sure sign that it is God's will. Others believe exactly the opposite. I've met people who open their Bibles and expect their finger to fall on God's guiding word, but others expect to use their brain and want me to check out their list of pros and cons. Discernment leads us into deep waters. What are we to make of "signs" and "open doors" and desire and self-sacrifice?

Biblical discernment involves more than good judgment, open doors and decision-making skills. Right discernment arises out of a relationship with God in prayer. It is founded on the reality of the Holy Spirit's presence within us. Jesus makes it clear the Holy Spirit is our Counselor and Guide into God's will and ways. The Holy Spirit can be counted on to

1. assure us of God's love, goodness and trustworthy nature (Romans 8:16)

2. convict us of sin, revealing the false self and all its agendas and attachments (John 16:8)

3. lead us into truth, opening us to the cleansing power of repentance and freedom Jesus brings (John 16:13)

4. bring glory to God (John 16:14) through everything that happens to us

5. nurture the fruit of the Spirit (Galatians 5:22-23)

To know God's will we must be assured of God's love. Discernment depends on a deep trust in God's good intentions toward us. Distrusting God's intentions and fearing that his will could be life-thwarting rather than life-giving can sabotage our ability to listen and wait for direction. Reveal the source of your distrust to God. Ask for help and healing. The Spirit does not beat us up for expressing our doubts and fears to God. He hears us out, assures us of God's love and leads us into trust.

To discern well we also need the Spirit of Truth to open our eyes to our attachments to things that influence our decision making: things like prestige, personal agendas, comforts, productivity and so on. We need to confess our agendas and honestly ask the Lord what must die in us for God's will to come forth. One of my favorite prayers for guidance is "Lord I am willing to receive what you give, release what you take, lack what you withhold, do what you require and be who you desire. Amen."

When our hearts are open to receiving whatever God says, we are in a place where we can wait and listen for a nudge from God. We rest in the confidence that we don't have to figure things out on our own. We become alert to the presence of the Spirit revealed in love, joy, peace patience, goodness, kindness, gentleness, patience and self-control. The presence of this fruit reminds us that we can't fall out of God's care or move beyond his notice. When praying for God to make his way plain, I often pray, "Lord Christ, take those things the evil one would use to discourage and destroy, and turn them to my good, my growth and your glory. Amen."

Suggestions for Listening to God

Take your time. It is best not to do all these steps at once. The brain gets tired, anxiety takes over, and you can end up trying to force the hand of God. Listening for God's direction takes time. Not every decision you make will need to incorporate all these steps. Some choices are easier than others.

1. Come into the presence of the holy One focusing your attention on his love and goodness. Thank God that you have a Guide who is on your side and wants to help you.

2. Consider what it means to be totally attached to God's agenda and will. Confess any idols of your heart that blocks your trust.

   - Acknowledge any compulsions and addictions that get in the way of freely surrendering to God.

   - How does this choice play into your persona and false self? Check out your motives.

   - Get some distance from your impulses, agendas and compulsion to decide now.

   - Pray to recognize and relinquish anything that takes priority over God's will. This kind of prayer is the "nevertheless" prayer Jesus prayed in Gethsemane. *Not my will but yours be done.* It is sometimes called the "prayer of relinquishment." Ask God to move in your will so you want to choose that which promotes his glory and spreads his love. If you can't pray this prayer, then pray for a desire to pray this prayer.

3. Lay your choice before God and examine the matter thoroughly. If it helps to journal the scope of the decision, commit your thoughts to writing.

4. Share your desires with God. What is it you want? Does your desire reflect some deeper desire? How does your desire or choice line up with love of God and others? How does the choice lead you deeper into faithfulness and goodness?

5. Use reason.

- How does this decision enable you to live out the fruit of the Spirit?
- Will this choice be experienced as a life-giving, loving choice for those it affects?
- Write your pros-and-cons list: weigh the advantages and benefits, the disadvantages and dangers of each option.
- Does the choice lead to a yes in your mind?

6. Attend to your feelings.

- What about this choice leads to *consolation:* life-giving feelings that bring in the Spirit's fruit of love, joy, faith and peace?
- What excites you and gives you hope?
- Picture yourself in this situation for a length of time. What do you sense?
- What about this choice leads to *desolation:* life-thwarting feelings of turmoil, confusion and anxiety? Desolation leaves us feeling chaotic, cut off from God. We feel demotivated by accusation, shame and fear.
- Does this choice lead to peaceful feelings?

7. Listen to God as you read Scripture. Pay attention to where the Word lights up and speaks to you (see "Devotional Reading").

8. Seek the counsel of those gifted in discernment who can listen to you and with you. Ask them:

- Am I being a good steward?
- Am I running away from or toward something rather than waiting?
- Am I open to a different path?
- Does this choice serve communion and community?

9. Offer your choice to God. Pray for wisdom and the freedom of the Spirit to blow through you. Wait. Ask God to bring your heart and head and spirit into agreement. Do they all confirm this course of action?

REFLECTION QUESTIONS

1. How does the way you spend your time and energy reveal what is important to you and reflect the deep desires of your heart?

2. When making decisions, do you procrastinate or become so uncomfortable with waiting that you jump in and decide so you don't have to endure uncertainty?

   How does this affect your discernment process?

3. Do you believe that God has only one perfect blueprint for your life? Why or why not?

4. What do you see as the role of the mind in making decisions?

5. What do you see as the role of the heart in making decisions?

SPIRITUAL EXERCISES

1. To discern where the Holy Spirit has been recently working in your life, answer the following questions:

   - For what am I longing?
   - What themes keep recurring in my life?
   - Where am I struggling?
   - What is most life-giving to me? What is least life-giving?

2. It is seldom wise to make a decision at a deep point of desolation, because it can provoke premature decisions. Name some causes of desolation in your life: fatigue, over-extension, sloth, fear, emotional blocks, loss of trust. • How do these things play into your decision-making process? • When you make a choice out of desolation, what is that like? • Ask God to enable you to wait through a time of desolation so as better to hear his voice.

3. Catalog major decisions in your life to date. Beside each one, write your decision-making process. • Which decisions felt best and worst? Why?

4. Divide your life into seven-year segments. For each period record the deepest desire of your heart. What desires resurface again and again? • How do you listen to these desires in your discernment process? • Talk to God about the desires of your heart.

Resources on Discernment

Listening to God in Times of Choice and *The Voice of Jesus* by Gordon T. Smith
The Spiritual Exercises of Ignatius Loyola

"Purity of heart is to will one thing."—Søren Kierkegaard

SECRECY

DESIRE	to follow the simple and often hidden way of Christ
DEFINITION	Secrecy is practicing the spirit of Christ reflected in hiddenness, anonymity, lack of display and the holding of confidences.
SCRIPTURE	"Do nothing out of selfish ambition or vain conceit, but in humility consider others as better than yourselves." (Philippians 2:3) "He must become greater; I must become less." (John 3:30) "But when you pray, go into your room, close the door and pray to your Father, who is unseen. Then your Father, who sees what is done in secret, will reward you." (Matthew 6:6)
PRACTICE INCLUDES	• finding acts of service that you can render without letting anyone know what you have done or why you have done it • holding confidences as secrets not to be shared • refraining from the compulsion to tell all you know • abstaining from revealing your good deeds, talents and qualities • consecrating intimate moments of your walk with God to him alone; speaking of them with no one else • being a safe place for others to share their secrets • celebrating the achievements of others without having to bring up your own
GOD-GIVEN FRUIT	• developing a secret place of intimacy with Jesus • maintaining confidences • practicing spiritual disciplines in secret • freedom from the hunger for notoriety, fame and recognition by keeping your achievements to yourself • governing self-centered conversation • bearing being misunderstood without seeking to justify yourself or rationalize your behavior • living from peace rather than competing for attention • demonstrating that what is important in life is not what is found on your résumé • receiving praise and recognition well and then moving on without needing to add any self-deprecating comments

SECRECY

IT IS NO SECRET THAT MOST OF US DO NOT BELIEVE IN SECRECY. Anonymity is not our thing. Recognition, accolades and the limelight are. We want people to *know* just how generous, smart, successful and popular we are. But we don't want to appear to be a braggart, so we come up with subtle and socially approved ways of promoting ourselves and our image. We give money to causes where our name gets out. We name drop about who we know. We let slip how and where we volunteer. Every good deed we do sees the light of day. And every juicy secret we know comes out in our next conversation.

Jesus valued secrecy. On more than one occasion he told people not to tell others about things concerning him (Mark 1:44; 9:9; Luke 8:56). He also told others to keep their own secrets about good things they did. He said, "When you give to the needy, do not let your left hand know what your right hand is doing, so that your giving may be in secret" (Matthew 6:3-4). A deed that exists for the sake of recognition is not for God; it's for you. Deeds designed to create an image or support an appearance can certainly bring about good—but they are not free gifts. They are deeds bound to what "I can get out of it." God knows the heart of your deeds. He understands motivations and intentions. This being the case, admitting what is inside seems the only sensible thing to do. Reveal your naked self and secret motivations to Jesus. Develop your own private love relationship with God. We often plan special and intimate things for those we love, things we don't share with others. Jesus invites us to do the same with him. We can do special and secret things for God alone—things that will delight his heart as pure, free gift.

Jesus was totally free. He gave gratuitously and graciously. He did not look for a return. He played to an audience of One—his Father. Secrecy stems from the desire to share confidences with God—to play to an audience of One.

Secrecy acknowledges that not all good deeds need public recognition. Furthermore, not all information is public information or appropriate for others to hear. We all have choices about what we say and don't say. Secrecy is a way we make distinctions that honor God and each other. It is a way we hinder the spread of gossip, slander and rumor. Through secrecy we create safe spaces where people can freely be who they are without fear or dis-ease. Through secrecy we learn to give freely rather than for kickbacks.

REFLECTION QUESTIONS

1. What is it like for you to keep secrets or maintain confidences?

   Talk to God about this.

2. How might the discipline of secrecy address an addiction to approval and image management?

3. What personal and secret words of love has God said to you alone?

   Do you treasure and remember them?

4. What is it like for you to savor something you learn rather than tell someone about it the first chance you get.

5. What is it like for you—and the person prayed for—when someone uses public prayer as a way to reveal secrets? (For instance, "Lord help Joe as he struggles with pornography.")

   How would the Lord have you pray for someone without betraying their confidence?

6. How do you feel about anonymous gifts and cards?

   Do you struggle with not knowing who has been good or generous to you? Explain.

SPIRITUAL EXERCISES

1. Covenant before God to keep confidences and secrets. When you are tempted to tell someone what you heard in confidence, confess that you have trouble keeping confidences and that you are trying to honor God in this matter. Then move on to another topic.

2. This week choose to do something for or give something to someone anonymously. Ask God to help you discover who you should choose. As you talk to people, pay attention to any need they might mention. Plan a way of following through on your desire without letting them know where the help or gift came from. • Talk to God about what this is like for you.

3. Savor secrecy. Let it be a way for you to love God and show him that he matters to you. • What can you do for God that no one will know about? Go and do it. • What is it like for you?

4. Choose to keep a spiritual discipline you practice a secret between you and God for a stipulated period of time. • What is that like for you?

Resources on Secrecy

Spiritual Letters to Women by François Fénelon
Service and Secrecy by Jan Johnson

"In a noise-polluted world, it is even difficult to hear ourselves think let alone try to be still and know God. Yet it seems essential for our spiritual life to seek some silence, no matter how busy we may be. Silence is not to be shunned as empty space, but to be befriended as fertile ground for intimacy with God."—Susan Muto

SILENCE

DESIRE	to free myself from the addiction to and distraction of noise so I can be totally present to the Lord; to open myself to God in the place beyond words
DEFINITION	Silence is a regenerative practice of attending and listening to God in quiet, without interruption and noise. Silence provides freedom from speaking as well as from listening to words or music. (Reading is also listening to words.)
SCRIPTURE	"But oh! GOD is in his holy Temple! Quiet everyone—a holy silence. Listen!" (Habakkuk 2:20 *The Message*) "After the earthquake came a fire, but he LORD was not in the fire. And after the fire came a gentle whisper." (1 Kings 19:12) "There was silence in heaven for about half an hour." (Revelation 8:1) "But Jesus often withdrew to lonely places and prayed." (Luke 5:16)
PRACTICE INCLUDES	• setting a period of time in which you don't speak but isolate yourself from sounds (other than perhaps the sounds of nature) • driving or commuting without the radio or CD player turned on • leaving the TV off; spending time in silence with God alone • exercising without attending to noise; listening to God • having personal retreats of silence
GOD-GIVEN FRUIT	• being attentive to the voice of Jesus • having freedom from negative habits of speech (deception, gossip, impulsive chatter, small talk, impression management, the need to express your opinion or critique) • freedom from addictions to noise or sound (radio, TV, phone, iPod, etc.) • receiving quiet from the chaos and the noise in your life • having deeper intimacy with God • growing in self-awareness as the silence invites the subconscious to move into deeper levels of knowing • developing increased listening skills

SILENCE

IT IS DIFFICULT TO FIND SILENCE IN AN AGE OF technology and information. Silence challenges our cultural addiction to amusement, words, music, advertising, noise, alarms and voices. Silence asks for patience and waiting. And both silence and waiting make us uncomfortable. They seem so unproductive. We can't tell if we are *doing* anything in them. So when we come upon silence, we fill it. We cram it with something else we can learn or do or achieve.

We break the silence of travel with an iPod, the silence of the evening hours with the TV or computer, the silence of sleep with an alarm clock. Every part of our life is inundated with words—urgent words, random words, trivial words, hurtful words, managing words, religious words and on and on. In the midst of so many words it becomes difficult to know which messages are really important and which ones we need to remember. To get through the flood of words we develop skills like skimming and scanning. We look for bullet points and bold print. We ask for summaries. We urge people to be brief and cut to the chase. And when we think they aren't saying anything significant, we simply block out their words to attend to our own internal flood of words.

This habit of glancing at words and people extends to our relationship with God. We want pithy, memorable sermons. We want more religious words to chew on. The trouble is there are so many other things we are trying to remember that the sermon evaporates by the time we reach the parking lot. Could it be that what we need is time alone with God and a lot fewer words? Do we need to put on the "Do Not Disturb" button and learn what it is to be available to God alone?

We need to realize that the world can go on without us for an hour or a day or even longer. We don't need to respond to every word and request that comes our way. The discipline of silence invites us to leave behind the competing demands of our outer world for time alone with Jesus. Silence offers a way of paying attention to the Spirit of God and what he brings to the surface of our souls.

In quietness we often notice things we would rather not notice or feel. Pockets of sadness or anger or loneliness or impatience begin to surface. Our own outer agenda looms larger than our desire to be with God in silence. And as the silence settles in and nothing seems to be happening, we often struggle with the feeling that we are wasting time. Everything we notice in this struggle can become an invitation to prayer. Like a can opener the silence opens up the contents of our heart, allowing us deeper access to God than we experience at other times. As we remain in the silence, the inner noise and chaos will begin to settle. Our capacity to open up wider and wider to God grows. The holy One has access to places we don't even know exist in the midst of the hubbub.

Jesus told his disciples, "I have much more to say to you, more than you can now bear" (John 16:12). It is Holy Spirit's job to keep the inner process of revelation underway. But in order for the Spirit to do his job, we need to cooperate and put ourselves in a place to deeply and reflectively listen. Be alone with God in the silence. Offer your body and your attention to God as a prayer.

As you quietly offer your body you can hone your listening reflexes. There is nothing you need to do here. This is not a time to come up with strategies for fixing your life. Silence is a time to rest in God. Lean into God, trusting that being with him in silence will loosen your rootedness in the world and plant you by streams of living water. It can form your life even if it doesn't solve your life. The anonymous author of *The Way of the Pilgrim* wrote, "I need peace and silence to give free play to this quickening flame of prayer." Let the silence lead you to prayer.

REFLECTION QUESTIONS

1. In Revelation 8:1 we read that there was "silence in heaven for about half an hour." What might be going on in heaven's silence?

2. How do you avoid or resist silence?

3. Do you like to fill silences with sound or learning—tapes, talk shows, news and so forth? What does this mean?

4. Where do you have silence with God in your life?

5. How much time each day do you give to silence (i.e., no words, printed or audible)?

6. Do you think God values time with you in silence? Explain.

SPIRITUAL EXERCISES

1. If silence is new for you, begin with ten minutes. Setting a timer can help a novice who keeps watching the clock. The timer lets you forget the time and settle into the quiet. Intentionally place yourself in the presence of God and become quiet. • As you become quiet what do you hear: voices, traffic, your breath, wind, your heart, distracting thoughts? Let the noise go. Continue to let the quiet deepen. Be with God. • After ten minutes, reflect on what it was like for you to simply become still enough to hear the background. • Try this several times a day. What happens to you? The benefits of being silent are often seen in the fruit it bears rather than in the experience of silence per se.

2. While doing a task, turn off any background noise and continue the task by offering it to God. Be in the present, doing what you are doing with a listening heart. • What is it like for you? • What distracts you?

3. Go into silence. Begin to mediate on Psalm 37:4—"Delight yourself in the LORD / and he will give you the desires of your heart." What does this verse say to you? • What desires has God put into your heart? What does God say to you about your desires? • Stay and wait. Ask for the freedom to delight in God and for ability to know and live out your God-given desires.

4. Go into silence, placing yourself in the presence of God with the words "Here I am." • As distractions come to mind, let them go by imagining they are boats floating down a river. Let the current take the distractions away. Don't follow the distractions. Gently return to God repeating "Here I am." Let the current of God's Spirit carry you. • What is this like for you?

5. Spend a half day in silence: no books (other than the Bible), no music, just listen. What surfaces? • How do you want to interact with God about his gift of silence? (See the appendix "Spending Time with God.")

6. If you struggle with silent time, bring a timer with you to prayer. Sit in a quiet and comfortable place where you can attend to the Lord. Take some deep breaths, relaxing your body and quieting your mind. • Put the timer on one minute. Become still before the Lord. When a distracting thought comes to mind, count it, but drop it into the river of God's peace. Let it float down the river. Count each thought that comes up and let it float down river. After one minute, how many thoughts have gone through your mind? • Set the timer for another minute. Repeat the same exercise. How many thoughts went through your mind this time? • Repeat the exercise one more time. Ride the river of God. • What do you find out about quieting your soul? • What was it like for you to do this? It takes time to quiet your thoughts; don't become discouraged. Practice will help you learn how to best quiet yourself.

Resources on Silence

Invitation to Solitude and Silence by Ruth Haley Barton
The Awakened Heart by Gerald May

"We are so afraid of silence that we chase ourselves from one event to the next in order not to have to spend a moment alone with ourselves, in order not to have to look at ourselves in the mirror."
—Dietrich Bonhoeffer

SOLITUDE

DESIRE	to leave people behind and enter into time alone with God
DEFINITION	The practice of solitude involves scheduling enough uninterrupted time in a distraction-free environment that you experience isolation and are alone with God. Solitude is a "container discipline" for the practice of other spiritual disciplines.
SCRIPTURE	"Very early in the morning, while it was still dark, Jesus got up, left the house and went off to a solitary place, where he prayed." (Mark 1:35) The LORD said, "Go out and stand on the mountain in the presence of the LORD, for the LORD is about to pass by." (1 Kings 19:11) "Let him sit alone in silence for the LORD has laid it on him." (Lamentations 3:28)
PRACTICE INCLUDES	• giving God time and space that is not in competition with social contact, noise or stimulation • taking a retreat • observing sabbath refreshment by abstaining from constant interaction with others, information and activities • addressing your addiction to being seen • communing with God alone while you walk or run by yourself • practicing disciplines alone: study, prayer, examen, journaling and so forth
GOD-GIVEN FRUIT	• freedom from the need to be occupied and stimulated • moving away from letting the world "squeeze you into its mold" (Romans 12:2) • liberation from constantly living your life in reference to other people • quieting the internal noise so you can better listen to God • giving yourself time and space to internalize what you already know • speaking only what you hear from God rather than out of your store of opinions • including solitude and retreat as part of your lifestyle

SOLITUDE

THOUGH WE MAY BE UNFAMILIAR WITH the discipline of solitude, most of us recognize it as something we wanted when we were first in love. It didn't matter if the time spent together accomplished anything very useful or important to the world at large. It was simply the way we let our beloved know that he or she mattered. In order to show love, we sought time alone together.

The Song of Songs is a mysteriously wonderful book of the Bible. It gives a glimpse of lovers who want to be alone so they can express the full range of their love for one another. The church regards this book as descriptive of human love as well as of divine love. God longs to commune with his children. He beckons, "Arise, come, my darling; / my beautiful one, come with me" (Song of Songs 2:13). In solitude the heart waits for God, and God alone. Here the soul opens wide to listen and receive.

Jesus began his ministry with forty formative days of solitude. No doubt Jesus intended to commune with God alone, but he also encountered the tempter in that desert place. Mark writes, "At once the Spirit sent him out into the desert, and he was in the desert forty days, being tempted by Satan" (Mark 1:12). Solitude is a formative place because it gives God's Spirit time and space to do deep work. When no one is there to watch, judge and interpret what we say, the Spirit often brings us face to face with hidden motives and compulsions. The world of recognition, achievement and applause disappears, and we stand squarely before God without props. In solitude Jesus did battle with the intoxicating possibilities of achieving his kingdom and identity in the power of the self. He faced down the self Satan offered and instead chose his true identity as the beloved Son. Throughout his three years of ministry Jesus returned again and again to solitude, where the rush of attention and the accolades of the crowds could be put into their proper perspective. Solitude with God was a way Jesus remained in touch with his true identity in God.

Most of us can identify with the intoxicating feeling that comes when we are the center of attention. Solitude is a discipline that gets behind those feelings to who we are when we feel invisible and unrecognized. Who are we when productivity and recognition fall away and God is the only one watching us? Some of us simply seem to lose our sense of self when there is no one to mirror back who we are. Without the oxygen of doing and the mirror of approval, our feelings of being real and important evaporate. Hollow places open up in our heart, and our soul feels empty and bare. We can feel agitated, scattered and distracted. These disconcerting feelings do two things for us. They reveal how much of our identity is embedded in a false sense of self. And they show us how easy it is to avoid solitude because we dislike being unproductive and unapplauded.

But we need solitude if we intend to unmask the false self and its important-looking image. Alone, without distractions, we put ourselves in a place where God can reveal things to us that we might not notice in the normal preoccupations of life. Solitude opens a space where we can bring our empty and compulsive selves to God. And no matter how well we "do" silence, God is there to accept, receive and love us. God longs for us to be our true self in Christ. He wants us to be who we are meant to be. In solitude we see how little we embrace our true identity in Christ. And we find the truth of who we are in Christ. We are the beloved, and God is pleased with us. This identity is given; it is not earned. Many other voices pull at us, seeking to own and name us, but in solitude we learn what it is to distinguish between the voice of God and the voices of the world. (This is sometimes called the "discernment of spirits" [1 John 4:1].) Times of solitude can be sweet times, but they can also be dark times when God seems to remain withdrawn and silent. We seek the Lord, but he doesn't seem to show up. These times of testing, or the "dark nights," like Jesus had in the wilderness, are well documented in the lives of the saints. Don't be afraid of the darkness or the solitude. Stay with God. The light will eventually dawn.

REFLECTION QUESTIONS

1. How and when do you resist or avoid being alone?

2. What tends to pop into your mind when you are alone?

3. What do you resort to doing when alone?

4. What troubles you or makes you antsy about being alone?

5. When have you felt most comfortable being alone?

   Most uncomfortable?

6. What sense of God do you have when you are alone?

SPIRITUAL EXERCISES

1. In a place where you can't be interrupted, intentionally place yourself in the presence of God. Recognize that the Lord is as near as your own breathing. Inhale God's breath of life; exhale all that weighs on you. Simply be alone with God. • When it is time to return to others, leave the presence of God gently. Carry the sense of being alone with God with you into the next thing.

2. Spend fifteen minutes or more alone with God. You can do an activity if you wish: walk, run, drive, iron. Dedicate the time ahead of you to God. • After the time is up, con-

sider how it was for you to be alone with God. Was it hard? Good? Did God speak to you in any way?

3. Make the time you spend in the shower each morning your alone time with God. Present yourself to your Creator—all of your body, all of the dirt that has accumulated in your soul, all that God has made you to be. Let the water from the shower remind you of the water of life that nourishes and changes you. Let the warmth touch you with love. If you like a cold shower, let the bracing impact call you to live your life to the full. Offer yourself to God for the day. Thank him for the alone time he spends with you.

4. Set aside half a day for time alone with God. Go to a retreat center, quiet chapel or park. Don't stay in your home. Take only your Bible. (See the appendix "Spending Time with God.")

Resources on Solitude

Invitation to Solitude and Silence by Ruth Haley Barton
Surrender to Love by David Benner

"The purpose of prayer, the sacraments and spiritual direction is to awaken us."—Thomas Keating

SPIRITUAL DIRECTION

DESIRE	to give caring attention to my relationship with God, accompanied by the prayerful presence of someone who helps me listen well to God
DEFINITION	Spiritual direction is "help given by one Christian to another which enables that person to pay attention to God's personal communication to him or her, to respond to this personally communicating God, to grow in intimacy with this God, and to live out the consequences of the relationship." (From *The Practice of Spiritual Direction* by William Barry and William Connolly 1982)
SCRIPTURE	"I have much more to say to you, more than you can now bear. But when he, the Spirit of truth, comes, he will guide you into all truth." (John 16:12) "Come near to God and he will come near to you." (James 4:8) "The Sovereign LORD has given me an instructed tongue, to know the word that sustains the weary. He wakens me morning by morning, wakens my ear to listen like one being taught." (Isaiah 50:4)
PRACTICE INCLUDES	• entering an intentional and regular relationship that fosters union with God • opening your prayer life and experience of God to another for the sake of shared listening • listening to your life and the desires God has placed in your heart • letting the Spirit set the direction of the discussion • living by what God is saying to you • allowing another set of eyes and ears to help you interpret your experiences and the voice of God
GOD-GIVEN FRUIT	• walking with a companion who can help you hold your soul before God • noticing your experiences of God • attending to and recognizing God's voice in your life • mending the split between your head and heart • fostering deeper union with God • growing in prayer • learning to better discern the Holy Spirit's movements in decisions you make • finding Jesus in the wounds as well as the joys of life • receiving deeper inner healing

SPIRITUAL DIRECTION

IN THE NEW TESTAMENT WE SEE A VARIETY of relationships in which one person gives spiritual guidance to another. John the Baptist exhorts people to prepare themselves to receive the coming Messiah. Part of preparing themselves involved confessing their sins, receiving baptism and receiving instruction from John, who taught them how to live out the changes confession would bring (Matthew 3:6; Mark 1:5; Luke 3:10-14). Paul also writes of the unique relationship that exists between spiritual children and their spiritual father (or guide). "Even though you have ten thousand guardians in Christ, you do not have many fathers, for in Christ Jesus I became your father through the gospel. Therefore I urge you to imitate me" (1 Corinthians 4:15-16).

Jesus' relationships to his disciples also reveals his personal attention to their growth. He did not treat everyone the same, nor give them all the same advice. He spoke to them personally, in ways that touched their souls. Notice how differently he speaks to Mary and Martha at the death of their brother (see John 11:1-44).

Spiritual direction is a relationship that allows one to assist another in discerning God's activity and presence in his or her life. This relationship assumes that we all need help to listen to God and live out his call. In the busyness of everyday life we can become blind and deaf to the river of life that flows in and around us all. A spiritual director listens with one ear to God and the other to the directee, always encouraging the directee to recognize where God can be found throughout the journey. At its core, spiritual direction attends to the faithfulness and initiative of God. The Holy Spirit is really the Director of the time together as both parties pay attention to God's movements and call.

Spiritual direction is for those longing to drink from the river of life and ready to reflect on their own journey. This usually assumes a certain amount of spiritual maturity as well as an understanding of the importance of noticing God's activity in the soul. Prayer, impressions, experiences and behavioral patterns all become part of the direction process that moves toward deeper intimacy with the Trinity.

Spiritual direction is offered at many retreat centers and through a variety of Catholic orders. But spiritual direction is becoming more popular in Protestant circles as well. If you are looking for a spiritual director, call a local retreat center and ask if they offer spiritual direction. Often spiritual directors are linked to each other through group supervision or Spiritual Directors International. Training centers for spiritual direction may also provide you with leads for spiritual directors in your area.

REFLECTION QUESTIONS

1. How would you describe where you are in your spiritual pilgrimage?
2. How does the idea of attending to the presence and work of God in your life with a spiritual director attract or repel you?
3. Where have you been aware of God's voice, movement or initiative in your life during the past six months or year?
4. Are you growing in recognizing and naming your blind spots? Explain.
5. How do you keep your finger on the pulse of what God is doing in your soul?

SPIRITUAL EXERCISES

1. A spiritual director might ask you to attend to the activity of God in your life through the following exercise. If this sort of exercise is beneficial to you, consider speaking about your experience with someone you know who listens well to God. Draw a lifeline and divide it into seven-year segments. In each segment put the initials of a person you trusted. What kind of people have you trusted? • How has this affected you? How has it affected your view of the trustworthiness of God? • Who do you trust right now with the last 10 percent about yourself?

2. The following questions weave their way in and out of the spiritual direction relationship.

    • What do you sense about your receptivity or resistance to God in general or in particular areas of your life? Bring these thoughts to God in prayer.
    • What is your operative image of God at this time in your life? Tell God how this image affects your behavior and choices.
    • Have you ever had a strange or unusual experience of God? What was it like for you? How did it affect your view of God?

3. If you want a spiritual director but are unable to find someone, ask God to give you insight into the people you know who are able to talk on the level of the soul. Ask someone with gifts in listening and attending to their spiritual journey to walk with you and help you listen to your life.

Resources on Spiritual Direction

The Art of Spiritual Listening by Alice Fryling
The Contemplative Pastor by Eugene Peterson
Holy Invitations by Jeanette Bakke
Toward God by Michael Casey
www.shalom.org
www.christosministries.org

"Never think in lowering yourself you have less power for good."—Charles de Foucauld

"The Christian is under both instruction and authority. . . . He believes what he believes because Jesus taught it, and he does what he does because Jesus told him to do it."—John Stott

SUBMISSION

DESIRE	to have Jesus as the Master of my life in absolutely every way
DEFINITION	Submission that leads to growth means aligning my will and freedom with God's will and freedom. God's will for us includes freely submitting to each other out of love and reverence for Christ.

SCRIPTURE	"Submit to one another out of reverence for Christ." (Ephesians 5:21)
	
	"Who being in very nature God,
	    did not consider equality with God something to be grasped,
	but made himself nothing,
	    taking the very nature of a servant,
	    being made in human likeness.
	And being found in appearance as a man,
	    he humbled himself
	    and because obedient to death—
	        even death on a cross!" (Philippians 2:6-8)
	
	"He must become greater; I must become less." (John 3:30)
	
	"Obey your leaders and submit to their authority. They keep watch over you as men who must give an account." (Hebrews 13:17)
	
	"Offer your bodies as living sacrifices, holy and pleasing to God—this is your spiritual act of worship." (Romans 12:1)

PRACTICE INCLUDES	• seeking God's will (no matter where it leads) and doing it • allowing others to mentor, disciple, teach, correct and guide you • being a good follower • laying aside the need to be in charge • willing and eager obedience to God and those to whom you owe obedience • being an eager learner, trainable and tractable
DESIRED OUTCOMES	• being free from the need to be in charge • teachability • esteeming and honoring others more than yourself • being free from a rebellious and autonomous spirit • surrendering and losing your life to find it • developing approachability, gentleness, humility • expressing a deep regard for others and what they might have to offer

SUBMISSION

SUBMISSION IS AN UNPOPULAR, REPUGNANT CONCEPT THESE DAYS. The notion of giving away power conjures up images of becoming a doormat, a weak-willed nonentity or a brainwashed cult follower. But this perception is miles away from the biblical model of submission. True biblical submission is not linked solely to hierarchy and roles. It begins in the very center of the Trinity where the Father and the Son and the Holy Spirit all mutually honor and defer to each other. Christ's submission to the Father did not make him less than the Father. It was a way the Son gave glory to the Father. (Philippians 2:5-10 wonderfully depicts the nature of biblical submission.)

Godly submission is rooted in God's good and loving intentions for each one of us. Submission is not something God forces down our throats—because forcing people to submit is oppression. Therefore, biblical submission does not trap people in abusive relationships that rob them of their freedom. Submission is a way we allow God's kingdom agenda to shape our choices, relationships and vocations. And it always works in conjunction with our personal freedom.

Scripture makes it clear that God has a plan and knows the best way for people to live. Submission is trusting that God's instructions concerning this life are good for us. Instructions to forgive, serve and love are not given to abuse us but to set us free to be who we were meant to be.

When Christians are instructed to submit to one another (Ephesians 5:21) they are called into relationships that reflect the Trinity. Each member of the body of Christ contributes to every other. Each part serves every other. Each one has a lead part that no other part can play. Together Christians freely choose to enter the divine dance of love. Steps change with seasons and rhythms. Sometimes submission means giving. Sometimes it means receiving. Sometimes submission means leading and at other times it means following. But in each case there is an element of self-giving.

The Catholic and Orthodox, as well as some Protestant, traditions include hierarchical relationships in which younger believers, or novices, submit to spiritual fathers and mothers. Paul encouraged Timothy to see that more mature believers receive, accept and help younger disciples on their journey. Seasoned saints bring experience, wisdom and perspective to new believers. In all Christian traditions and institutions abuses of power exist. However, this is not a reason to invalidate the good that can come out of relationships where godly submission is practiced. It is, rather, a plea to discern when authority figures misuse their power and influence to harm others. Submission to abusive people is never the biblical model for relationships.

REFLECTION QUESTIONS

1. What is your reaction to the word *submission?*

2. What submitting experiences have you had?

3. Who is an example of someone who knew how to practice healthy, biblical submission? How has his or her life influenced you?

4. Do you have to have a submissive temperament? Why or why not?

5. What does it look like for a leader, an activist or an achiever to be submissive?

6. If you have questions about the biblical concept of submission, how might you educate yourself on the topic?

SPIRITUAL EXERCISES

1. Arrange a small group discussion on the topic of submission. Ask people to share their positive or negative experiences of submission to each other. How does understanding these experiences inform your understanding of Ephesians 5:21—"Submit to one another out of reverence for Christ"?

2. Who today do you submit to in the normal events of your life: boss, teachers, parents, colleagues, friends, spouse? What does healthy submission look like in each of these relationships? Pray for grace in these relationships.

3. Consider a character flaw you would like to have transformed in your life. What spiritual discipline might help you cooperate with God in his transforming work? • Willingly practice this discipline for a stipulated period of time. Submit your process to a trusted friend. What is this like for you?

Resources on Submission

Absolute Surrender by Andrew Murray
Life Together by Dietrich Bonhoeffer
Community & Submission by Jan Johnson

Part Four

SHARE MY LIFE
WITH OTHERS

ROBERT MULHOLLAND SUGGESTS THAT SPIRITUAL FORMATION is about being transformed into the image of Christ "for the sake of others." Keeping company with Jesus is not just a private spiritual act, it is the way we share the trinitarian life of God with others. We are meant to live in community in the same way God does. In the company of others we make our journey and learn to tell the truth about ourselves. Interacting with others we learn the vulnerability of giving and receiving love. The *S* disciplines connect us with this loving-one-another life of Christ's body.

The body of Christ is not something we create. It already is. Paul says, "Because there is one loaf, we, who are many, are one body, for we all partake of the one loaf" (1 Corinthians 10:17). Sharing our lives with others is always a risk. Authenticity, interdependence and being known come with a cost. But the alternative to paying the cost of living a one-another life is to live cut off from God. By appropriately opening ourselves to each other in the presence of Christ we discover ways to "lay down our lives for our friends." We learn how to become safe people who bring God's welcoming embrace to others.

"The pace of life and our preoccupation with unimportant things take so much of our attention. The significant things, like taking time to develop friendship, to read and pray, . . . to listen to God—these all get sacrificed on the altar of good works and Christian busyness."—Luci Shaw

ACCOUNTABILITY PARTNER

DESIRE	to give a regular and honest account of my choices, priorities and temptations to a godly and wise companion who points me to Christ
DEFINITION	Having an accountability partner means that I appropriately and reciprocally disclose struggles, failures and temptations to a godly friend who is committed to asking hard questions, willing to challenge, and given to encouragement and prayer.
SCRIPTURE	"Therefore confess your sins to each other and pray for each other so that you may be healed." (James 5:16) "Brothers, if someone is caught in a sin, you who are spiritual should restore him gently. But watch yourself, or you also may be tempted. Carry each other's burdens, and in this way you will fulfill the law of Christ." (Galatians 6:1-2) "But encourage one another daily, as long as it is called Today, so that none of you may be hardened by sin's deceitfulness." (Hebrews 3:13)
PRACTICE INCLUDES	• authentic self-revelation and confession • giving and receiving correction and input • praying for one another • contacting one another in times of temptation and need
GOD-GIVEN FRUIT	• keeping company with Jesus no matter what happens • honoring the truth of being a beloved child of God, in community with another • loving the truth and living in freedom • experiencing God's love and forgiveness more fully through the love and acceptance of a faithful friend • being aware of how denial, rationalization and blame take over your life when left to your own self-assessment • being free from pretense and dishonesty • being humble • sharing your motivations, goals and priorities with another who can help you keep these things in line with biblical values • having appropriate interdependence, self-disclosure and trust

ACCOUNTABILITY PARTNER

WE WERE NOT MEANT TO LIVE AS SELF-RELIANT, INDEPENDENT OPERATORS. Yet many of us choose to live this way because we are afraid of vulnerability. Being known scares us. Admitting feelings or failures shames us. Somewhere, life taught us that openness was dangerous, so self-protection becomes huge. Fences and defenses keep people at arms length. Being competent and in control keeps our weaknesses and struggles out of the reach of others. No wonder we feel alone when we struggle with loneliness, temptation and pain. The walls around us are thick. Furthermore, the effort we pour into image maintenance separates us from who we really are. Hiding the "real me" from others sadly hides the "real me" from me! Image management, pretense—it is a lonely, diseased road.

Clearly we were not designed to journey alone. Without trusted friends we wither and sometimes die. God created us for community and interdependence—with him and with others. God is never alone. He is Trinity. And we are created in his interdependent image. We need others. We need their wisdom in unmasking defense mechanisms that keep the truth at bay. Many of us cannot get through a day or a relationship without falling back on rationalization, denial and blame. And our blind spots hinder us from recognizing how manipulative and hurtful these defenses are. However, what we cannot see is often blatantly visible to others. Without their help and love and truth, we will never know the taste of real freedom.

Not long ago I was challenged by a psychologist to ask several people I worked with how I came across to them. His suggestion proved to be enlightening. I didn't see clearly how I affected people. I made erroneous assumptions about myself as well as others. And I needed that information if I was ever to change.

Accountability partners help us face into the truth of who we are in Christ. They help us face down the lies that shape us, and they orient us in the direction of God's patient love. Together, accountability partners walk into the temptations and difficulties of life. They share the last 10 percent of themselves with each other. They let their secrets out. And together they focus on living holy and responsible lives, fueled by desire for God. Regular and prayerful companionship becomes a life-changing vehicle of God's grace. Accountability partners are particularly valuable for those who (1) are reticent to share struggles, (2) feel stuck in the faith journey, (3) need help facing temptations, (4) tend to journey alone, (5) want to grow in appreciating the love of the body of Christ.

REFLECTION QUESTIONS

1. Who do you talk to about your spiritual life?

   Are you comfortable sharing your faith journey with another?

2. Who has helped you grow in loving and trusting God?

   How has he or she helped you?

3. Where are the growing edges of your faith?

   How do you pray about them and live them out?

4. What are your besetting weaknesses? Addictions? Fears? Temptations?

   Who is praying with and for you about these things?

5. How do you celebrate and share God's work in your life with others?

SPIRITUAL EXERCISES

1. If you would like to have an accountability partner, begin by asking God to bring some-one to mind. An accountability partner does not have to be older and wiser than you. He or she simply needs to share the desire to cooperate with the Holy Spirit in the transformation process. • When a name comes to mind, approach the person(s) with your desire. Decide how often you will meet together. Begin by sharing your stories, temptations and desired areas of growth. Pray for each other.

2. Think back over the last three decades about the people that have shaped your faith. List their initials on a piece of paper. Beside each initial describe how they helped you grow. What did they give you? What did they not give you? • What patterns do you see? • Discuss your observations with your accountability partner. • Discuss what you would like to be for one another.

3. Mutually share your struggles and temptations with your accountability partner. • When faced with temptation, covenant to contact them for encouragement and help.

4. Study the parable of the prodigal son (Luke 15) with your accountability partner (or read *The Return of the Prodigal Son* by Henri Nouwen). • Share how you are like both the younger and older son. How are you becoming like the Father?

5. Get a box of colorful adhesive bandages and meet with your accountability partner or group. Put a bandage on every part of your body that has been wounded physically or emotionally. Share when and how you received these wounds. Pray for each other. • In the following weeks discuss how your wounds affect your lifestyle. Where do they send you into rationalization, denial and blame? • Confess your sins and pray for each other.

6. If you are someone who responds well to rewards or incentives, consider what sort of rewards motivate you to persevere. Are there particular incentives that could help you in cultivating godly patterns of thought and behavior? • How could your accountability partner help you celebrate times when you resist temptation or hold your tongue or encourage your spouse and so forth?

Resources for Accountability Partners

Lost and Found Ministries <www.lostandfoundministries.org>
Finding a Spiritual Friend by Timothy Jones

"Casual recreational sex is hardly a feast—it's not even a good, hearty sandwich. It is a diet of fast food served in plastic containers. . . . The tiger of desire has to be tamed, not chained, nor mounted and ridden, but trained. Love never storms the gates."—Joyce Huggett

CHASTITY

DESIRE	to revere God by receiving and honoring my body and the bodies of others with purity of thought and action
DEFINITION	Healthy chastity is rooted in a deep acceptance of, respect for and protection of the glorious body God has given me and all other human beings. Chaste behavior cultivates sexual purity and nourishes trust.
SCRIPTURE	"You, my brothers, were called to be free. But do not use your freedom to indulge the sinful nature; rather, serve one another in love. The entire law is summed up in a single command: 'Love your neighbor as yourself.' " (Galatians 5:13) "No one ever hated his own body, but he feeds and cares for it, just as Christ does the church—for we are members of his body." (Ephesians 5:29-30) "You shall not commit adultery." (Deuteronomy 5:18)
PRACTICE INCLUDES	• fidelity in marriage and all relationships • not using sex as a test of love • not engaging in sexual behavior that leaves anyone with shame, distress or guilt • accepting your gender and expressing your sexuality in life-giving, God-honoring ways • dressing and acting with modesty • refraining from demeaning sexual jokes and practices • loving rather than using people
GOD-GIVEN FRUIT	• keeping company with Jesus in the midst of met and unmet desire • maintaining healthy, life-giving relationships • developing deep self-acceptance • rooting your own gender in biblical truth rather than in sexual practices • practicing purity • having a healthy sexual relationship in marriage • celebrating yourself as a sexual being

CHASTITY

GOD NOT ONLY MADE THE BODY SACRED, but God himself has come in person, in bodily flesh. The body of Jesus was not some asexual spiritual shell. Jesus was a red-blooded Jewish male with appetites, drives, hormones, temptations and relationships with women. Being 100-percent human, he had the *freedom* to make choices about what to do with his body.

The truth is that real freedom always puts us in a place of responsibility. If I want the freedom to play Mozart, I will have to abide by the laws of music. If I want freedom to raise horses, I will have to build some fences. Freedom put Jesus in a place of responsibility. And Jesus never abrogated responsibility for his behavior. He always shouldered his freedom in a way that honored and cherished the bodies of others. He was free to let the sinful woman massage his feet. He was free to hold children and bless them. He had intimate friendships with both men and women. And these relationships were sexually pure. Jesus is a remarkable example of a man who was comfortable in his own skin and totally free to love. He wasn't emotionally shut down. He was free to go to parties and to hang out with prostitutes. And he was not judgmental or uptight around sexually promiscuous people.

God's boundaries regarding chastity always bring responsibility. But the responsibility to honor another's body actually brings freedom to love. Loving behavior always nurtures, encourages, protects, brings freedom, develops intimacy and supports biblical truth. It never leaves another with cause for shame or embarrassment.

Jesus was fully alive and truly pure. He was no innocent. Purity is not the same thing as innocence. Innocence has not yet been tested. Purity is the product of testing. And no matter what your past has been, the possibility of becoming pure is always an option. It is won with every decision you make to honor God with your body and the body of others. When you stumble in the area of sexuality, begin again. Return to the God who made you and confess that you no longer want to deal with your weakness in the power of the self. Seek forgiveness and help from the Holy Spirit to change. Ask him to free you to shoulder the responsibilities of loving as Jesus did. Help may come to you through a friend or a support group that walks with you as you seek to live in freedom to love in Christ's way.

God's intention is not to spoil your fun but to help you grow into all he intends for you to be. His commands concerning sexuality always serve your best interests. They are life-giving commands, not life-thwarting regulations. God calls adultery and sexual promiscuity bad because these behaviors are destructive to your life. These behaviors do not serve wholesome, healthy relationships, and they don't bring true freedom.

Chastity is based on the awareness that God loves bodies. He came in a body—in Jesus. And now he continues to come to this world through our bodies. We are the temple of God on earth. The Holy Spirit inhabits our bodies, and Christ lives in us. Your whole being is made to be filled with God's trinitarian life.

REFLECTION QUESTIONS

1. Who have been your examples of healthy sexuality and relationships?

   What have they taught you?

2. How have unhealthy models for sexuality influenced or harmed you?

3. What impact do movies, magazines and easy access to pornography have on you?

4. How has your faith helped or not helped you face issues of your own sexuality?

SPIRITUAL EXERCISES

1. Read through Psalm 139:11-18. What is David's opinion of his body? • What is God's view of the body? • What is your own view of your body? Talk to God frankly about how you feel about your body. Listen to what he wants to say to you.

2. Plan a quiet time in a safe place, where you can thank God for your body. Stand before a mirror (naked if you can) and thank God for every part of you. • What wounds does this touch? • What is it like for you to do this?

3. Make a life confession of the sins of your body to a trusted friend or confessor. Prepare by dividing your life into seven-year periods. Write down what you need to confess in each time period. Make your confession. Receive the words of God's forgiveness and absolution to you. • When you are plagued with guilt, return to the love and forgiveness offered you in the discipline of life confession.

4. Form or join an accountability group that is willing to support and be a companion to you in your desire to live a life of purity. Give them freedom to discuss the personal nature of your relationships and pray for you (see "Accountability Partner").

5. When you see a beautiful man or woman, thank God for him or her. Ask to see men and women through God's eyes. Even if you don't know who they are, pray that they will know God and will let their beauty serve him. Lift them to the Father, and thank him for yourself as well.

Resources on Chastity

The Mystery of Marriage by Mike Mason
Real Sex by Lauren Winner

"We go to church so as not to be alone—alone in our joys, alone in our suffering, alone in the everydayness of our lives, alone in the important passages of our lives. . . . We go to church to tell people we love them, and hopefully, to hear them tell us the same thing."—Ronald Rolheiser

COMMUNITY

DESIRE	to express and reflect the self-donating love of the Trinity by investing in and journeying with others
DEFINITION	Christian community exists when believers connect with each other in authentic and loving ways that encourage growth in Christ. They engage in transparent relationships that cultivate, celebrate and make evident Christ's love for all the world.
SCRIPTURE	"I am writing you these instructions so that . . . you will know how people ought to conduct themselves in God's household, which is the church of the living God, the pillar and foundation of the truth." (1 Timothy 3:14-15) "Let the peace of Christ rule in your hearts, since as members of one body you were called to peace. And be thankful. Let the word of Christ dwell in you richly as you teach and admonish one another with all wisdom, and as you sing psalms, hymns and spiritual songs with gratitude in your hearts to God." (Colossians 3:15-16)
PRACTICE INCLUDES	• practicing the biblical "one anothers" • cultivating authentic relationships that connect you to God and his plan to serve and love this world • exercising your gifts in fellowship with others • engaging in hospitality that promotes honest sharing and caring • participating in a small group or covenant group • sharing life with an accountability partner or prayer partner • engaging in mission with others
GOD-GIVEN FRUIT	• keeping company with Jesus in everything that does and doesn't happen in community • working against the spirit of isolation and independence that cripples the church by practicing the "one anothers" within the body of Christ • moving from independence and self-absorption to others-centeredness • growing in love and concern for others • having a relational rather than a functional definition of identity • practicing Matthew 18:15 by offering and receiving forgiveness and reconciliation • revealing God's love through caring for others • speaking the truth in love • participating in a small group where you are known and encouraged to grow in faith • becoming part of a community that is larger than yourself and your own goals, possessions and achievements

COMMUNITY

RESIDENTS OF THE UNITED STATES LIVE IN A NATION founded on a Declaration of Independence. Independence is a wonderful gift so long as it does not keep us from the right sort of dependence. Jesus taught his followers that they were part of the family of God. They were not meant to be lone rangers but part of a living organism, Christ's body, the church (1 Corinthians 12). No part of the body functions by itself, nourishes itself or serves itself alone. Every part is for every other part—whether hurting or rejoicing. I am amazed how hitting my thumb with a hammer can send my whole body to the rescue. My mouth opens, my eyes, water, my neurons run back and forth with messages from thumb to brain that says, "This hurts! Help the thumb."

The family of God is not simply a utilitarian concept; it is a loving organism where every part belongs and finds its health in right relationship to every other part. No part is meant to function alone. Paul vividly describes this reality of belonging in 1 Corinthians 10:17: "Because there is one loaf, we, who are many, are one body, for we all partake of the one loaf."

We belong together, not apart. God is not a bachelor who lives alone. He is a holy community of three. And we express his nature best when we are in a community committed to growing and being transformed into Christlikeness.

Henri Nouwen writes in *Making All Things New:* "Community as discipline is the effort to create a free and empty space among people where together we can practice true obedience. . . . To create space for God among us requires the constant recognition of the Spirit of God in each other."

God's family is meant to be the "show and tell" of what true belonging and love looks like. Sadly, our Christian life together can be a disappointing misrepresentation of who Christ is. Nevertheless, God's one plan for reaching the world is rooted in the community of broken people who gather with a desire to love him and bring in his kingdom. We will never be perfect people; but imperfect people committed to a radical Spirit-empowered love can change their relationships and their world.

The discipline of community can be practiced in many ways. You will find material on small groups, covenant groups, hospitality, spiritual friendship and prayer partners in this book. Each of these is a unique expression of body life.

REFLECTION QUESTIONS

1. What is appealing or unappealing to you about being an independent operator?

2. How do you respond to the words

   - dependent
   - independent
   - interdependent

   How does your response affect your experience of Christian community?

3. What kind of connection does Christ want you to have with Christian brothers and sisters?

4. How does the life you are leading reflect the value Christ places on belonging to the family of God?

5. When has the body of Christ nurtured and sustained you?

   What was it like for you?

6. What gifts do you bring to the body of Christ?

SPIRITUAL EXERCISES

1. Choose one of the "one anothers"—"love one another," "serve one another," "pray for one another," "forgive one another"—(see appendix 6, "One Anothers"). Practice living one particular "one another" every day for a week. • What is this practice like for you?

2. Have a "We Celebrate Your Birth, O Beautiful Child of God" party. Write notes of gratitude to the person. Write prayers of desire for his or her life. Put all these in a scrapbook.

3. Ask someone to tell you their story. Listen to the story as deeply as you can. Tell the person how much it means to you to hear the story. • How does the story give you a deeper understanding of your friend, of God and of yourself?

4. Include others in family gatherings. Practice what it is to belong to God's family—not just your nuclear family.

5. Begin a thank-you list. Thank God for the people in your life who have helped you grow. • Write a song or poem about God's good gift of family.

6. If you have something against a brother or sister in Christ, go to that person and make peace with them. • Meditate on Romans 12:18. Journal your response.

7. Join a church, a small group, a mission group. Become part of a community of faith and see how this imparts Christ to you in new and deep ways.

Resources on Community

The Safest Place on Earth by Larry Crabb

"No one person can fulfill all your needs. But the community can truly hold you. The community can let you experience the fact that, beyond your anguish, there are human hands that hold you and show you God's faithful love."—Henri Nouwen

COVENANT GROUP

DESIRE	to enter into authentic, confidential and healing relationships with a committed group of fellow pilgrims
DEFINITION	A covenant group is composed of people who commit themselves to helping and encouraging one another, as each prayerfully seeks to live out God's will in their lives.
SCRIPTURE	"Be devoted to one another in brotherly love." (Romans 12:10) "For as long as it's still God's Today, keep each other on your toes so sin doesn't slow down your reflexes." (Hebrews 3:13 *The Message*) "Let us not give up meeting together, as some are in the habit of doing, but let us encourage one another." (Hebrews 10:25)
PRACTICE INCLUDES	• sharing your story and your authentic self with a small group who listens with you for God's word for your life • confessing the truth to others who can encourage and help you stay the course • practicing the "one anothers" of Scripture in the context of a committed community • having ongoing, long-term prayer for others and their transformation • allowing others to know you well enough to speak the truth to you • gathering with others who help you live by intentional rhythms that shape your character into the image of Christ
GOD-GIVEN FRUIT	• keeping company with Jesus and others • journeying with others in transparent and authentic ways that lead deeply into the reality of being God's family • experiencing the gifts of the body of Christ in ministry to one another • building appropriate interdependence on others • gathering around the person of Christ and sharing his Word and Spirit with others • merging into community rather than emerging into independence • committing to a long-term journey with others • practicing the biblical "one anothers" • developing discernment

COVENANT GROUP

WE ARE A NATION ON THE MOVE. People switch jobs, leave communities and turn over their relationships at an astonishing rate. Consequently we are a society with acquaintances, colleagues and allies, but no real friends. We may know how to work together to get things done, and we may be gifted in small talk, shop talk and weather talk, but we trust no one with the last 10 percent of ourselves. In a crisis we don't know who to call in the middle of the night. There is no one we trust with our lives.

Covenant groups are a particular kind of small group designed to take participants to deep levels of the soul with one another. They provide a vehicle for continuity and development of relationships that attend to peoples' stories as well as the hard questions concerning lifestyles, priorities, goals and spiritual well-being. Because the trust and safety needed for this kind of self-revelation takes time, covenant groups tend to be long-term and closed to people dropping in to try it out. My own covenant group has been going at least twelve years, though I have been a member for only ten of those years. (Covenant groups decide together when they want to bring in new members or split.)

As trust builds, members learn how to listen deeply to one another in the presence of Christ. They promise to encourage, help, support, challenge and pray for one another. Intentional spiritual nurture, care and listening are primary reasons for gathering. Therefore, the major portion of group time is devoted to authentic sharing by and prayer for each member.

Covenant groups may sign a written covenant that addresses availability, prayer, openness, honesty, confidentiality, accountability and so forth. Or the covenant may be a verbal promise to remain faithfully engaged with others on the journey. In either case the deliberate and intentional nature of covenant groups requires shared commitment. My covenant group has challenged me, corrected me, cried with me and held me in my pain. I need them to keep me on track.

At times covenant groups take on projects or ministries together. My covenant group consists of women involved in different ministries in the Chicago area. We decided that one thing we could do together that would incorporate our gifts and desires would be to lead a spiritual pilgrimage. So in 2003 we took thirty folks to visit the sites of the Spanish mystics. As we traveled together, we introduced them to spiritual practices of Ignatius of Loyola, Teresa of Ávila and John of the Cross.

REFLECTION QUESTIONS

1. Do you prefer task groups or relational groups? How have your past experiences and temperament so inclined you?

   Is there a group of people who really knows you and cares about you? What is that like for you?

2. Which do you prefer: one on one, small groups, large groups? Where is your growing edge in each of these settings? How do you experience God in each of these settings?

3. Can you imagine Jesus spending his life on a cell phone, rushing to meetings and never having time to answer a question he didn't refer to his secretary?

4. What kind of group relationships did Jesus value?

5. Why did Jesus do develop a small band of disciples?

SPIRITUAL EXERCISES

1. Take an inventory of your relationships. Divide a piece of paper into columns titled "Allies," "Colleagues," "Acquaintances," "Friends," "Close Friends." Name those who you know in each category. • What did you find out about your relationships? • What is God saying to you about this?

2. Who would you like to grow with in your spiritual life? Pray for God to bring a few names to mind. Contact these people and see if they are willing to meet together regularly to share the journey.

3. Take a closer look at how you interact in groups. How do you think others would describe your group participation: a good team player, a good listener, an authentic participant, a control person? Ask people who are in small group settings with you to give you their perspective on what you are like in a group. • Offer yourself to God and ask to become a growing, teachable participant rather than an independent operator.

Resources on Covenant Groups

A Spiritual Formation Workbook by James Bryan Smith
Companions in Christ by Adele Gonzalez, E. Glenn Hinson, Rueben P. Job, Marjorie J. Thompson, Wendy M. Wright and Gerrit Scott Dawson

"Spiritual discipline, then, is developing soul reflexes so that we know how to live. We discipline ourselves to develop soul memory in normal times so that we'll be equipped for the times of high demand or deep crisis."—Douglas Rumford

DISCIPLING

DESIRE	to be in a relationship where I am encouraged or where I encourage another to become an apprentice of Jesus
DEFINITION	Discipling is the process of equipping, training and encouraging another in his or her apprenticeship to Jesus. It means journeying with and helping another to grow in knowledge as well as in the virtues and character of Christ.
SCRIPTURE	"So then, brothers, stand firm and hold to the teachings we passed on to you, whether by word of mouth or by letter." (2 Thessalonians 2:15) "Make it your ambition to lead a quiet life, to mind your own business and to work with your hands, just as we told you, so that your daily life may win the respect of outsiders and so that you will not be dependent on anybody." (1 Thessalonians 4:11) "Go out and train everyone you meet, far and near, in this way of life, marking them by baptism in the threefold name: Father, Son, and Holy Spirit." (Matthew 28:19 *The Message*) "I no longer call you servants, because a servant does not know his master's business. Instead, I have called your friends, for everything that I learned from my Father I have made known to you." (John 15:15)
PRACTICE INCLUDES	• meeting with another to study the Bible, pray and encourage his or her spiritual growth • teaching and equipping another so he or she can teach others also • instructing and modeling of Christian virtues and disciplines • attending to the worship, faith and obedience of a younger believer by a more seasoned saint • intentionally investing in the life of an apprentice to Christ • using gifts and talents to help another grow in Christ
GOD-GIVEN FRUIT	• keeping company with Jesus as you fulfill his command to go and make disciples • becoming a model of service, faith, obedience and worship of Christ • becoming a trainer, equipper and encourager of others • using your gifts for the sake of the kingdom • obediently following Jesus in making disciples • investing in what lasts—the growth and fruitfulness of others • passing on what you have been given • becoming a lifelong learner and a lifelong lover

DISCIPLING

IN MATTHEW 28:19-20 JESUS TELLS HIS FOLLOWERS that they are to "go and make disciples of all nations, baptizing them in the name of the Father and of the Son and of the Holy Spirit, and teaching them to obey everything I have commanded you." Making disciples is the God-given agenda for the church. That agenda is more than "saving souls." It involves helping people make the transformational journey into Christlikeness. Disciplemakers give light and hope and help to those willing to be intentional about their growth.

Discipling typically happens when believers meet around the Word of God to spur one another on to love and good deeds. Often a more mature Christian disciples a younger one in a Paul-Timothy relationship. But it is also possible for a group of two or three peers to disciple one another through meeting and studying together. Though the Holy Spirit is ultimately responsible for a disciple's growth, the disciplemaker has a part to play. Disciplemakers seek to help others grow in loving God with all their heart, soul, strength and mind. Discipling someone includes introducing them to a number of spiritual practices, relationships and experiences that can help them mature in their faith. A discipling relationship may focus on Bible study, *lectio,* book discussions; varieties of prayer; lifestyle choices; mentoring in areas of service, stewardship, hospitality, self-care and witness.

Just as parents long to see their children reach their potential, so disciplemakers long for the world to experience the impact of lives apprenticed to Jesus. The book of Acts records how the Holy Spirit "turned the world upside down" through the lives of Jesus' first disciples. Jesus is still looking for disciples. And the Holy Spirit is still able to turn the world around through the lives of people committed to keeping company with Jesus.

REFLECTION QUESTIONS

1. What do you think the difference is between being a Christian and being a disciple?

2. Talk to God about the desires and fears you have related to being a dedicated disciple of Jesus.

3. *Discipline* and *disciple* come from the same root. What sort of reaction do you have to the word *discipline?*

4. Does being a disciplined apprentice of Jesus appeal to you? Why or why not?

5. Who do you want to become? What do you want to be remembered for when you die?

6. How are you intentionally partnering with God to become who he intended you to be?

SPIRITUAL EXERCISES

1. To discover where you are in your discipleship journey, draw a lifeline marking out seven-year segments. In each segment write down the factors that shaped your growth in Christ. • Are there particular disciplines that formed you? Have the disciplines changed with the seasons of your life? Where are there gaps in knowledge or experience in your journey?

2. What disciplines resonate with the desires of your heart today? • Do you sense God calling you into a new practice, relationship or experience that can help you grow as a disciple?

3. How would you describe the people who have helped you grow in your spiritual journey? What particular gift did they give to you? What have you learned from them about yourself and God? • What do you want to say to God about each person? • How can you express your thanks to each of these people?

4. Who have you intentionally given yourself to for the sake of their growth in Christ? List their names. Beside each name write what it was like for you to walk with them. Where were you challenged? How did you experience God in each relationship? • Spend some time praying for each of these people.

5. If you have children at home, consider how you are reflecting the life of Jesus in your interaction at home. What would you like for them to learn about Jesus from you? • Imagine Jesus in each of the rooms of your house. What is he enjoying? Who is he caring for? • How can you thoughtfully model the virtues of Jesus' life in your relationships with your children?

Resources in Discipling

Discipleship Essentials by Greg Ogden

"The essence of hospitality is a heart open to God, with room prepared for the Guestness of the Holy Spirit, that welcomes the presence of Christ. This is what we share with those to whom we open our doors. We give them him."—Karen Burton Mains

HOSPITALITY

DESIRE	to be a safe person who offers others the grace, shelter and presence of Jesus
DEFINITION	Hospitality creates a safe, open space where a friend or stranger can enter and experience the welcoming spirit of Christ in another.
SCRIPTURE	"Welcome one another, therefore, just as Christ has welcomed you, for the glory of God." (Romans 15:7 NRSV) "Love the Lord your God with all your heart and with all your soul and with all your mind and with all your strength. . . . 'Love your neighbor as yourself.'" (Mark 12:30-31) "Stay on good terms with each other, held together by love. Be ready with a meal or a bed when it's needed. Why, some have extended hospitality to angels without ever knowing it!" (Hebrews 13:1-2 *The Message*) "Do not let your hearts be troubled. Trust in God; trust also in me. In my Father's house are many rooms; if it were not so, I would have told you. I am going there to prepare a place for you." (John 14:1-3)
PRACTICE INCLUDES	• sharing your home, food, resources, car and all that you call your own so that another might experience the reality of God's welcoming heart • reaching out to and receiving the stranger or the enemy with the hope that he or she might be transformed into a friend • loving, not entertaining, the guest • welcoming others into your clique, group, club, life • spontaneously inviting people for meals • reaching out beyond your nuclear family to include others • hosting exchange students
GOD-GIVEN FRUIT	• keeping company with Jesus; offering his welcoming heart to others • displaying God's welcoming heart to the world (children, foreign students, neighbors, teachers, colleagues) • living the truth that all you have belongs to God • providing safe places for people in an unsafe world • loving people rather than impressing them • developing conversational skills that put others at ease • opening your home to others • expressing your love for God through celebrating and honoring others

HOSPITALITY

THE WORLD SEEMS TO BECOME MORE DANGEROUS EVERY DAY. People feel vulnerable in their own homes and on guard in the presence of others. Many environments are competitive, hostile and unsafe. Safe places and safe people are few and far between. True welcome and nurture seem a long-lost dream. Because we have been welcomed into the love of Christ and received as dearly loved children, we can offer the world a place of safety and healing. We can incarnate the welcoming heart of God for the world. God welcomes strangers, inviting them to share his home and get to know his family. During World War II an entire French village risked their lives to welcome and shelter Jews. When pastor Andre Trocmé was asked why the village responded as they did, he replied, "I could not bear to be separated from Jesus." That is hospitality at its core—offering the welcome of Jesus to any and all.

Hospitality is not about impressing others with well-decorated homes and gourmet cooking. It's not simply for the gifted or those with clean homes. Neither is it just for women. Hospitality is a way of loving our neighbor in the same way God has loved us. In *To Know as We Are Known,* Parker Palmer describes hospitality as a way of "receiving each other, our struggles, our newborn ideas with openness and care. It means creating an ethos in which the community of truth can form."

The early church shaped their life together around the practice of hospitality. "They broke bread in their homes and ate together with glad and sincere hearts, praising God and enjoying the favor of all the people" (Acts 2:46-47). Our world desperately needs safe people and safe places. Hospitality is one way we become God's welcoming arms in a big and often hostile world.

REFLECTION QUESTIONS

1. When have you been so deeply received that the welcome touched your soul?

2. When have you been wounded because you were not welcomed and received?

   How has the welcome of Jesus touched your life and your wounds?

3. How comfortable are you with being the host or hostess?

4. Who models hospitality and welcome for you?

5. How do you feel about having guests come to visit?

   Where do you struggle with doing everything perfectly?

6. How might Jesus want to use your heart and home as a shelter for others?

SPIRITUAL EXERCISES

1. Remember a time you have been deeply welcomed and received. Recount the circumstances and the way people reached out to you. Picture where Jesus was in this event. Let God touch you again with his welcome and love.

2. Develop the practice of praying for the people you invite to your home. Pray for them as you invite them. Pray for them the day they come. Pray for them as they leave your driveway. • How has sharing your home with them given you deeper ways to hold them before the Lord? • Send a note with your prayer to your guests.

3. Be spontaneous. Hold a "craving potluck." Ask everyone to bring something they crave. Don't try to make it perfect. Focus on the guests.

4. Hospitality is not something we do all by ourselves. It invites others in. When you offer hospitality, let your guests help. • If you have trouble letting people help you, make this a matter of prayer. What in you needs to be touched to make you receptive and open?

5. When strangers or guests arrive, welcome them with all your heart. Everyone in the home should go to the door to greet the guests. Tell them how glad you are that they have come. • Then when they leave, stay in the driveway until they are gone from view. Treat each guest as though he or she were an angel in disguise, "for by so doing some people have entertained angels without knowing it" (Hebrews 13:2).

6. Have a "left-overs" gathering. Invite people to bring what is in their refrigerator. See what kind of meal happens. Tell your guests the main point is just to be together!

7. Develop a list of standard conversational questions (other than "What do you do?") that can open people up to one another. How do the questions you ask bring welcome rather than comparison?

8. Help your children grow in understanding God's hospitable heart. Help them plan a party for their friends. Encourage them to think about what will make each one feel most welcome.

Resources on Hospitality

Open Heart, Open Home by Karen Mains
Opening Our Hearts and Homes by Karen Mains and Adele Calhoun
Making Room by Christine Pohl

"Ask me not where I live and what I like to eat. Ask me what I am living for and what I think is keeping me from living fully for that."—Thomas Merton

MENTORING

DESIRE	to accompany and encourage others to grow to their God-given potential
DEFINITION	Mentoring is a relational experience in which one person empowers another by sharing his or her life, experience and God-given resources. A mentor nurtures an apprentice's personal development, faith and skill.
SCRIPTURE	"But Barnabas took him and brought him to the apostles. He told them how Saul on his journey had seen the Lord and that the Lord had spoken to him." (Acts 9:27) "Timothy, my son, I give you this instruction in keeping with the prophecies once made about you, so that by following them you may fight the good fight, holding on to faith and a good conscience." (1 Timothy 1:18) "Likewise, teach the older women to be reverent in the way they live. . . . Then they can train the younger women to love their husbands and children, to be self-controlled and pure." (Titus 2:3-5)
PRACTICE INCLUDES	• guidance, encouragement and modeling given by a more mature believer to a younger one • training that equips another to better use their gifts • building authentic relationships that provide support, encouragement and help in specific areas. • providing or receiving influence, instruction, training and perspective
GOD-GIVEN FRUIT	• learning from example • practicing teachability and humility • building others up in Christ • opening my calling, vocation, gifting and limits to a mentor's wise attention • garnering the wisdom of those who have walked with God for many years • developing and encouraging new leaders and disciples • seeing others grow and change

MENTORING

WE DON'T AUTOMATICALLY CHANGE OUR IDEAS, attitudes and behavioral patterns just because we learn something new that is good for us. Most of us need more help in transformation than that. We need examples, relationships, hands-on experience, support and empowering. We need mentors. In Christian theology the Holy Spirit is the mentoring nuclear reactor of transformation. And one of the tools in his hand is the body of Christ. Barnabas is a wonderful example of a believer who risked mentoring a wildcard named Paul. Barnabas's investment in Paul reached farther than either of them could have imagined. Paul's teaching and life helped shape the early church, and his letters became part of Scripture.

Throughout church history people have been shaped and guided by mentors and teachers. Gregory (A.D. 213-270) wrote of his teacher Origen:

> He stimulated us by the acts he performed more than by the theories he taught. . . . Less obvious, but more important . . . was the fellowship with this man. Where I was blind he guided me. He taught me the truth concerning the Word. It was like a spark dropping into my inmost soul and catching fire there. (Bruce Shelley, *Church History in Plain Language*)

Godly mentors help people grow. They believe in others. They recognize raw potential and willingness to be taught. Mentors often see more in the mentee's gifts than the mentee does. A mentor's confidence and equipping skills can motivate a mentee to try new things and take risks he or she would never try alone. Mentors are not competitive; they eagerly empower others—even if it means empowering them into their own position. Mentors believe that by giving away their gifts, time, treasure, teaching and power they can influence and shape others for the sake of the kingdom.

Mentoring does not need to be simply a professional and structured enterprise. Parents can mentor their children in skills and behaviors. Teachers can mentor their students. Students and friends can mentor one another when they have a skill someone wants. More mature married couples can mentor younger married couples, and older parents can mentor younger parents. Mentoring is passing on what you have. It does not require you to be responsible for more than you know.

Few of us remember who won the last five Heisman trophies. We don't remember who wins the Nobel or Pulitzer prizes each year. But we all remember those mentors who believed in us and equipped us to become more than we ever could have been on our own.

REFLECTION QUESTIONS

1. Reflect on the kind of person you want to be at age thirty, at fifty, at eighty.

2. Who do you know now that is an example of where you want to head?

3. What are you doing now to become the person you long to be?

4. How has the presence of someone in your life enabled you to do something or become someone you could never have on your own?

5. Is there something you wanted to do and no one ever believed you could? How did that affect you?

6. How does being competitive affect your ability to mentor others?

7. When have you empowered another person to succeed, grow or develop?

   What was that like for you? For the other person?

SPIRITUAL EXERCISES

1. Take a mentor review. Think back over your life, writing down the names of those who have believed in you and mentored you. What happened to you because of their presence in your life? • Write them a letter telling them what they mean to you.

2. "Pay it forward." Think over your job and the colleagues you work with. Who needs someone to believe in them and mentor them? Ask the Lord if he intends for you to mentor this person. Offer to be a mentor for the next year.

3. Ask God to give you his heart for others and their transformation. Then pay attention to the mentoring nudge the Holy Spirit gives. Take the initiative to help someone grow.

4. Where do you feel stuck spiritually? Who could help you? Ask for help!

5. If you are an older married couple, take on a newly married couple and share your lives with them. • If you are young at heart, find some young people to share your heart with. • If you are gifted at hospitality, tutor someone who isn't. • If you are gifted in prayer, become a prayer partner of a young person. • Pass on the gift of you to another. (Remember, you don't have to offer something spiritual—just offer who you are and what you know.)

6. What keeps you from mentoring another? • Talk to God about your hesitations. What is he calling you to do?

Resources on Mentoring

A Resilient Life by Gordon MacDonald
Finding a Spiritual Friend by Timothy Jones

"God has created me to do Him some definite service; He has committed some work to me which He has not committed to another. . . . I have a part in a great work; I am a link in a chain, a bond of connection between persons. He has not created me for naught. I shall love as Christ loved, I shall do his work."—John Henry Newman

SERVICE

DESIRE	to reflect the helping, caring and sharing love of God in the world
DEFINITION	Service is a way of offering resources, time, treasure, influence and expertise for the care, protection, justice, and nurture of others. Acts of service give hands to the second greatest commandment: "Love your neighbor as yourself."
SCRIPTURE	"This is the kind of fast day I'm after: to break the chains of injustice, get rid of exploitation in the workplace, free the oppressed, cancel debts. What I'm interested in seeing you do is: sharing your food with the hungry, inviting the homeless poor into your homes, putting clothes on the shivering ill-clad, being available to your own families." (Isaiah 58:6-7 *The Message*) "Whoever serves me must follow me; and where I am, my servant also will be. My father will honor the one who serves me." (John 12:26) "Love the Lord your God with all your heart and with all your soul and with all your mind. This is the first and greatest commandment. And the second is like it: 'Love your neighbor as yourself.' " (Matthew 22:37-39)
PRACTICE INCLUDES	• walking the talk; being what you profess • doing service projects: Habitat for Humanity, mission trips, volunteerism, foster care, prison ministry • mentoring, gifts of mercy and helps • using your influence to better the lives of others • using your gifts to build the kingdom of God
GOD-GIVEN FRUIT	• giving yourself to others in the service of Jesus • seeing your neighbors as real and important; loving them as you love yourself • recognizing the difference between a Messiah complex and knowing how to love others well and sacrificially • walking your talk • rooting out injustice • seriously caring for widows, orphans and the oppressed • receiving interruptions as opportunities to do good • volunteering time, talents and treasure for the good of others • being free to leave your comfort zone and risk yourself in service

SERVICE

MANY AMERICANS SPEND THEIR LIVES WORKING THEMSELVES into a place where they can be served more than serve. As the saying goes: "It's good to be queen [or king]!" Our culture sees the blessed ones as those who get waited on and served. And few among us aspire to be the maid with the job of serving and blessing others.

In Genesis 18:18 the Lord says, "Abraham will surely become a great and powerful nation, and all nations on earth will be blessed through him." God's trajectory is to bless the earth through his people. And to show them exactly what he has in mind, he comes to earth as one who serves (Luke 22:27). Jesus is God with us. And he calls us to serve (Matthew 22:37-39). This is not religious rhetoric that we simply endorse as a good rule of thumb. The Christian discipline of service is the way the world discovers the love of God. We are the way God blesses the earth.

Jesus' attention to the blessing God intended to bring to the nations never wavered. When he finds the temple in Jerusalem clogged with buying and selling, he takes the whole religious establishment to task—running them out of the temple with a whip of cords. God's people were to be a blessing; his temple was not supposed to be a place of business but "a house of prayer for all nations" (Mark 11:17). God intends to bless the nations through us and our lives of service. Christians are the very presence of God to others. We become God's vehicle of blessing on planet earth.

We will never really serve others unless we see that the needs of our neighbors are as real and important as our own. This may seem obvious. But the truth of the matter is many of us look right through others and never see them, let alone care about what they need. When we are preoccupied with our own concerns, much of the world is simply invisible to us. Service is rooted in *seeing*—in seeing others as God does. God cares about productive and nonproductive people, poor people and rich people, educated and noneducated people. God cares about everybody. And if we harbor hatred that breeds neglect of any of God's people, we are hindering the Spirit of Jesus. The Spirit of Jesus is a compassionate, serving Spirit that always works for the good of others. Jesus maintains that radical love for others demonstrates whether we know God or not.

Martin Luther King Jr. said, "Everybody can be great because anybody can serve. You don't have to have a college degree to serve. You don't have to make your subject and verb agree to serve. You only need a heart full of grace, a soul generated by love." It is enough to make a truly great difference in someone's life.

REFLECTION QUESTIONS

1. What is it like to be loved by someone as he or she loves him- or herself?

2. Do you like to be served or to serve? How does this affect the way you live?

3. When do you live out of an entitlement mentality rather than love of neighbor?

SPIRITUAL EXERCISES

1. Every morning for the next two weeks ask your spouse, roommate or a colleague, "What can I do for you today?" Then do it. • Talk to God about what this is like for you. What do you see about yourself?

2. Develop a yearly practice of involving yourself in one intentional service, mission or relief project. Consider which type of project speaks to some of the longings of your own heart.

3. Divide a paper into three columns. Above one column write, "For Me." Above the second column write, "For Others." Above the third column write, "For God." Review the past week or month. Jot down in each column the things you have bought and done for yourself, others and God. What does this inventory reveal about your life? • Take time to read Luke 23. Gaze at Jesus on the cross. What has God given because he loves you? • How would you like to see the answers in your columns change over the next months? Listen to your longings and God's promptings.

4. Spend some time meditating on the story of the good Samaritan found in Luke 10:25-37. Become quiet and ask the Lord to speak to you. Give your imagination to God. Read the slowly story and aloud, savoring the words. • What stood out to you? • Read the passage a second time, imagining you are the Levite. What are your concerns? Why are you in a hurry? • Then put yourself in the place of the priest. What are your concerns? Why do you pass by? • Imagine you are the Samaritan. Why do you stop to help? How do you feel about incurring all the expenses for another's care? • Who of these three characters do you tend to be like? • Who in your life receives your care: family? friends? Who else?

5. Sign on to set up or take down an event. This part of event planning is the least sought after. • What is it like for you to do a simple task that doesn't require your skill or expertise? What does this tell you about your acts of service?

6. Ask those who know you to give you their take on what your spiritual gifts are. Plan a way of using your gifts to benefit others in the next week and month.

7. Get to know some missionaries or a faith-based organization. Find out what they need.

Ask them how you could serve. Do something that helps them help others.

Resources on Service

Service and Secrecy by Jan Johnson

An Intrusive Gospel? Christian Mission in the Postmodern World by C. Norman Kraus

www.thesimpleway.org

"In our world full of strangers, estranged from their own past, culture and country, from their neighbors, friends and family, from their deepest self and their God, we witness a painful search for a hospitable place where life can be lived without fear and where community can be found."
—Henri Nouwen

SMALL GROUP

DESIRE	to make my spiritual journey with a community of trusted friends
DEFINITION	Small groups intentionally connect people, regularly gathering them together to help one another grow in loving God and doing his will.

SCRIPTURE	"How good and pleasant it is
	    when brothers [and sisters] live together in unity!" (Psalm 133:1)
	
	"Though one may be overpowered,
	    two can defend themselves.
	A cord of three stands is not quickly broken." (Ecclesiastes 4:12)
	
	"Let us not give up meeting together, as some are in the habit of doing, but let us encourage one another—and all the more as you see the Day approaching." (Hebrews 10:25)

PRACTICE INCLUDES	• regularly gathering with others to study Scripture, pray and support one another • connecting with others through support groups, discernment groups, covenant groups, Bible study groups, outreach groups, mission groups, book clubs, discipleship groups, prayer groups • intentionally opening myself to others and listening to their insights about my life and journey • developing a hospitable community in which strangers can become known • blessing others in my small group through my gifts
GOD-GIVEN FRUIT	• keeping company with God and others • being known in a safe and supportive community • being part of something larger than your own independent journey • growing in personal transformation • caring for others beyond my personal family and immediate friends • increasing openness to people who are different from you

SMALL GROUP

Jesus was never a lone ranger. He has always been part of a divine community with the Father and the Holy Spirit. And when he came to earth, he continued to live his life in small groups. He began his ministry by choosing twelve disciples to be with him (Luke 6:13). Then he spent three years pouring himself into this small group. He taught them truth about God and about themselves. He modeled spiritual practices for and with them. He introduced them to experiences of service, witness and healing prayer. And day after relentless day, in the messy, hard-to-control center of community, he gave them the gift of his full presence.

Spiritual transformation is not a solo event. God works in us through others. Dan Meyer suggests that babies should have a tag attached to their toe that reads, "Life is hard. Do it in groups." We all need a circle of friends to encourage, support and speak the truth to us. Without their authentic voices, we may never see who we are. It is the unconditional love of a small group that can give us the courage to name the good, the bad and the ugly about ourselves. Small groups can help us press into God's love when it seems beyond us.

Many of us recognize that small groups are a good idea. We can even identify places of loneliness and times when we feel invisible or unknown. But the pace and activity in life overwhelms us. And a longing for meaningful relationships does not necessarily translate into intentionally making room for them in our busy schedules. Still, the discipline of doing the spiritual journey in the company of others remains Jesus' model for discipleship. As seasons of activity shift, reexamine your priorities. How might life in a small group replace a night in front of the TV or computer?

Small groups are a simple means of connecting people and offering them a place for self-disclosure and meaningful interaction. Within this context each group decides their purpose, duration, number and so on. Purposes range from therapeutic to recreational and from social to instructional. Small groups exist for Bible study, prayer, social action, support, games, meals, hobbies, tasks and projects. Small groups come in a variety of shapes and sizes: study groups, support groups, ministry groups, training groups, covenant groups (included in this book) and triads.

There is no one right way to do small groups. Small groups take on their own particular personalities based on the participants and their goals. Some groups are highly structured and have a designated leader. Other groups share the leadership and have a more laid-back approach. Still, the best small groups tend to include (1) an intentional purpose and agreement to make the group a priority, (2) a structure that supports the purpose and people in the group, and (3) facilitators who help keep the group on track.

Generally, small groups go through definitive stages of development. Not all small groups make it through every stage. During my time as a staff member with InterVarsity Christian Fellowship I remember being taught four stages of small group development.

- Forming—a group begins and decides its purpose, content, structure and covenant.

- Storming—a group runs into conflict, difficulties and personality quirks. Different ideas about what it means to journey together emerge. Control issues surface. Some people dominate while others clam up. Often if a group disintegrates, it is during this stage.

- Norming—the group makes it through the "storming" stage and settles into the gifts and struggles of the journey for the long haul.

- Transforming—the group accomplishes its goal or mission and in the process grows and becomes more of who God created them to be.

REFLECTION QUESTIONS

1. How have small group experiences affected your spiritual journey?

2. If you have been in a small group that went through the stages mentioned above, what was that like for you?

3. What would your dream small group look like?

SPIRITUAL EXERCISES

1. If you have never been part of a small group experience, ask the Lord if now is the time to join one. Consider what kind of small group you would like to be involved in: an outreach group, a Bible study group, a book club, a covenant group, a support group. Ask God to help you start or find a group you can journey with.

2. Three people are enough to begin a triad, or small group. So if you are not a group lover, ask two other people to join you in a triad. Meet to discuss your expectations, content and structure you wish to have.

3. Many books are available to aid the small group process. Spend some time at a bookstore looking into the variety of tools that could help you in the content or process of forming a small group.

Resources on Small Groups

Discipleship Essentials by Greg Ogden
Small Group Leaders' Handbook: The Next Generation by Jimmy Long, Ann Beyerlein, Sara Keiper, Patty Pell, Nina Thiel and Doug Whallon
www.emergentvillage.com

"The Creator arranged things so that we need each other."—Basil of Caesarea

SPIRITUAL FRIENDSHIP

DESIRE	to develop a friendship that encourages and challenges me to love God with all my heart, soul, strength and mind
DEFINITION	Spiritual friendship involves cultivating a covenant friendship where I can naturally share about my life with God. It is grounded in relationship to God and a commitment to support, encourage, and pray for one another.
SCRIPTURE	"A friend loves at all times, and a brother is born for adversity." (Proverbs 17:17) "Instead, I have called you friends, for everything that I learned from my Father I have made known to you." (John 15:15) "Accept one another, then, just as Christ accepted you, in order to bring praise to God." (Romans 15:7) "As iron sharpens iron, so one man sharpens another." (Proverbs 27:17)
PRACTICE INCLUDES	• journeying with another so you mutually grow in faith, hope and love • covenanting to pray for and receiving one another in love • playing together and praying together • knowing another well enough to be a support, encouragement and word of God to them • developing a healthy, interdependent friendship that encourages and grows the soul • inviting a friend into the journey of recognizing your blind spots
GOD-GIVEN FRUIT	• gaining the perspective and support of a trusted Christian friend • being open about your highs, lows, temptations and joys • experiencing God's love through the love of a friend • appreciating and being thankful for the giftedness of your spiritual friend • allowing a trusted friend to stretch and challenge you • laying down your life for love of another • having more than allies, colleagues and acquaintances in your journey

Spiritual Friendship

Jesus Christ himself was the model friend. He walked the complicated path of interdependence, giving and receiving as he went. Jesus was not an independent mover and shaker. He lived his life in community. He could often be found in the company of twelve chosen companions. Together they shared good times and bad times, meals and money, work and rest. Among the Twelve, Jesus had three closer friends: Peter, James and John. Jesus invited these three men to share high points, like the transfiguration, and low points, like Gethsemane. Though he could have experienced these events alone, he included others in what was both sweet and costly. Jesus was not a friendless male or a man unable to connect with women friends. Mary and Martha held significant places in Jesus' life. Ultimately, it was friendship with us that moved Jesus to embrace the cross. In John 15:13 he says, "Greater love has no one than this, that he lay down his life for his friends." To die for a friend—that's just not ordinary, everyday friendliness.

Friendliness is common currency today. We are told to "Fly the friendly skies." User-friendly software always helps. Seeker-friendly churches make everyone feel welcome. And if you are in the eastern United States, you can eat at Friendlys. Friendliness doesn't require loyalties or major investments of time and energy. Friendliness may grease the wheels of human interaction, but it is not the same thing as friendship. Friends are not a dime a dozen. They are not the same thing as allies, colleagues, neighbors, relatives and acquaintances. Friends require a degree of intentionality and self-donating love that goes beyond friendliness and supporting each other in some act or enterprise. Friends know our being as well as our doing. Friends mutually and naturally supply support, sharing, counsel, fun, encouragement, growth and a sense of being uniquely chosen and valued.

Spiritual friendship adds another dimension to the wonderful gift of friendship. As friends open their spiritual journeys to one another in the presence of Christ, they both step onto holy ground. Spirit connects with spirit. And the deep place where our spirit touches the Spirit of God becomes shared territory. Spiritual friends donate themselves to one another in love. They go out of their way to practice the biblical "one anothers" together (see appendix 6, "One Anothers"). Because of the bond of love, friends can hear truths from each other that they can't with nonfriends. Furthermore, loyal spiritual friends help one another experience their true belovedness. Spiritual friendship is not an easy path. It winds through the rigors of giving and receiving love to the very end. It lays down convenience and dies to self for the sake of the friend.

While spiritual friends are chosen and unique, they do not cut themselves off from others, refusing to invite them into the depths of their friendship. Spiritual friends want their relationships to reflect the love of the Trinity. The Father, Son and Holy Spirit invite others in to their divine community. So true spiritual friends invite others into their shared loving and knowing. Loving another doesn't create less love to share out—it creates more.

REFLECTION QUESTIONS

1. When has God taken the initiative to be a friend to you?

2. What sort of friend are you to God and others?

3. Who do you talk to about your spiritual life?

   How has a discerning, encouraging and challenging friend helped you in your journey?

4. Do you turn to someone in a time of crisis, or do you wait until the crisis is over to talk to someone? What does this tell you about yourself?

5. Do you need to be needed and appreciated? How does this affect your friendships?

SPIRITUAL EXERCISES

1. Take a friend inventory: draw a lifeline and divide it into seven-year segments. Put the initials of friends who have been important to you in each segment. What do you notice about your friendships? What kind of friends do you tend to gather around you? • What does this tell you about yourself?

2. Draw two columns on a piece of paper. Title one "Characteristics of a Spiritual Friend." Title the other "Characteristics of Myself as a Friend." Now fill the columns with your observations. • What did you learn about yourself?

3. We can never be perfect as a friend. We have limitations and flaws. List your current limitations (physical, time, emotional, etc.). • Do you want a spiritual friend enough to rearrange your life to have one?

4. When friends are taking a hit in your hectic life, develop one of the following disciplines: (1) write postcards while on the airplane, (2) read the same book together, (3) send flowers, balloons, cookies, (4) take a retreat together.

5. Where do you want and need balance? Complete the following.

   • Friends for the heart . . .

   • Friends for the head . . .

- Friends for the hand . . .
- Friends for the soul . . .

Resources on Spiritual Friendship

Sacred Companions by David Benner
Soultalk by Larry Crabb
Spiritual Friendship by Aelred of Rievaulx

"In essentials unity. In nonessentials liberty. In all things charity."—Rupert Meldinius

UNITY

DESIRE	to live in harmony with Christ's desire for the church to be one; to be a bridge-builder and peacemaker in the body of Christ
DEFINITION	Unity is the mark that demonstrates to the world that the body of Christ is one organism, with one faith, one hope, one baptism and one God and Father of all. Unity lives out the reality that Christ has already reconciled all things to himself. So in him we belong to one another.

SCRIPTURE	"How very good and pleasant it is
	    when brothers live together in unity." (Psalm 133:1)
	
	"There is one body and one Spirit—just as you were called to one hope when you were called—one Lord, one faith, one baptism; one God and Father of all, who is over all and through all and in all." (Ephesians 4:4-6)
	
	"The goal is for all of them to become one heart and mind—
	    Just as you, Father, are in me and I in you,
	        So they might be one heart and mind with us." (John 17:21 *The Message*)
	
	"And through him to reconcile to himself all things, whether things on earth or things in heaven, by making peace through his blood, shed on the cross." (Colossians 1:20)

PRACTICE INCLUDES	• working with believers from various traditions to achieve kingdom purposes • having dialogue that bridges understanding between Catholic, Orthodox and Protestant denominations • sharing worship services with other Christian denominations in your community • finding points on which you agree with others, not simply points on which you disagree • refraining from speaking unkind, slanderous and divisive things against others in the body of Christ • distinguishing between biblical principles and your personal convictions regarding those principles
GOD-GIVEN FRUIT	• having fewer divisions between and more love among Christians • focusing on the essentials, being gracious in the nonessentials • growing in appreciation for the diversity of the body of Christ • living by Jesus' prayer for the church in John 17 • continually praying for peace and unity within the church

UNITY

IN THE HOURS BEFORE HIS DEATH JESUS PRAYS A REMARKABLE PRAYER. He says, "I pray also for those who will believe in me, . . . that all of them may be one, Father, just as you are in me and I am in you. May they also be in us so that the world may believe that you have sent me" (John 17:20-21). Jesus' longest recorded prayer is all about oneness with God and one another. Oneness with another is a lot different than simply knowing another. Oneness is a participation in the core of another's being. Peter explains oneness with God as participation in the divine nature (2 Peter 1:4). Paul calls this mysterious oneness "Christ in you, the hope of glory" (Colossians 1:27). The life of God is riding in us, coursing through out bodies.

Beyond calculating God lives in us. And our own human nature is caught up in the dance of the divine nature. We are one with others not because we get along or share the same nationality or socioeconomic status—our unity doesn't depend on the quality of our lives. We are one because we belong to and are one with Christ. He has reconciled us to himself, and not just us alone but the whole world (2 Corinthians 5:18-19)! Christians are to live the radical unity-reality Jesus inaugurated. In a world defined by conflict, believers are to be recognized by a love that unifies. We are to display the unity of the triune God— because we are part of it.

But God has left us free to resist this reality. We can hold prejudices and grudges. We can be racist and sexist and break unity at every turn. But when we do, we absolutely quench the Spirit and disfigure the face of Christ in the world. The gospel is that we are one in Christ. And when we are born again we share in God's DNA of love.

So what do we say about the divisions and splits within church history? How are we to think about all who have suffered for the church and from the church? First, there is no way of getting around the grief this brings to God. And second, unless you grant that God is at work in the church, there is no way to explain how a small Jewish cult called "the Way" survived the first century, let alone the following twenty centuries of persecutions, divisions, heresies and all manner of political and religious intrigue. God has built his church on Christ, and the gates of hell cannot stand against it.

God reconciled the world to himself. And the multiethnic, socially diverse community of faith that still names Jesus as Lord is a miracle.

So let's heed the Holy Spirit's call to live as children of God, brothers and sisters of Jesus, and as family of our Father who is in heaven. "As far as it depends on you, live at peace with everyone" (Romans 12:18).

REFLECTION QUESTIONS

1. Are there fellow believers you would rather prove wrong than accept as brother or sister? What does that tell you about your heart?

2. What are your attitudes toward ecumenism, unity and oneness in the body of Christ?

3. When have you experienced a unity of reconciliation that is supernatural? What was that like for you?

4. How does competition among churches affect unity?

SPIRITUAL EXERCISES

1. Study the "one anothers" (see the "One Anothers" appendix) found in Scripture. • Begin living out one of the "one anothers" this week. • The following week choose another "one another." • Which "one another" is most difficult for you? Explain.

2. The body of Christ is to "rejoice with those who rejoice; mourn with those who mourn" (Romans 12:15). Look back over the past year. Who has rejoiced with you? Who has wept with you? Talk to God about what this meant to you. • What is it like for you to rejoice or weep with another? Find someone to rejoice or weep with today.

3. Looking for God in other churches: Once a year, go for a God hunt in a church tradition that is different from your own. How does this body of Christ reflect the Lord? What do they have to give you as part of the body?

4. As much as it depends on you, make peace with a fellow believer you are separated from. • How does what you are doing reflect Jesus' prayer in John 17? • What is it like for you to make peace?

5. Imagine what it will be like when every tribe and tongue and nation gather to worship God. Consider what might surprise you. Who will be there that you didn't expect?

6. Study Jesus' prayer in John 17. How does his prayer challenge your thoughts about unity?

7. Create a "one another" collage. Draw a number of circles on a piece of paper and label each of them with a "one another." For example, there could be a circle for "love one another," "serve one another," "pray for one another," "stir up one another to love and good works," etc. • Pray for God to speak to you about relationships that you need to attend to in each circle. Write the name of one or two people in each circle. Make a plan to attend to a circle a week.

Resources on Unity

Building Unity in the Church of the New Millennium by Dwight Perry

God's Dream Team: A Call to Unity by Tommy Tenney

Making Peace with Conflict by Carolyn Schrock-Shenk and Lawrence Ressler, eds.

www.buildingchurchleaders.com

"Our communication of the gospel depends not on human strategies or well-polished techniques or even brilliantly reasoned arguments but on divine initiative. It is the hidden work of the Holy Spirit that gives our words meaning and power and that produces changed hearts."
—Rebecca Manley Pippert

WITNESS

DESIRE	to reveal the life-changing love of Jesus to others
DEFINITION	To witness means modeling and telling of the difference Jesus has made in one's life.
SCRIPTURE	"You will receive power when the Holy Spirit comes on you; and you will be my witnesses in Jerusalem, and in all Judea and Samaria, and to the ends of the earth." (Acts 1:8) "Therefore go and make disciples of all nations, baptizing them in the name of the Father and of the Son and of the Holy Spirit, and teaching them to obey everything I have commanded you." (Matthew 28:19-20)
PRACTICE INCLUDES	• living in the presence of Christ in a way the world finds compelling and desirable • intentionally engaging in life with people of different beliefs • serving others at points of need and in times of pain • inviting others to investigate the claims of Christ and the community of faith • sharing the good news of Jesus at the appropriate time in the appropriate way • becoming involved with an Alpha course • leading a Bible study or GIG (Group Investigating God) with God seekers • comfortably expressing my Christian journey in words that appropriately connect with others • addressing the fears and sins that harm my witness
GOD-GIVEN FRUIT	• leaving others with the fragrance of Christ wherever I go • expressing God's heart for the world • seeing people around me come to know Jesus

WITNESS

THE VERY LAST THING JESUS TOLD HIS FOLLOWERS WAS, "you will be my witnesses" (Acts 1:8). A witness is simply someone who tells what they saw or heard or experienced. A witness tells the story of what happened to them. Anyone who follows Jesus has a story to tell. And no story is boring or uneventful. Every disciple has the very life of God pulsing through his or her body. Every disciple has been set free, released, redeemed, forgiven, made new and inhabited by the Holy Spirit. All disciples have stories of God's work in their lives that are meant to help set others free. Testifying to this good news requires no strategy or program. It depends on responding to the Spirit's nudge to open your mouth and heart for the sake of others.

Paul, the first great missionary of the church, told his story in myriad ways, suiting his message to his audience. In Athens, Paul argued with Greeks, quoting philosophers and using apologetics to present the good news of Jesus (Acts 17). In Corinth, Paul lived in community with Priscilla and Aquila. He supported himself by making tents so he could stay long enough to plant a church. In Rome, Paul spent two years in his own rented house "and welcomed all who came to see him. Boldly and without hindrance he preached the kingdom of God and taught about the Lord Jesus Christ" (Acts 28:30-31). In Jerusalem, Paul told the story of his conversion (Acts 22). When on trial before Felix, Paul defended himself and gave an account of his belief in the "resurrection of the dead." Paul suited what he said to who he was with. He didn't have a formula for witnessing. But he did have a desire to share the life-changing love of Jesus that couldn't be shut down.

Still Paul knew that it was not up to him to convert anyone. In 1 Corinthians 3:6 he writes, "I planted the seed, Apollos watered it, but God made it grow." God is the one who draws people to himself, and he is pleased to use us in the process.

The early church continued to follow Paul's and Jesus' example. Believers committed themselves to living the Christ-in-me life in the midst of the world. Writing to non-Christians, the early church father Tertullian said in *The Apology*, "We live in the world with you. We do not forsake forum or bath or workshop, or inn, or market, or any other place of commerce. We sail with you, fight with you, farm with you." Witness to the life-changing

Jesus happens on the job and in the everyday comings and goings of life. The litmus test for witness is not simply an ability to explain the good news. It is the way you live the good news.

REFLECTION QUESTIONS

1. What is it like for you to share your faith with others?

2. What would make it easier and more comfortable for you to talk about what Christ has done for you?

3. What is it like for you to interact with people who have different beliefs than you?

4. If you feel your own "redemption story" is uneventful or uninteresting, how does that affect your ability to share the good news with others?

5. What things do you think someone needs to know about Jesus before they can become his follower?

SPIRITUAL EXERCISES

1. God changed the course of Israel's life when he rescued his people from slavery in Egypt. Their redemption story is found in the book of Exodus. Read the story of Israel's rescue. • You also have a "redemption story" about how God has found and rescued you. Write an account of your redemption story. How might God use this story to set others free? • Share the story of your journey to freedom in Christ with a friend.

2. There are wonderful evangelism tools and training programs that can assist you in learning how to share your faith. Check out <www.saltshaker.org> or <www.alpha.org>.

3. Make a list of the people you are praying will respond to God. Beside each name list one intentional way you can be the face of God to them in the next month.

4. Write an account of how God has been at work in your life in the past six months. Ask the Holy Spirit to make you sensitive and open to an opportunity to share your experience with a seeking friend.

Resources on Witness

Out of the Saltshaker by Rebecca Manley Pippert
Evangelism and the Sovereignty of God by J. I. Packer
Saltshaker Ministries <www.saltshaker.org>
The Alpha Course <www.alpha.org>

Part Five

HEAR GOD'S WORD

GOD IS A GOD OF COMMUNICATION AND WORDS. Throughout the ages he has spoken to us through the written Word, the spoken word and the incarnate Word. The *H* disciplines address our need and desire to hear a word from God. Our world of printed as well as verbal noise can drown out the reality and wonder of God's Word. There are always other books to read and speakers to listen to. Of course God does use books and people to speak to us. But Scripture is a primary way that the Holy Spirit opens us up to the God who is beyond us.

In the Bible God reveals to us both our sin and our belovedness. Our desires for nourishment, strength, comfort and joy are all addressed in Scripture. Reading God's Word, listening to Scripture on tape or singing biblical texts all put us in a place to attend to the God who speaks. Though there is no new word of revelation today, God is still speaking and guiding us personally and intimately through the Word. Regularly being with God in his Word is a way we open ourselves to truths and guidance outside us.

"In the Bible God gives us revelations of himself which lead us to worship, promises of salvation which stimulate our faith, and commandments expressing his will which demand our obedience. This is the meaning of Christian discipleship. "—John R. W. Stott

BIBLE STUDY

DESIRE	to know what the Bible says and how it intersects with my life
DEFINITION	Bible study involves engaging the mind and focusing attention on Scripture in an attempt to understand and apply truth to every part of my life.
SCRIPTURE	"Every part of Scripture is God-breathed and useful one way or another—showing us truth, exposing our rebellion, correcting our mistakes, training us to live God's way." (2 Timothy 3:16 *The Message*) "Let the word of Christ—the Message—have the run of the house. Give it plenty of room in your lives. Instruct and direct one another using good common sense. And sing, sing your hearts out to God!" (Colossians 3:16 *The Message*) "I have hidden your word in my heart that I might not sin against you." (Psalm 119:11)
PRACTICE INCLUDES	• attending to biblical instruction (oral or written) with an open mind and heart in order to grow in love and understanding of the truth • systematically studying Scripture to gain the big picture of what God is doing on planet earth • using study guides, manuscript studies, small group Bible studies, etc.
GOD-GIVEN FRUIT	• keeping company with Jesus no matter how little or much God speaks to me through his Word • loving God with my mind • learning and internalizing what Scripture teaches about God • having Scripture shape and form my thinking and lifestyle so they are increasingly redemptive and life giving • using my understanding to build the community of faith • putting myself in a place where God can instruct and correct my behavior and attitudes • growing in my ability to rationally defend and express my faith

BIBLE STUDY

THE BIBLE IS DIVINE REVELATION. God's own word to us. It reveals who God is, who we are and why we are here. Through Bible study we gain insights into God, human nature and creation.[†] Studying the Scripture can equip, guide and reveal how to live in life-giving ways that deepen our friendship with God and others. Both Old and New Testaments encourage regular study, meditation, contemplation and memorization of God's Word. The benefits of Bible study are directly related to how open, attentive and obedient we are to what we read.

Jesus exemplified the love of God's Word in every area of his life. He used Scripture to answer those who tested him, resist temptation, find guidance, encourage his heart, comfort others, explain his actions and ultimately face his own death.

Several Ways to Study the Bible

Artist method. Read a passage of Scripture, considering three questions as you read:

1. What speaks to my heart? Draw a heart beside the word that speaks to your heart.

2. What new thought or idea comes to me? Draw a light bulb beside the new thought or idea.

3. What does Scripture move me to do? Draw a hand beside the action you want to take.

Consider how you can apply one of your insights today. Share your insights with a friend.

Detective method. Read a short narrative passage from one of the Gospels. Let the story take shape in your mind's eye. Imagine the scene. Observe all the facts. Ask the *who, when, where, what* questions. Once you have the facts, *interpret* the facts. Ask the *why* and *wherefore* questions. What meaning did the actions have for the characters? What meaning do the actions have for you? Then *apply* your study to your own life. Ask *how* will this change my life? What do you take away from the story?

Treasure-seeker method. When reading Scripture consider the following application questions:

[†] I owe my understanding of Bible study to Ada Lum and Ruth Siemens. These two wonderful IFES staff mentored me in inductive study, fueling my desire to study the Scriptures.

Is there an example here for me to follow? Is there a promise to claim or a command to obey? Is there a truth to be applied? Is there a prayer for me to pray? Is there a sin to be confessed? Is there a question God is asking me?

Jesus' apprentice method. If you are unfamiliar with Scripture and don't know where to begin, choose one of the Gospels (Mark or Luke) and study to discover all you can about Jesus. Ask yourself the following questions: What seems important to Jesus? What sort of questions does he ask people? What sort of questions do people ask him? What is Jesus inviting me to be and do?

REFLECTION QUESTIONS

1. How has God spoken to you through the study of his Word?

   How has Bible study affected your life?

2. When the Word of God seems dry to you, what do you make of this season in your life?

3. What are you looking for when you read Scripture—information, comfort, understanding, guidance, a word from God, communion with God?

4. How does what you are looking for influence how you study?

SPIRITUAL EXERCISES

1. Experiment with different ways of listening to Scripture.

   • Read the Bible out loud. Savor the words. Which words stand out for you? Keep these words with you all day.

   • Listen to the Bible on tape or CD while driving or exercising.

   • Print a verse on a card and place it where you will see it throughout the day. Put a verse on your screen saver.

2. To enhance your understanding of the biblical context and meaning the text may have had to its original audience, invest in a Bible commentary, a Bible dictionary or go online and type in places, cultures and peoples you are reading about in your Bible study.

3. Go to a Christian bookstore and look through the array of Bible study guides available. Does one of the study guides intrigue you? Let your desire guide you in choosing one for further study.

4. If systematic Bible study appeals to you, consider joining a Bible study at your church or in your community. Or begin your own neighborhood Bible study.

5. Study the questions Jesus asks people in the Gospels. What do you learn about Jesus and the importance of questions?

Resources on Bible Study

How to Lead a Seeker Bible Discussion by Rebecca Manley Pippert
How to Study the Bible by Jack Kuhatschek
Discovering the Bible for Yourself by Judson Poling

"Our desire to know more, read more and study more can be another expression of our culture and its acquisitive nature. Knowing God, not knowing more, is the goal."—Richard Rohr

DEVOTIONAL READING

DESIRE	to prayerfully encounter and surrender to the living God through attending to Scripture
DEFINITION	Devotional reading or hearing of Scripture requires an open, reflective, listening posture alert to the voice of God. This type of reading is aimed more at growing a relationship with God than gathering information about God.

SCRIPTURE	"Turn my heart toward your statutes. . . .
	Oh, how I love your law!
	    I meditate on it all day long. . . .
	How sweet are your words to my taste,
	    sweeter than honey to my mouth! . . .
	Your statutes are my heritage forever;
	    they are the joy of my heart." (Psalm 119:36, 97, 103, 111)
	
	"For the word of God is living and active. Sharper than any double-edged sword, it penetrates even to dividing soul and spirit, joints and marrow; it judges the thoughts and attitudes of the heart. Nothing in all creation is hidden from God's sight." (Hebrews 4:12-13)
	
	"The word is very near you; it is in your mouth and in your heart so you may obey it." (Deuteronomy 30:14)

PRACTICE INCLUDES	• prayerfully dwelling on a passage of Scripture • listening deeply God's personal word to you • reading not to master the text but be mastered by it • staying with one text until the Lord prompts movement to another • reading for depth, not breadth • contemplative and formational reading of Scripture or other devotional texts
GOD-GIVEN FRUIT	• keeping company with Jesus whether or not he speaks to you • seeking and listening for a personal word from God • dwelling in a text until it begins to live in and master you • responding to God's Word with your heart and spirit, not just your rational, cognitive and intellectual prowess • softening of your heart so that the head-heart schism is mended and you live more and more out of love • having Scripture guide your dialogue with God • a growing receptivity and submission to God's Word

DEVOTIONAL READING

WE UNDERSTAND WHAT WIND IS BY FEELING IT BLOW IN OUR FACE. We know what snow is like when we make a snowball or watch snowflakes collect on our mittens. This sort of knowing transcends the intellect; it is direct, sensate and experiential. Devotional reading, or *lectio divina*, invites us into this kind of knowing. It is the kind of knowing for which Paul prayed when he said,

> I pray that you, being rooted and established in love, may have power, together with all the saints, to grasp how wide and long and high and deep is the love of Christ, and to *know this love that surpasses knowledge*—that you may be filled to the measure of all the fullness of God. (Ephesians 3:17-19, emphasis added)

The first 1,500 years of church history were characterized by the practice of *lectio divina*. Since many people were illiterate and many that could read didn't have Bibles, *lectio divina* offered a way of attending to Scripture as it was read in church, with an ear to hearing a word from God. Some brief and memorable word or phrase became bread for the soul throughout the week. Devotional reading is not an exercise in mentally critiquing or exegeting the text. It exists to further divine companionship. *Lectio divina* invites us into God's presence to listen for his particular, loving word *to me* at this particular moment in time. In *lectio* one listens to the word as it is read aloud, or you read the text aloud for yourself.

Devotional reading of Scripture is rooted in the assurance that every part of the biblical story—letters, parables, Gospels, Prophets, history—is inspired and can give voice to God's particular word to us.

Devotional reading was traditionally made up five movements:

1. *Silencio*—quiet preparation of the heart. Come into God's presence, slow down, relax, and intentionally release the chaos and noise in your mind to him.

2. *Lectio*—read the word. Read a Scripture passage slowly and out loud, lingering over the words so that they resonate in your heart. When a word or phrase catches your attention, don't keep reading. Stop and attend to what God is saying to you. Be open to the

word. Don't analyze it or judge it. Listen and wait.

3. *Meditatio*—meditate. Read the Scripture a second time out loud. Savor the words. Listen for any invitation that God is extending to you in this word. Reflect on the importance of the words that light up to you. Like Mary, who pondered the word in her heart, gently explore the ramifications of God's invitation.

4. *Oratio*—respond, pray. Read the Scripture a third time. Now is the moment to enter into a personal dialogue with God. There is no right or wrong way to do this. The important thing is to respond truthfully and authentically. What feelings has the text aroused in you? Name where you are resistant or want to push back. Become aware of where you feel invited into a deeper way of being with God. Talk to God about these feelings.

5. *Contemplatio*—contemplate, rest and wait in the presence of God. Allow some time for the word to sink deeply into your soul. Yield and surrender yourself to God. Before you leave, you might consider a reminder that can help you dwell on or incarnate this word throughout the day.

REFLECTION QUESTIONS

1. How has your faith journey been characterized by a head-heart split?

   How has God's love moved from being a matter of belief to a real and lived experience?

2. How would you characterize the way you tend to read?

   How has the way you read Scripture been influenced by reading habits in general?

3. What are the strengths and weaknesses of scanning and hurrying through material in search of the main idea?

4. How and when have the Scriptures been the voice of God to you?

   How have they brought you into the presence of Christ?

SPIRITUAL EXERCISES

1. Using Mark 10:46-52

   • *Silencio.* Put yourself in the presence of God. Become quiet and offer yourself to God.

   • *Lectio.* Read Mark 10:46-42 out loud, slowly allowing the words to resonate and settle in your heart. Linger on the word or phrase that catches your attention and lights up for you. Sit with the word or phrase and savor it as a word of God for you.

   • *Meditatio.* Read the passage again and listen to where the word connects with your life right now. Enter into the scene in your imagination. Imagination is a God-given gift. Envision the scene. Carefully watch the people. Listen to how they interact. What do you hear and experience as you watch and listen?

   • *Oratio.* Read the passage one more time, listening attentively. Has God addressed you in this Word and invited you to respond? Allow the Scripture to lead you into a prayer response. Do not censure your thoughts or requests. Let them flow out spontaneously and freely before the Lord who loves you. Hold nothing back. Respond to God's invitation to you.

- *Contemplatio.* Deeply receive God's Word and rest in his presence and love. Give yourself some time to wait and be still before you reenter life as usual. Take God's Word to you with you throughout the day. Return to it and remember it all day long. Stay with God until you feel prompted to leave.

2. Before reading Scripture, open yourself to the presence of God. Say something like "Here I am, Lord" or "Open my eyes to see wonderful things in your Word." • Read slowly until a word or phrase lights up for you. When you sense a word lighting up for you, attend to this word. Do not read any further. Listen to your feelings and God's nudging around this word. Let this word summon you into prayer. • Reflect on this word throughout the day.

3. In your Bible reading, ask God to give you a prayer response to his Word. As a word or phrase lights up for you, consider the prayer God may be calling you to pray. Then pray that prayer for the coming week.

4. When you read Scripture, insert your own name into the pronouns that stand for *you*. What is it like for you to read Scripture in this personal way? • For example read Isaiah 43:1-3. Insert your name in the blank space.

> But now this is what the LORD says—
>
> he who formed you O _____,
>
> Fear not, for I have redeemed _____;
>
> I have summoned _____ by name; _____ is mine.
>
> When _____ passes through the waters,
>
> I will be with _____;
>
> and when _____ passes through the rivers,
>
> they will not sweep over _____.
>
> When _____ walks through the fire,
>
> _____ will not be burned;
>
> the flames will not set _____ ablaze.
>
> For I am the LORD, _____'s God,
>
> the Holy One of Israel, _____'s Savior.

What is this experience of reading Scripture like for you?

5. Choose a biblical character with whom you identify. Turn to Scripture passages in which this character shows up. Read the passage aloud, placing yourself in the story as

an onlooker. Let the story settle deeply into you. Listen for similarities between you and this biblical character. Where do you struggle like he or she does? How do his or her circumstances give deeper meaning to your journey? Listen to what the Lord is saying to you through this character and his or her story. • How does this story help you understand your own story and where God is in that story? Talk to God about what it is like to have his Word speak to you.

Resources on Devotional Reading

Gathered in the Word by Norveen Vest
Shaped by the Word by Robert Mulholland

"A spiritual kingdom lies all about us, enclosing us, embracing us, altogether within reach of our inner selves, waiting for us to recognize it. God Himself is here waiting our response to His Presence. This eternal world will come alive to us the moment we begin to reckon upon its reality."—A. W. Tozer

MEDITATION

DESIRE	to more deeply gaze on God in his works and words
DEFINITION	Meditation is a long, ardent gaze at God, his work and his Word. Slowing down and giving one's undivided attention to God lies at the core of Christian mediation.

SCRIPTURE	"Do not let this Book of the Law depart from your mouth; meditate on it day and night, so that you may be careful to do everything written in it. Then you will be prosperous and successful." (Joshua 1:8)
	
	"If I'm sleepless at midnight,
	    I spend the hours in grateful reflection." (Psalm 63:6
	    The Message)
	
	"I'll ponder all the things you've accomplished,
	    and give a long, loving look at your acts." (Psalm 77:12
	    The Message)
	
	"May the words of my mouth and the meditation of my heart
	    be pleasing in your sight,
	    O LORD, my Rock and my Redeemer." (Psalm 19:14)

PRACTICE INCLUDES	• reading creation as "a most elegant book, wherein, all creatures great and small, are as so many characters leading us to see clearly the invisible things of God" (Belgic Confession) • mulling over, chewing on and ruminating over God's Word and its application • meditating on people; seeing them as God sees them and expressing delight in them as he does • paying attention to God with your body by slowing down, relaxing and breathing deeply • meditating on Jesus and on Scripture
GOD-GIVEN FRUIT	• developing sight for the interior things of God in the natural and external world • seeing beyond a first glance and first impression to the heart of God • developing depth of insight • developing a love for gazing on God • experiencing calmness, serenity and quietness stemming from an awareness of the nearness of God

MEDITATION

MEDITATION IS NOT SIMPLY A DISCIPLINE OF Eastern religions and New Age gurus. Meditation rests at the core of Judeo-Christian spirituality; it's an invitation to apprehend God. In *The Pursuit of God* A. W. Tozer writes, "God dwells in His creation and is everywhere indivisibly present in all His works." And Psalm 139:7 asserts, "Where can I go from your Spirit? / Where can I flee from your presence?" God is near. In the words of C. S. Lewis in his *Letters to Malcolm: Chiefly on Prayer:* "God walks everywhere incognito." Clues to his presence can be found in creation, in history, in human beings, in worship and in Scripture. But we must stop and pay attention. Meditation runs counter to our busy culture, where speed reading, first impressions and skimming are as deep as we go. In meditation we gaze at something or someone long and longingly. We seek the treasure and truth of what we see. Just as moving a prism reveals different bands of color, meditation allows God to shine his truth and light into our hearts.

Meditation is not about emptying the mind so there is nothing there. Christian meditation opens us to the mind of God and to his world and presence in the world. As we enter times of mediation, it is important to let go of our preoccupations so we can focus our minds and become present to God. Our minds are naturally designed to make associations and follow tangents. Meditation is a way we train the mind to stay put so it can explore appropriate associations. Simple physical exercises like stretching, sitting comfortably and breathing deeply can help us pay attention, listen deeply and even curb our distractibility. These exercises are not an end in themselves. They simply seek to put body, mind and spirit on the same page so we can better pay attention to God and treasure what he reveals.

To meditate on Scripture choose a verse, chapter or book of the Bible. Don't hurry. Listen to the Scripture. Write down your questions. Use your imagination. You may wish to memorize a short part of the text to keep it clearly before you. Like a cow chewing the cud, keep returning to your text with your mind and heart. When you are distracted, gently return to your text. Express once again your desire to pay attention. The impact of meditating on Scripture can show up later in our interactions with others. (See "Devotional

Reading," "Praying Scripture" and "Memorization.")

To meditate on God's good creation, attend to what God has made. Open yourself to the beauty around you and drink deeply. Let the Spirit move you into praise. Meditation on creation is meant to lead us into the arms of our Creator. (See "Care of the Earth.")

REFLECTION QUESTIONS

1. How would you characterize your ability to pay attention?

2. When do you find it easiest to focus your mind or heart?

3. How might the tendency to do everything quickly affect your ability to meditate?

4. What is your gut reaction to the word *meditation*?

SPIRITUAL EXERCISES

1. Prepare yourself to meditate on Scripture by choosing a comfortable and quiet place. Do not rush. Stretch, arrange your chair, take off your shoes. Sit in a position that you can maintain without effort or attention. Place yourself in the presence of God. Release your anxieties and to-do list to the Lord. Ask him to open your heart to his Word.

   Read Psalm 139, Psalm 86, Psalm 42 or another short passage from Scripture.

   Take your time, and when a word "lights up" for you stop and attend. Let the word or phrase roam around in your mind and heart. What do you hear? What feelings do you notice in yourself? Write down any questions that surface. You can attend to these at another time.

   - When your mind wanders, gently bring it back and continue your meditation. Do not feel you have to finish anything. Take your word with you. • Begin again tomorrow with the same passage.

2. Take a walk in nature, meditating on the handiwork of God. The lilies of the field and the birds of the air spoke to Jesus of God's care (Matthew 6:26-31). How does God speak to you in his creation?

3. Meditate on the news. How is God speaking to you through current events? Is he inviting you to see the world through his eyes in some new way? Is he inviting you into prayer in a new way?

4. Meditate on the great truths of the faith using the Apostles' Creed, the Nicene Creed or a confession of faith. Spend time deeply entering into the words and their meaning. • The following is a quote from the Heidelberg Confession of Faith and is a lovely truth for meditation:

   Question: What is your only comfort in life and in death?

   Answer: That I belong body and soul, in life and death, not to myself, but to my faithful Savior Jesus Christ, who at the cost of his own blood has freely paid for all my sins and has completely freed me from the dominion of the devil.

5. Meditate on the work of God in the lives of individuals throughout the ages. Listen to what they can teach you and how they can shape you.

Resources on Meditation

The Apostles' Creed and the Nicene Creed

Devotional Classics by Richard Foster and James Bryan Smith

"If I had to find one word to describe how belief came to take hold in me, it would be 'repetition.' "
—Kathleen Norris

MEMORIZATION

DESIRE	to carry the life-shaping words of God in me at all times and in all places
DEFINITION	Memorization is the process of continually remembering the words, truths and images God uses to shape us. Memorization provides us with a store of learning, which can be accessed anywhere and anytime.

SCRIPTURE	"Oh, how I love your law!
	    I meditate on it all day long." (Psalm 119:97)
	
	"I have hidden your word in my heart
	    that I might not sin against you." (Psalm 119:11)
	
	"Then they remembered his words." (Luke 24:8)
	
	"I think it is right to refresh your memory. . . . And I will make every effort to see that after my departure you will always be able to remember these things." (2 Peter 1:13, 15)

PRACTICE INCLUDES	• memorizing Scripture, hymns, poems, quotes, etc. • rereading portions of Scripture until they are committed to memory • memorizing Scripture verses that clearly reveal God's plan of salvation • memorizing the books of the Bible, particular dates and times as well as where various verses are found • learning by heart portions of Scripture that encourage you when you are tempted
GOD-GIVEN FRUIT	• keeping company with Jesus by hiding his Word in your heart • recollecting God-given encouragement and exhortation • developing a habit of remembering that anchors your life in biblical truth • committing to memory Scripture, hymns, poems and quotes that God is using in your life • knowing where well-loved portions of Scripture are located

MEMORIZATION

FOR MILLENNIA, COMMITTING THINGS TO MEMORY served as the foundation for religious, political and educational instruction. Memorized matter was known to have staying power. It was not at the mercy of being relevant or hip and didn't depend on books or literacy. Words, stories and prayers known by heart could be stored deep in the mind, pop up out of the blue and amuse, comfort, and educate others.

But the world has changed. The printing press, the increasing accessibility of books, the flood of information, the World Wide Web—all these make memorization less important. If we want to know something, we can just Google it. If we like a poem by Emily Dickenson or want to know who the Chaldeans were, we type in a few words and have it on our computer in a heartbeat.

No doubt the ability to read and access to books and computers are wonderful gifts. But a mind so overwhelmed with information that nothing is known by heart can leave the soul at the mercy of the last mental image that took our fancy. Memorization allows us to choose words and images that shape our minds and hearts. It gives the mind somewhere to go when all the media is turned off. Furthermore, memorizing God's Word allows us to access divinely inspired thought and wisdom. And it works in us even when we are not conscious of its doing so.

If you are someone who forgets birthdays and can't remember why you opened the refrigerator door, the whole notion of memorization can seem ludicrous. Don't be too discouraged. Consider the things you have already memorized without trying. What songs do you know by heart? What proverbs or sayings or Bible verses? Memorization depends on repetition. Choose what you want to memorize and tape it where you constantly see it. Return to it again and again.

REFLECTION QUESTIONS

1. What is your attitude toward memorization?

2. What do you believe the benefits of memorization can be?

When have you experienced the benefits of memorization?

3. What sort of things have you memorized without trying? What was that like for you?

4. If you were put in solitary confinement, what sort of things would you have learned by heart to nourish your soul?

5. Do you find yourself memorizing sporting statistics, line-ups or world records; recipes; phone numbers; e-mail addresses; directions?

   How does memorizing these things help you or encourage you in memorizing words that can nourish your soul?

SPIRITUAL EXERCISES

1. Begin by memorizing some of the choruses or songs that you enjoy. Sing the bits you remember. Listen again to the bits you forget. Write them out if it helps you. • When you have committed the song to memory, notice when the song simply pops into your mind. Let the song be a way God enters into your life and speaks to you.

2. When you find yourself captivated by a Scripture, write it on a card that you can tape to a mirror, a window or even the shower wall. Every day read the verse, rehearsing it in your mind and heart. On a daily basis remind yourself of the Scripture until you know it by heart. Only then are you ready to move on to another portion of Scripture.

3. Memorize a chapter of the Bible. Take your time with this. Let the words sink into your soul. If singing helps you to remember things, don't be afraid to sing the words.

   Memorize a book of the Bible.

4. Develop a group that memorizes the Scripture passages for worship services. Work together to dramatically speak God's Word.

Resources on Memorization

Delighted by Discipline by Mark R. Littleton
Spiritual Disciplines for the Christian Life, chapter 2, by Donald S. Whitney
The Topical Memory System by NavPress

Part Six

INCARNATE
THE LOVE OF CHRIST

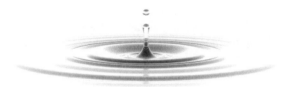

THE *I* DISCIPLINES STEM FROM A DESIRE TO OFFER others a taste of God's life-changing love. The Son of God came to earth and took on flesh (was incarnate) to show us the face of God's love. While on earth Jesus called his followers to incarnate this show-and-tell love in their own bodies. With the love of Jesus resident within us, our capacity to love grows. Love always gives birth to more love. It is not a depletable quantity but an eternal quality of God. In Christ we are rooted into the depths of God's love. We cannot run out of it.

The incarnating disciplines open us to God's heart. They invite us to participate in God's kingdom agenda: his love of justice, his concern for the poor and the oppressed, the widow and the orphan. The *I* disciplines are ways we express our faith, hope and love in the midst of a selfish, entitlement world. Incarnation took Jesus to the last breath of self-donating love. And if we intend to follow him, we can expect that truly "loving our neighbor as ourselves" will take us to depths of self-donating love. In those depths we are in the heart of worship.

"This land that gives us our food, our water; these trees that clean the air for us to breathe; all these green and growing things that bless our bodies with their beauty—these are not resources. They are fellow creatures, with their own rights and responsibilities before God. They have their own sacred duties to perform, if only we will let them."—Barbara Brown Taylor

CARE OF THE EARTH

DESIRE	to honor the Creator by loving, nurturing and stewarding his creation
DEFINITION	Caring for the earth is a way of expressing God's delight in his very good creation. By engaging in loving care of the earth, the environment, the plants and the animals, we honor the gifts and treasures of our Creator.
SCRIPTURE	"For the creation was subjected to frustration, not by its own choice, but by the will of the one who subjected it, in hope that the creation itself will be liberated from its bondage to decay and brought into the glorious freedom of the children of God." (Romans 8:20-21) "GOD claims Earth and everything in it. God claims World and all who live on it. He built it on Ocean foundations, laid it out on River girders." (Psalm 24:1-2 *The Message*) "Then God said, 'I give you every seed-bearing plant on the face of the whole earth and every tree that has fruit with seed in it. They will be yours for food. . . . God saw all that he had made, and it was very good. . . . The LORD God took the man and put him in the Garden of Eden to work it and take care of it." (Genesis 1:29, 31; 2:15)
PRACTICE INCLUDES	• all actions that lead to making the earth more and more like God's original Garden of Eden • protecting the earth's natural resources, with a concern for future generations and what they inherit • working against pollution of air, water and land • treating animals humanely • advocating and practicing crop rotation and soil enhancement rather than land depletion • using energy supplies wisely • recycling • not littering • riding a bike or walking rather than driving a car
GOD-GIVEN FRUIT	• keeping company with Jesus no matter what this planet undergoes • honoring the Creator and celebrating his handiwork • contributing to the beauty of and mending the brokenness of this planet • sharing God's earth—my yard, the harvest from my garden, my flowers, my private property—with others • witnessing to Christ through wise stewardship of our ecological resources • growing in the realization that all created things belong to God and not ultimately to humans

CARE OF THE EARTH

WHILE IN GRADUATE SCHOOL, A NUMBER OF US decided to organize a morning to care for the land beside the roads in our town. Students were given big black garbage bags, and they walked the streets that curved around our campus. Beer cans, wine bottles, fast-food containers, cigarette packs, plastic and paper bags, moldy food, sanitary products, un-paired shoes and gloves, they all went into the bags. That day the rubbish that clogged the shoulders of roads, collected in culverts, and snaked through the grass and weeds filled hundreds of bags. It was not a large effort, but it marked my attitude toward litter forever. Caring for the earth begins where we are, with the stuff we have and use and want to get rid of.

Scripture makes it clear that we are caretakers and stewards of all that God has made. In the Old Testament, God's people were to make sure the land *and* animals had a sabbath rest (Leviticus 25). Just because land could yield crops every year and animals could work every day did not mean that they should. God has asked us to respect the created order. For when we exploit this beautiful world we harm not just land and animals and air but ourselves as well. Environmental degradation increases the labor of those who already struggle to find water and collect natural resources. Economic productivity is never the last word when we are dealing with limited natural resources.

Often we believe that land owners have the right to determine what happens on their land. If the owners want to fill wetlands, if the owners want to build a huge concrete park-ing lot, if the owners want to post "No Trespassing" signs, if the owners want to cut down rain forests, it is their land and they can do as they please. This mindset neglects the truth that this planet does not belong to us but to God. "The sea is his for he made it, / and his hands formed the dry land" (Psalm 95:5). This world belongs to the Creator, and it is ours only in trust and by divine delegation. Genesis 1:28 and 2:15 recount God's cultural man-date to Adam and Eve: "God blessed them and said to them, 'Be fruitful and increase in number; fill the earth and subdue it.' . . . The LORD God took the man and put him in the Garden of Eden to work it and take care of it."

Creation is God's gift, and it is to be nurtured and maintained with love and care.

Christians are to exercise loving dominion that honors scriptural values and leaves future generations what they will need.

REFLECTION QUESTIONS

1. How does God view the resources you use?

2. How does God view your use of natural resources and your due diligence in taking care of planet earth?

3. How do you feel about environmentalists, developers, animal rights activists, vegetarians, factory farms, etc.?

   What do your hot buttons reveal about your view of dominion?

4. Where have you taken for granted God's good gifts in this world?

   Who goes without these gifts?

5. What is God asking of you? Listen and journal a response.

SPIRITUAL EXERCISES

1. Plan a way to make the earth more beautiful. Plant flowers in the inner city or around a school. • Sponsor or take care of a stretch of road. • Work to remove billboards. • Share your motivation with others.

2. Plant a garden. Share the produce or plants with others.

3. Invite children to play in your yard. • Teach a child how to garden. • Take a child on a nature walk and point out environmental goods and ills.

4. Become familiar with some part of our distressed environment. (Do a Web search on the environment and you will find dozens of ways to participate in good stewardship of the earth.) Commit yourself to stewardship of some earthly resource.

5. Walk or ride a bike rather than drive your car. • Recycle. • Use cosmetics that aren't tested on animals.

6. Take a resource walk. Thank God for the sheep who give you wool, for the cows who give you milk, for the trees that give you furniture, etc.

7. Take a walk through God's beautiful world. What characteristics of God are revealed in earthly beauty? • Journal your discoveries.

8. Become conscious of the litter in the places you live and work. Organize an hour or morning when volunteers pick up litter.

Resources on Care of the Earth

The Environment and the Christian by Calvin DeWitt
Under the Bright Wings by Peter Harris
www.arocha.org
www.ausable.org
www.creationcare.org

"There are times when nothing holds the heart but a long, long look at Calvary. How very small anything that we are allowed to endure seems beside that cross."—Amy Carmichael

COMPASSION

DESIRE	to become the healing presence of Christ to others
DEFINITION	Compassion means feeling with and for others as well as extending mercy and help to them in extravagantly practical ways. Compassion is part and parcel of sharing in God's heart for an aching and wounded world.
SCRIPTURE	"Filled with compassion, Jesus reached out his hand and touched the man." (Mark 1:41) "I have compassion for these people." (Matthew 15:32) "Be sympathetic, love as brothers, be compassionate and humble. Do not repay evil with evil or insult with insult, but with blessing, because to this you were called so that you may inherit a blessing." (1 Peter 3:8-9)
PRACTICE INCLUDES	• finding the opportunity and means to comfort, encourage and support those who struggle, suffer and are oppressed • seeking to heal wounds rather than react to the wounded • showing mercy rather than passing judgment • reading the newspaper or listening to the news as a call to prayer and compassion • volunteering for some form of community-based service of compassion • visiting those who are sick, hospitalized, unable to drive and attending to their needs and desires with patient love
GOD-GIVEN FRUIT	• keeping company with Jesus and showing his compassion whether or not it is received or recognized • learning what it means to have a love that keeps no record of wrongs, does not delight in evil, always protects, always trusts, always hopes, always perseveres • becoming a source of comfort and encouragement to others • understanding and supporting those you are quick to judge • loving others, not just in word but in deed and in truth • opening your heart and God's heart to others • sharing your resources and time with others who are in need • noticing those who are ill, hurting and in need of jobs; praying for them with a willingness to meet their needs as God directs

COMPASSION

THE WORLD IS A COMPETITIVE PLACE. We compete over resources, opportunities, education, jobs, relationships and the basic necessities of life. In the process it becomes patently obvious that life in this world can be a cutthroat business that inflicts an incredible amount of pain. Daily we rub shoulders with the "walking wounded." Sometimes these wounds come from others; sometimes they are self-inflicted; sometimes they come from abusive and competitive systems. No matter how the injuries occur, suffering people need to meet the compassion of Jesus.

Jesus showed compassion to outcasts, prostitutes, IRS agents, crowds, beggars, women, foreigners, societal outcasts as well as those with communicable diseases. He saw the people that others overlooked. And he was quick to feel for them rather than label them as lazy, promiscuous, self-destructive or a "piece of work." When a neglectful religious leader passed judgment on a woman he didn't know, Jesus said to him, "Simon, do you see this woman?" (Luke 7:44). Simon saw only appearances. He didn't feel for the woman because he did not *see* her. Jesus really sees the hungry, the poor, the grieving, the physically impaired, the mentally deranged, the demonically oppressed and the culturally marginalized. And what he sees moves him to compassion. But it doesn't stop there. For Jesus, compassion was a call to action, to healing and to restoration.

The early church took Jesus' example of compassion very seriously. History recounts how the infant church shocked the Roman world with its compassion for others in the midst of plagues, war and persecution. Some historians claim that the compassion of Christians was one reason why Roman religion gave way to Christianity within a space of three hundred years.

Christ is still longing to touch this suffering world through the compassion of his church, and his apprentices are people of compassion. They know how to look for pain in the eyes of others. They know that labels don't help people change. They believe that love always has hands and feet.

It is our choices that will reveal whether the church today becomes known as a wellspring of compassion or a place where no one particularly cares.

REFLECTION QUESTIONS

1. When is compassion deserved or undeserved?

2. What attitudes and emotions surface when you relate to emotionally needy or dysfunctional people?

3. What experiences in your past make it easy or difficult to be compassionate with yourself?

4. Do you think the attitude that "people just need to work harder and show more initiative in order to get on in life" affects relationships? How?

5. What is it like for you when people are compassionate toward you?

SPIRITUAL EXERCISES

1. Become quiet and still. Get in touch with your desire to see Jesus. • Read the crucifixion account in one of the Gospels. As you read, become one of the watchers: Mary, a disciple, a soldier or a thief. What did you see from this person's perspective? • What is it like for Jesus to be abandoned by those he counted on? What is it like for Jesus to find that God is silent? What is it like for him to submit to the aloneness, the pain, the nakedness? What desire drives Jesus to the cross? • Let Jesus summon you into prayer.

2. Construct a timeline of your losses. At each point record how you responded (e.g., anger, denial, blame, withdrawal, depression, etc.). How did moments of compassion come or not come into these moments? • Dialogue with Jesus about what you see.

3. Choose one way you can show compassion to someone this week. After you have done so, talk to someone about what it was like for you to do this.

4. Draw up a list of the people whose services you receive: teachers, pastors, caretakers and so on. Next to each name write down any needs you know they have (e.g., personal, financial, physical, etc.). What is God calling you to do? Listen, journal, act.

5. Consider who the outsiders and disenfranchised are in your community. Choose one of these groups and find out something about them. What do they need? What do they have to give? Where is God calling you to walk in his compassion?

6. Ask three people who are close to you if they will honestly answer some questions: "How do I come across?" "What is it like to be with me?" "Do I show an interest in others?" "Do I mostly talk about myself?" • What do you learn about the way you come across?

Resources on Compassion

Comforting One Another by Karen Mains

"In themselves Spiritual Disciplines can do nothing; they can only get us to a place where something can be done."—Douglas Rumford

CONTROL OF THE TONGUE

DESIRE	to turn the destructive way I use words into authentic, loving and healing speech
DEFINITION	Control of the tongue involves an intentional awareness and governance of words as well as tone of voice in all communication.

SCRIPTURE	"We get it wrong nearly every time we open our mouths. If you could find someone whose speech was perfectly true, you'd have a perfect person, in perfect control of life. . . .
	
	A word out of your mouth may seem of no account, but it can accomplish nearly anything—or destroy it!
	
	It only takes a spark, remember, to set off a forest fire. A careless or wrongly placed word out of your mouth can do that. By our speech we can ruin the world, turn harmony to chaos, throw mud on a reputation, send the whole world up in smoke and go up in smoke with it, smoke right from the pit of hell.
	
	"This is scary: . . . With our tongues we bless God our Father; with the same tongues we curse the very men and women he made in his image. Curses and blessings out of the same mouth! . . .
	
	My friends, this can't go on." (James 3:2, 5-7, 9-10 *The Message*)
	
	"A fool's mouth is his undoing,
	    and his lips are a snare to his soul." (Proverbs 18:7)
	
	"Gracious speech is like clover honey—
	    good taste to the soul, quick energy for the body." (Proverbs 16:24 *The Message*)

PRACTICE INCLUDES	• speaking the truth in love • not speaking out of anger or irritability • using words to encourage and build others up • speaking life rather than death into others lives • not yelling, cursing or belittling others • refusing to take part in gossip, slander or backstabbing • curbing half-truths used to create impressions and manage your image • using verbal and body language in a godly way • addressing your critical nature as revealed in your critical tongue
GOD-GIVEN FRUIT	• keeping company with Jesus in all your speech • building others up through words • noticing how the words you speak affect others • apologizing and forgiving with words • meaning what you say and saying what you mean; no double meanings • letting go of verbal defense mechanisms • revealing Christ in the use of your tongue

CONTROL OF THE TONGUE

WORDS ARE SMALL THINGS THAT HOLD INCREDIBLE POWER. With them we make both love and war. James says, "A word out of your mouth may seem of no account, but it can accomplish nearly anything—or destroy it!" (James 3:5). We may rarely think about lexicons and grammar, but lexicons and grammar shape our lives, our memories, our past, present and future.

Everyone has tasted the power of words spoken in deep love and deep hate. We know that long after a speaker is dead and gone, their blessings and curses remain. Words are powerful! They mark us forever. No wonder James exhorts believers to attend to their words. Governing our words, refraining from labels that judge and taking responsibility for our meanings is part of growth in godliness. Evagrius wrote, "Better a gentle worldly man than an irascible and wrathful monk." Words give away what is really happening in our hearts. What James says is true: "No man can tame the tongue. It is restless evil, full of deadly poison" (James 3:8). We need help to change our use of words.

When I was in college I went to a church that cared deeply about how people used words. Within our fellowship we had people who were attempting to address their addiction to criticism and critiquing. When they were in situations where the spirit of criticism began to take over, they would say, "I am addicted to criticism. If this discussion continues in a critical way, I will need to be excused because I cannot stop myself once I get going." We need help to change our patterns of speech.

Thank God that we are *inhabited beings*. The Spirit of God lives in us and partners with us to change our verbal outbursts. Indeed God intends to so renovate our tongues so that we become God's own word of blessing, truth and love for others. Healing and blessing others with our lips is one way God heals our world.

REFLECTION QUESTIONS

1. Do you recognize when you are controlling a conversation, holding forth, pontificating, dissembling?

Where does the need to do this come from?

2. How do you feel about and respond to conversations where others dominate or outshine you?

3. How do you or don't you listen and draw others out in conversations?

4. In conversations when do you feel the need to appear well-informed, spiritual or witty?

5. Are you ever aware of taking on a teaching role even in social conversations? What is that about?

6. When and how are you most likely to speak a harsh or impatient word?

7. What is your fallback conversational posture?

   Are you defensive, critical, open or able to give the benefit of the doubt?

8. How do you speak about others when they are not around?

SPIRITUAL EXERCISES

1. If you are not good at giving praise or expressing thanks, intentionally create a word list. Divide a piece of paper into four columns headed with the words "Thank You," "I'm Sorry," "I Made a Mistake" and "You Did a Good Job." In each column write all the ways you know to convey each truth. Put this list where you can see it and revisit it. Intentionally use these words and phrases for a week. • What do you notice about yourself and your relationships?

2. Before you jump to conclusions about what somebody means, check out their meaning with a phrase like, "What I hear you saying is . . ." Keep using this phrase until you have their meaning right. What is it like for you to do this?

3. Never use words like "You always . . ." and "You never . . ." These are fighting words. • As you remove these words from your speech, what happens to your relationships?

4. Devise small strategies that can give you space to gain control of your tongue. For example, you might count to ten, take a time-out or leave the room before you lose your temper. When you notice you are about to yell, take a deep breath and say quietly to yourself, "Turn down the volume." • Practice one of your strategies for a week. What is it like for you? Small strategies like these can offer you a moment to refocus on what really matters and how you want to say it.

5. Since Scripture tells us that we will give an account for every word we have said, spend some time praying about how you use words. • Imagine that all the words you speak are picked up and stored in a receiver somewhere out in outer space. Then imagine all your words being played back to you. What do you hear? • Give the Lord an account of today's words. Confess with your mouth the sins of your mouth. Receive God's gift of forgiveness.

6. It supposedly takes at least three weeks to break an old habit. Choose a habit of speech

you wish to break. Consider what new habit you want to replace the old one. Ask two or three people to pray with you in the next three weeks while you attend to this habit. • When you sense yourself moving into the speech pattern you wish to change, say "stop" to yourself. Learning to recognize a trigger to a speech pattern and then actually saying "stop" is a huge step in addressing your habit. • Ask God to help you put your new habit into practice. When you goof up, confess and gently begin again.

Resources on Control of the Tongue

Patterns by Mel Lawrenz, chapter 12

Renovation of the Heart by Dallas Willard, chapters 6-8

"Humility and honesty are really the same thing. A humble person is simply a brutally honest person about the whole truth. You and I came along a few years ago; we're going to be gone in a few years. The only honest response to life is a humble one."—Richard Rohr

HUMILITY

DESIRE	to become like Jesus in his willingness to choose the hidden way of love rather than the way of power
DEFINITION	Humility is not thinking less of yourself but thinking of yourself less. Humble people let go of image management and self-promotion. They honor others by making the others' needs as real and important as their own.

SCRIPTURE	"Be especially careful when you are trying to be good so that you don't make a performance out of it. . . .
	    Just do it—quietly and unobtrusively. That is the way your God, who conceived you in love, working behind the scenes, helps you out." (Mathew 6:1, 4 *The Message*)
	
	"My dear friends, don't let public opinion influence how you live out our glorious, Christ-originated faith." (James 2:1 *The Message*)
	
	"Therefore, as God's chosen people, holy and dearly loved, clothe yourselves with compassion, kindness, humility, gentleness and patience." (Colossians 3:12)
	
	"For this is what the high and lofty One says— . . .
	'I live in a high and holy place,
	    but also with him who is contrite and lowly in spirit,
	to revive the spirit of the lowly
	    and to revive the heart of the contrite.' " (Isaiah 57:15)

PRACTICE INCLUDES	• refraining from image management • deliberately keeping silent about accomplishments and talents • refusing the impulse to name-drop • backing away from becoming the center of attention; drawing others out • avoiding favoritism; honoring others as God does • choosing downward mobility so others have more
GOD-GIVEN FRUIT	• keeping company with Jesus so your identity rests with him alone • having Jesus increase and you decrease • being liberated from the need for others' approval • taking your identity from being God's dearly loved child rather than from possessions • being free from ostentation and pretense • loving your neighbor as yourself; taking as much interest in others as in yourself and your opinions • living an authentically grateful life • becoming like Jesus, "who made himself of no reputation"

HUMILITY

IN A WORLD OF CORPORATE, POLITICAL, ECONOMIC and social hierarchies, humility is a hard sell. After all, who wants to be on the bottom of the heap, last in line or out of the loop? People scramble to have others realize how gifted, qualified, valuable and productive they are. Folks compete so they won't be overlooked and underutilized.

It's a normal human longing to want to be appreciated, valued and recognized for our potential. And humility does not mean thinking demeaning and low thoughts about ourselves. It's not denying the truth of our achievements or thinking less of ourselves. Humility stems from an honest understanding of who we are. However, longings to be appreciated and valued can motivate us to establish our identity in secondary things—things we are proud of but can lose. Personas and the false self are cobbled together by identifying with the grandiosity of secondary things. It is easy to tell when the false self is in place, because it is always afraid of looking little and inadequate. It takes offense at slights and is horribly sensitive to being overlooked. The false self is turned in on itself.

Humility stems from having someone besides yourself as the center of your attention. Apprentices to Jesus are chosen, loved, appreciated and important to the Creator of the universe. The Holy Spirit inhabits them. They are free to be who they are—no more and no less. A true Christ-in-me self is deeply at home in God and in its own skin. Such a self humbly receives its identity as a gift and feels no need to justify its existence. The mirror of public response doesn't matter. He or she isn't out to prove something or sell him- or herself. Awards, accolades and notoriety are not the center of identity. Regardless of how little or how much people "know" who he or she is, the humble person is truly free. And because the humble are free, they don't think less of themselves, they think of themselves less.

Jesus is the consummate example of humility and greatness. Jesus knew he was God's own Son. No one born of flesh will ever be greater than he. But Jesus laid down his divine power and greatness and appeared on earth as we all do. He was born the helpless son of the virgin Mary. The mind boggles at the depth of Christ's descent. Jonathan Edwards put it well when he suggested that even as Christ is infinitely greater than us, he is also infinitely more humble.

REFLECTION QUESTIONS

1. Who in your life tells you the truth without praise or blame?

   What is this like for you?

2. Does humility appeal to you or not? Explain.

3. What do you admire about humble people?

4. How do you recognize true humility?

5. Do you tend to believe you have earned everything you have? Do you act like your achievements are simply a tribute to raw talent?

   Let what you discover about yourself lead you into confession.

SPIRITUAL EXERCISES

1. Write a résumé of your character, not your expertise. What does this reveal about who you are becoming? Are you on the path to humility? • Begin to pray for the character you long to have.

2. If you are quick to draw attention to your good works, begin to do some things anonymously. What is it like for you? • What does it mean to you to have only God know?

3. What things are sources of pride to you? What about these things makes you proud? How do humility and pride fit together as you think about these things? • How do you think God is calling you to think about the things that bring you pride?

4. In Matthew 11:29 Jesus says, "Take my yoke upon you and learn from me, for I am gentle and humble in heart." What are the characteristics of a gentle and humble heart? • How are you cultivating a gentle and humble heart?

5. Assess your own image-management quotient: Spend a week intentionally listening to how you speak about yourself to others. Journal when you spin the truth to put yourself in a better light. Can you hear yourself saying, "I never watch TV, but yesterday I saw . . ."? Why is it important for you to be known as someone who doesn't watch TV? • When introduced to others, note what you say about yourself and what you want to come out about you. • Journal how you respond to another's praise or blame. What would it mean to speak more simply and truthfully about yourself? Ask God to root you in his love and set you free to simply be who you are.

Resources on Humility

Humility by Andrew Murray

The Gift of Being Yourself by David Benner

"Grace only exists where someone is paying the price, not where error is overlooked."—Udo Middleman

JUSTICE

DESIRE	to love others by seeking their good, protection, gain and fair treatment
DEFINITION	Justice seeks to help others through correcting and redressing wrongs. It treats others fairly and shows no favoritism.

SCRIPTURE	"Seek good, not evil ,
	      that you may live. . . .
	Hate evil, love good;
	      maintain justice in the courts." (Amos 5:14-15)
	
	"But let justice roll on like a river,
	      righteousness like a never-failing stream!" (Amos 5:24)
	
	"Remember those in prison as if you were their fellow prisoners, and those who are mistreated as if you yourselves were suffering." (Hebrews 13:3)
	
	"Real religion, the kind that passes muster before God the Father, is this: Reach out to the homeless and loveless in their plight, and guard against corruption from the godless world. . . .
	      Don't let public opinion influence how you live out our glorious, Christ-originated faith." (James 1:27—2:1 *The Message*)
	
	"Complete the Royal Rule of the Scriptures: 'Love others as you love yourself.' But if you play up to these so-called important people, you go against the Rule and stand convicted by it." (James 2:8-9 *The Message*)

PRACTICE INCLUDES	• being responsible to God and others • being a good steward of what you own • supporting just causes with time, action and financial support • treating others impartially and fairly • providing for the poor, needy and oppressed through the means available to you • volunteering for prison ministry, food-bank work and ministries that serve needs in the local community • refusing to buy products of companies that take advantage of the poor
GOD-GIVEN FRUIT	• keeping company with Jesus, living out his concern for the poor and oppressed • living sacrificially in order to bring justice and freedom to others • having concern and praying for the oppressed • being able to see others through Jesus' eyes of love • being other-centered rather than self-centered

JUSTICE

I SOMETIMES WONDER WHY JUSTICE SEEMS such a reach for us. If we submitted to the great commission, "teaching them to obey everything I have commanded you," and if we obeyed the great commandment, "love God and your neighbor as yourself," issues of justice could not be avoided. Our journeys would be characterized by Micah's great requirement: "What does the LORD require of you? / To act justly and to love mercy / and to walk humbly with your God" (Micah 6:8). We would be people who fought unemployment with job training, illiteracy with education, pollution with technology, oppression with legal protection, disease with medicine, danger with safety, poverty with help, chaos with order, fear with love, hunger with food, and on and on. We would grieve over injustice and oppression. We would courageously use our gifts and talents to oppose the results of the Fall.

Unfortunately, justice is not something we can take for granted among Christians. We, like the world around us, like our comforts and balk at sacrifice or inconvenience. While we endorse the notion of justice, our time and energy goes into personal development and material accomplishments. What is fulfilling to us at any given moment has more bearing on our life than the call to create a society in which justice and love visibly reflect God's nature.

We never outgrow the need for prophets who remind us of the "great requirement." We need to search our hearts and see where putting our own agenda first makes us part of the problem. Eugene Peterson suggests that a faith that doesn't serve justice can end up making us worse instead of better. It can actually separate us from God and his ways instead of drawing us to him.

Truth and holiness are always matters of substance, not appearance. Issues of justice consistently involve allocation of real and substantive resources: money, time, opportunities, goods and services. At the 2004 Spiritual Formation Forum in L.A., John Perkins claimed, "Justice is always about what one owns." The Christian life is not a game where the one with the most toys wins. What we have and own is never simply ours. We are stewards of what God has given us. God holds us responsible for what we do with what we have.

Followers of Jesus are to share their resources and work against the evil that robs the world of God's care and love. Lifestyles and choices that love and value people more than things is the litmus test of faith. A high school group in my church continually reminds me of this truth with their prophetic name "Get over Yourself!"

REFLECTION QUESTIONS

1. Where does concern for the injustices of this world fit into your thoughts and life?

   What is your general reaction to volunteering time to causes in your community that serve the poor, oppressed and needy?

3. What is it like for you to be treated unfairly? What difference can an advocate make?

SPIRITUAL EXERCISES

1. Become more aware of justice issues in your community through fact-finding excursions. Take your children or a small group with you. Call ahead and arrange a time to meet with folks involved in food banks, housing for the poor and elderly, shepherding homes, halfway houses, etc. What kinds of needs are represented by these organizations? What kind of help are they seeking? Volunteer to help.

2. Go on a short-term mission trip. Expose yourself to needs of the world.

3. Begin reading about justice issues. Sign up for the Internal Justice Mission weekly e-mail update.

4. Consider your responsibility before God for what you own. What effect does God's view of the gifts he has given you have on you? • How could you share your gifts with others? Could you tutor? Could you help settle a refugee family? Could you teach someone English? Could you provide training opportunities for first-time legal offenders?

5. Start a prayer group that prays through the concerns of the newspaper. Pray for peace and justice issues. Be open to what God might want you to do.

Resources on Justice

International Justice Mission <www.ijm.org>
John M. Perkins Foundation for Reconciliation and Development <www.jmpf.org>
Let Justice Roll Down by John Perkins
Send My Roots Rain: A Spirituality of Justice and Mercy by Megan McKenna

"I do not believe one can settle how much we ought to give. I am afraid the only safe rule is to give more than we can spare. In other words, if our expenditure on comforts, luxuries, amusements, etc., is up to the standard common among those with the same income as our own, we are probably giving too little away. If our charities do not at all pinch or hamper us, I should say they are too small."—C. S. Lewis

STEWARDSHIP

DESIRE	to live as a steward of God's resources in all areas of life; to live out of the awareness that nothing I have is my own
DEFINITION	Stewardship is the voluntary and generous offering of God's gifts of resources, time, talents and treasure for the benefit and love of God and others.
SCRIPTURE	"Remember this: Whoever sows sparingly will also reap sparingly, and whoever sows generously will also reap generously. Each man should give what he has decided in his heart to give, not reluctantly or under compulsion, for God loves a cheerful giver." (2 Corinthians 9:6-7)
	"You may say to yourself, 'My power and the strength of my hands have produced this wealth for me.' But remember the LORD your God, for it is he who gives you the ability to produce wealth." (Deuteronomy 8:17-18)
	"The earth is the LORD's and everything in it, the world, and all who live in it." (Psalm 24:1)
	"Do not store up for yourselves treasure on earth. . . . But store up for yourselves treasures in heaven." (Matthew 6:19-20)
PRACTICE INCLUDES	• a systematic, intentionally generous lifestyle flowing from love of God and others • living in a way that exemplifies that your life, your time, your money, your home, your family are not your own • making offerings that go beyond the tithe • thoughtfully investing resources and spiritual gifts to benefit the body of Christ • generous sharing of the resources God has given you: physical, mental, natural, economic and spiritual
GOD-GIVEN FRUIT	• being liberated from greed, self-centeredness, money and other things so that the generous spirit of Jesus grows in you • embracing generous hospitality toward those in need • modeling God's goodness and generosity • awareness of your selfishness and lack of love for others • living from the conviction that nothing belongs to you; you didn't deserve it or earn it; it all came from God • investing in the kingdom of God, building up treasure in heaven • loving God with all your heart, soul, strength and mind, and loving your neighbor as yourself • stewarding the earth and all your resources; freedom from the toxic disease of affluenza

STEWARDSHIP

WORSHIP HAS ALWAYS INCLUDED SHARING what God has given us with others. Justin, an early Christian teacher and martyr, wrote of the practice of stewardship within the church in *The Apology of Justin the Martyr:*

> The well-to-do and those who are willing give according to their pleasure, each one of his own as he wishes, and what is collected is handed over to the president [pastor], and he helps widows and orphans, and those who are needy because of sickness or for any other reason, and those who are in prison and the strangers on their journeys.

Stewardship means recognizing that nothing we have really belongs to us. Everything we own belongs to God. We are simply the stewards of his wealth, his gifts, his opportunities, his houses, his cars and his computers. Sharing is to be in our DNA. Yet much of the world identifies the Christian West as consumers rather than people who are good stewards. Fifty years ago Americans consumed half as many goods and services per person as they do today. During the same amount of time the size of homes tripled. Every day we buy more clothes, appliances, cars, books, televisions, computers and so forth simply because we can (and often when we can't). Some sociologists have named this propensity to continually purchase and consume more, "affluenza."

God intends for the body of Christ to battle affluenza and reach the world with his loving care. He does this through people who steward his wealth by sharing their resources and gifts. Stewards distinguish between building their own kingdom and building the kingdom of God.

The practice of stewardship will reveal what is in our heart. Stewardship shines its light into our entitlement mentality and on our need to impress others with what we have. Stewards ask hard questions:

- What do we need to have to be content?
- Are we willing to share?
- Will we live on less so that others might have more?
- Can we enjoy the public beach rather than own a beach of our own?

- Will we take public transportation or invest in a hybrid vehicle rather than buy another internal combustion engine?
- Can we downsize rather than trade up?

Exodus recounts the story of the building of the tabernacle. Moses asked the people to give to this cause with their talents, gold and time. So many people wanted to give that Moses had to order the people to stop giving: "And so the people were restrained from bringing more, because what they already had was more than enough to do all the work" (Exodus 36:6-7). How different would it be if we had such a desire to give?

Stewardship poses hard questions about the unique intentions of our hearts. The questions are always aimed at us personally, and we cannot read the heart of another. So let us refrain from judging others' choices and attend to God's question, "Are you doing all I would have you do with what I have given you?"

REFLECTION QUESTIONS

1. How does the knowledge that all you have belongs to God affect your life?

2. When have you gone without so someone else could have?

   What was that like for you?

3. What are your current addictions? For example, shopping, technology, keeping up with the Joneses, watching TV?

   How do these addictions affect your use of your resources?

4. What would it mean to you to begin to downsize so you could give more to others?

5. What would it be like for you to consider helping brothers and sisters in your community with their financial needs?

SPIRITUAL EXERCISES

1. Ask God to speak to you about being a steward of his gifts to you. Decide to give God a percentage of your income rather than a dollar amount. Then as your income rises and falls, give appropriately. Begin to increase this percentage as you earn more.

2. Take a look at the people who regularly are in and out of your life. Do you feel any sort of responsibility to know their needs? How does knowing a need affect you? • How could you be the loving hands of God's provision to someone you know?

3. Think back over your life. When have you given something that brought you great joy? What did you give? Why did it touch you so deeply? • How might you continue to give in the area that gives you joy?

4. How does the way you were brought up affect your stewardship? List the strengths or weaknesses that have been bequeathed to you. • Then consider the legacy you are passing on to others. What do you want people to say about your stewardship of your resources once you are gone?

5. Form an investment club that gives all of its profits to the cause of Christ. Enjoy discovering where you want to give. Invest in the kingdom of heaven.

6. Give a deserving person a "bonus."

7. Practice giving a tithe (typically 10 percent) of your God-given income back to God. • Increase the tithe to a larger percentage as your salary increases.

8. Set aside a "shepherd's purse." Collect all your quarters and put them in the purse. Then when you hear of a need, offer what is in your "shepherd's purse." Children can begin a "shepherd's purse" with nickels or even pennies.

Resources on Stewardship

Casting a Vision for Good Sense by Dick Towner
Good Sense Series by Dick Towner
www.generousgiving.org

"Holiness is not a condition into which we drift."—John Stott

TRUTH TELLING

DESIRE	to live an authentically truthful life
DEFINITION	Truth telling involves speaking in a way that does not exaggerate, minimize, deny, rationalize or manage the truth.

SCRIPTURE	"Simply let your 'Yes' be 'Yes,' and your 'No,' 'No'; anything beyond this comes from the evil one." (Matthew 5:37)
	
	"Likewise the tongue is a small part of the body, but it makes great boasts. Consider what a great forest is set on fire by a small spark. The tongue also is a fire, a world of evil among the parts of the body. . . .
	    Out of the same mouth come praise and cursing. My brothers, this should not be." (James 3:5-6, 10)
	
	"Truthful lips endure forever,
	    but a lying tongue lasts only a moment. . . .
	The LORD detests lying lips,
	    but he delights in men who are truthful." (Proverbs 12:19, 22)

PRACTICE INCLUDES	• refusing to spin events and experiences in order to impress others • not exaggerating • not cheating on tests, taxes, insurance forms, etc. • keeping promises and following through • repenting, and informing others of when you have lied to them • speaking the truth in love • refusing to flatter or dissemble • saying what you mean and meaning what you say • refusing to slander another • refusing to gossip or pass on gossip and rumor
GOD-GIVEN FRUIT	• having integrity and being honest • being freed from rationalization, denial and blame • being aware of when and how you manipulate the truth • being sensitive to the convicting work of the Holy Spirit in your conscience when you lie or stretch the truth • telling the truth even when it hurts • not taking your bearings on the truth from what the culture finds acceptable

TRUTH TELLING

IN THE BEGINNING GOD TOLD ADAM AND EVE that they were free to eat of every tree in the Garden of Eden but one (Genesis 2:16-17). One tree belonged to God alone. If they ate of this forbidden tree, they would die. That was reality! Eventually Adam and Eve decided they couldn't live with God deciding the nature of what was good and bad. They wanted to choose what was good and bad for themselves. They wanted to determine their own reality. So Adam and Eve became the first truth "spinners." It began with lying to themselves about the true nature of the tree and God's command concerning it. In effect, the spin was, "God is holding out on us." That spin led to other spins, and before you know it they were hiding from and lying to God and one another. But God refuses to let lies have the last word. God looked for Adam and Eve in an attempt to reconcile their broken relationship, reclaim truth and restore reality (Genesis 3:9, 15). The rest of the Bible is the story of how God mends the tear in the fabric of creation who began with a lie about reality.

Like Adam and Eve before us, we are truth spinners who want to define our own realities. We pad expense accounts with rationalizations and denials. We back out of commitments with blame and deceit. Advertisers, corporations, nongovernment agencies, educational and religious institutions spin the truth. Everything from ruining the environment to insider trading gets the spin. It's not hard to understand why people don't know who or what to believe. But lies that substitute for reality don't last forever.

Truth alone has staying power. Jesus says telling the truth begins with small things. Don't say yes when you intend to back out of it: "Simply let your 'Yes' be 'Yes' and your 'No,' 'No'; anything beyond this comes from the evil one" (Matthew 5:37). Begin to reclaim the truth about yourself and your words by honoring the Creator and reality as he defines it.

REFLECTION QUESTIONS

1. How do you live out God's reality about the goodness of telling the truth?

2. When do you use a sliding scale of honesty, exaggeration or partial truths to get what you want?

3. How has someone's honesty or lack of it affected you?

4. When has it cost you to be honest? What as that like for you?

SPIRITUAL EXERCISES

1. Take some uninterrupted time to assess your honesty. Think back over the past week. Where have you been tempted to stretch the truth, take advantage of a privilege, break a commitment or gossip? What do you see about yourself? Where is it hardest for you to tell the truth? • Write a prayer of confession in your journal. Or confess your sin to a trusted friend. Ask him or her to pray for you.

2. Practice one of these habits for the coming week: (1) not exaggerating, (2) not gossiping or (3) not rationalizing. • What is it like for you to do this?

3. What lies do you tend to tell yourself? What tapes do you play in your head that make you feel worthless, inadequate and unloved? Talk to God about what it is like to give space in your head and heart for these lies. • Turn to Psalm 139. What sort of thoughts does God have about you? Replace the lies you listen to with the truth of what God says about you.

4. When you become aware of having told a lie, apologize and make amends. This sort of attention to confession softens the heart to the reality of truth.

Resources on Truth Telling

Everything Belongs by Richard Rohr

Invitation to a Journey by Robert Mulholland

Part Seven

PRAY

PRAYER IS A WORD THAT DESCRIBES A RELATIONSHIP. Disciplines of prayer provide patterns for attending to God throughout the day. They open us to the divine dialogue through intentional encounter with the Trinity. The *P* disciplines open our gaze and hearing to God. In his book *The Way of the Heart*, Henri Nouwen quotes Theophan the Recluse: "To pray is to descend with the mind into the heart, and there stand before the face of the Lord, ever-present, all seeing, within you." Prayer is sustained less by duty than by a desire to connect and grow in intimacy and communion with the holy Three. But prayer also moves us up and out into our world. In *Love in a Fearful Land*, Nouwen also writes, "Prayer is the way to both the heart of God and the heart of the world—precisely because they have been joined through the suffering of Jesus Christ. . . . Praying is letting one's own heart become the place where the tears of God's children merge and become tears of hope."

The *P* disciplines provide a number of ways of entering into prayer. Often the exercises invite you to sit comfortably in a chair and become present to God. Though the posture of sitting for prayer is not necessarily rooted in biblical examples, it is the posture most of us in Western culture assume in order to concentrate on something or someone. Posture is an important part of prayer. The ancient Jews believed that prayer began with an intentional awareness of God's presence: know "before whom you are standing" (Berakhot 28b). The inward posture of the heart preceded all outward postures for prayer. If you wish to explore or substitute one of the many biblical postures of prayer, please feel free to do so (see "Postures for Prayer," appendix 7).

"Think often on God, by day, by night, in your business and even in your diversions. He is always near you and with you; leave him not alone."—Brother Lawrence

BREATH PRAYER

DESIRE	to pray a simple, intimate prayer of heartfelt desire before God
DEFINITION	Breath prayer is a form of contemplative prayer linked to the rhythms of breathing: (1) breathe in, calling on a biblical name or image of God, and (2) breathe out a simple God-given desire.
SCRIPTURE	"Be joyful always; pray continually; give thanks in all circumstances, for this is God's will for you in Christ Jesus." (1 Thessalonians 5:16-18) "His divine power has given us everything we need for life and godliness. . . . [H]e has given us his very great and precious promises, so that through them you may participate in the divine nature and escape the corruption in the world caused by evil desires." (2 Peter 1:3-4)
PRACTICE INCLUDES	• repeating a simple one-sentence prayer that begins with a biblical name of God that is meaningful to you; follow the name with a word or phrase expressing your deep God-given desire; connect the prayer to your breathing and return to it throughout the day until it becomes a soul reflex • saying a traditionally scriptural breath prayer known as the "Jesus Prayer": "Jesus, Son of David, have mercy on me, a sinner"; breath prayers include phrases of Scripture: for example, "My soul glorifies the Lord" (Luke 1:46), "My souls finds rest in God alone" (Psalm 62:1); breath prayers can be short prayers of love and desire, for example, "Shepherd, lead me by still waters," or "Come, Holy Spirit, come."
GOD-GIVEN FRUIT	• keeping company with Jesus whether or not you feel his presence • abiding in Christ, opening yourself to constant union all day long • putting into a phrase the deepest desire of your heart and praying out of that desire • reminding yourself that God is present and living in you • guarding self-talk so your thoughts, feelings and behavior flow from an ongoing dialogue with God • regulating your imagination and fantasy life • breathing in the life of Christ and breathing out the work of Christ • developing a rhythm of turning to God at any time of the day • developing a constant, inner, unbroken, perpetual habit of prayer

Breath Prayer

Breathing is an unconscious thing. And breath prayer reminds us that just as we can't live on one breath of air, we can't live on one breath of God. God is the oxygen of our soul, and we need to breathe him in all day long. After all, it is in him that "we live and move and have our being" (Acts 17:28). Breath prayer reminds us that each breath we are given is God's gift and that God's Spirit is nearer to us than our own breath.

Breath prayer or "prayer of the heart" has been practiced in the church for millennia. The Eastern Orthodox Church in particular has seen breath prayer as way of living out Paul's instruction to "pray without ceasing." The "Jesus Prayer" is a breath prayer described in *The Way of the Pilgrim:*

> Take a seat in solitude and silence. Bend your head, close your eyes and breathing softly, in your imagination, look into your own heart. Let your mind, or rather, your thoughts flow from your head down to your heart and say, while breathing: "Lord Jesus Christ, have mercy on me." Whisper these words gently or say them in your mind. Discard all other thoughts. Be serene, persevering and repeat them over and over again.

The Jesus Prayer combines "Son of David, have mercy on me" (Luke 18:39) with "God, have mercy on me, a sinner" (Luke 18:13). Breathing in, you pray "Jesus, Son of David," breathing out, you say, "have mercy on me, a sinner." This short repetitive prayer frees you from linear thought and allows you to begin to pray in your body, not just your mind. It is meant to be a lived, breathing rhythm of surrender. And it is a constant reminder of the One in whose presence you stand.

To practice breath prayer, ponder the nearness of God. Settle deeply into the truth that Christ is in you. Deeply breathe in, repeating any name of God that is dear to you (see "Names for Worshiping God," appendix 5). As you exhale, voice a deep desire of your heart. When you exhale, offer up the desire of your heart. The brevity of the prayer allows it to be repeated over and over throughout the day.

Examples of breath prayers are

- breathe in "Abba," breathe out "I belong to you."
- breathe in "Healer," breathe out "speak the word and I shall be healed."
- breathe in "Shepherd," breathe out "bring home my lost son."
- breathe in "Holy One," breathe out "keep me true."
- breathe in "Lord," breathe out "here I am."
- breathe in "Jesus," breathe out "have mercy on me."

REFLECTION QUESTIONS

1. How do you practice Paul's injunction to pray without ceasing?

2. How do you pray in a way that keeps you as conscious as possible of Christ's presence within you?

3. How does the thought of repetitive prayer strike you?

4. What are the up sides and down sides of repetitive prayer?

5. How might a breath prayer be shorthand for a longer prayer of your heart?

SPIRITUAL EXERCISES

1. Become comfortable. Breathe deeply. Intentionally place yourself before God. In rhythm with your breathing, gratefully inhale the breath of life. Exhale remembering that Jesus gave his last breath for love of you. Gently and thankfully repeat, "Breath of life, breathe on me."

2. Decide to pray the Jesus Prayer or some other scriptural breath prayer as often as you are able during one day. If you worry about forgetting, set a clock at every hour to remind you, or put the prayer on your car mirror. Reminders should be gentle and not forced. • In the evening spend time telling the Lord what it means to you to be able to return to him again and again during the day with one particular prayer.

3. Is there someone for whom you wish to pray ceaselessly? Listen deeply to what Jesus' desire for this person might be. • Form a breath prayer naming God's adequacy and your desire for the person. Throughout the day as they come to mind, offer up your prayer. Don't allow yourself to be drawn into long prayer dialogues about what you want God to do in this person's life. Let the breath prayer carry all your desire to God.

4. Begin and end each day with your breath prayer. Let it be the word that comes to mind as you wake and as you fall asleep.

5. Tell someone what breath prayer means to you.

6. Help a child form a breath prayer to say while at school or at play.

Resources on Breath Prayer

Soul Feast, chapter 3, by Marjorie Thompson

The Way of the Pilgrim translated by Helen Bacovcin

"In prayer we seek God. We do not seek peace, quiet, tranquility, enlightenment; we do not seek anything for ourselves. We seek to give ourselves . . . to God. He is the all of our prayer."
—M. Basil Pennington

CENTERING PRAYER

DESIRE	to quiet the heart and rest in God alone
DEFINITION	Centering prayer is a form of contemplative prayer where the pray-er seeks to quiet scattered thoughts and desires in the still center of Christ's presence.
SCRIPTURE	"For in him we live and move and have our being." (Acts 17:28) "If anyone loves me, he will obey my teaching. My Father will love him, and we will come to him and make our home with him." (John 14:23) "I slept but my heart was awake. 　　Listen! My lover is knocking." (Song of Songs 5:2) "My soul finds rest in God alone." (Psalm 62.1)
PRACTICE INCLUDES	• resting in and gazing on Christ • waiting before the Lord in open attentiveness • attending to the presence of the Holy Spirit within • taming scattered thoughts by attending to Christ through the use of a prayer word • releasing distractions into the hands of God and returning constantly to his presence within
GOD-GIVEN FRUIT	• keeping company with Jesus, trusting that he is working in you while you pray • living in more awareness of your union with Christ • bringing stillness into the busyness of life • learning to listen to God • seeking God's presence and assistance in all things • learning to hold Scripture in your heart • resting in God's will rather than your own agenda • developing a quiet center within that is not attached to outcomes

CENTERING PRAYER

CENTERING PRAYER IS NOT SOMETHING NEW. Nor is it a New Age thing. It is an ancient form of prayer that joined meditation on a word of Scripture with prayer. It provided a simple way to center one's life in God's presence. In the 1960s and 1970s three Cistercian monks, Thomas Keating, Basil Pennington and William Meninger, sought to revive this ancient form of meditative prayer. Centering prayer is distinctively different from practices of Eastern meditation that attempt to clear the mind of all thoughts. Centering prayer allows for the recognition of thoughts and gently releases them into the hands of God. This form of prayer relies on the awareness that the Holy Spirit resides in the one who prays, connecting them heart to heart with God.

This prayer may seem mysterious to some because it depends so little on words. We do not give God information about all our needs, projects, ideas, programs, plans and agendas. We don't suggest things we would like him to do. We sit in the presence of God and give him our undivided love and attention. Generally, the only words that are spoken in centering prayer are the prayer words that continually bring our drifting attention back to God. The prayer word is a simple word like *Jesus, love, peace, Father,* or a phrase from Scripture that encapsulates the intent of the heart to be with God. With this word we linger with God and open ourselves to his presence.

Because centering prayer is a way of being with Jesus that doesn't cover prayer concerns, some people wonder if it counts as real prayer. Furthermore, if it doesn't make you feel or experience something particular, what does it do? It is never possible to judge the value of any prayer based on feeling or experience alone. Experiences are not the point. In centering prayer the goal is to so dwell in Christ that the fruit of this dwelling begins to show up in your life. Centering praying may "do" nothing at the moment. You sense no rapture, no mystical bliss. But later, as you move out into the busyness of life, you begin to notice that something has shifted. Your quiet center in Christ holds. Centering prayer trusts that being with Jesus brings transformation. The words of Isaac of Stella capture the heart of centering prayer: "May the Son of God who is already formed in you, grow in you, so that for you He will become immeasurable, and that in you He will become laughter, exultation, the fullness of joy which no one can take from you."

A Short Method for Centering Prayer

1. Set aside a minimum of fifteen minutes (increase the time as you can). Set a timer if that helps you to be less concerned about when to stop.

2. Settle into a comfortable position.

3. Intentionally place yourself in the presence of God, in the center of his love.

4. Choose a simple word, phrase or verse from Scripture that expresses your desire for God (e g , love, peace, grace, Jesus, great Shepherd). Let this word guard your attention.

5. Take time to become quiet. It is not unusual for the first minutes to be filled with many noisy thoughts. Don't worry about them or pay attention to them. Let them go. Gently return your attention to the center of God's presence and love by repeating your word. When your thoughts wander let them drop to the bottom of your mind. Don't go after them. Gently return to the presence of Christ through repeating your word. Let the word draw your attention back to Jesus. *Be* with Jesus. Listen. Be still. When distractions persist let one of the following images help you return to Jesus.

   - Imagine that God's river of life runs through you. Deep down, the river is calm and slow. But on the surface there is rushing and debris. Imagine your distracting thoughts are part of the debris floating in the current. Don't try to capture these thoughts; release them and let the river of God's life carry them away. Anytime you are distracted, let the distractions go with the river. Gently return to the presence of Christ with your prayer word.

   - Imagine that you are visiting a friend who lives on a busy city street. Because it is a warm day, the windows are open and all the noise and bustle of life float into the room through the window. At times you are conscious of sirens or people talking or children laughing, but your attention is devoted to your friend and you do not let your mind follow the sounds outside. As you meet with Jesus, acknowledge the noisy distractions that pull at your attention, but continually return to the moment with Jesus through your prayer word.

6. Rest in the center of God's love. Trust that the Holy Spirit who abides in the depths of your spirit to connect you with God.

7. Take several minutes to come out of prayer. Don't hurry. Breathe in the presence of Christ. Offer yourself to God for the tasks awaiting you (e.g., "I am yours," or "Remain with me").

REFLECTION QUESTIONS

1. How do you express your desire for God?

2. Is praying your desire and love for God difficult?

   What does this tell you about yourself and your view of God?

3. What is it like for you to spend time with God when you are not speaking to him?

4. What happens inside you when you are quiet with God?

SPIRITUAL EXERCISES

1. *Sacred word.* Choose a prayer word as the symbol of your desire to let Jesus' action and presence form you. The word could reflect a deep desire of your heart (e.g., love, grace, peace), or the word might be a name or title of God (e.g., Jesus, great Shepherd, Counselor, Healer of my soul, Defender). Become still and offer yourself and your love to God. Let this word or phrase draw you into the presence of Christ. When you are distracted, return gently to your word and to the Lord. At the end of the prayer, remain still for several minutes. • Throughout your day return to your word and remind the Lord of your love for him.

2. Sit comfortably in a position that allows you to stay alert and attentive. Read a short passage of Scripture slowly and out loud. Choose a word from the text as your centering word. Then follow the directions given in exercise one. Let the word lead you into the presence of Jesus. When thoughts distract you, return to Christ by repeating your word. Simply be with Jesus. Offer yourself to him. Wait in his presence.

3. Set aside twenty minutes every day for six days. Follow the steps in "A Short Method for Centering Prayer." Practice centering prayer each day. • After a week reflect on your experience. Do you sense any internal shifts? • In the weeks ahead slowly stretch your times with God.

5. Do you know others who might appreciate this sort of prayer? Begin a centering prayer group.

Resources on Centering Prayer

Centering Prayer by M. Basil Pennington
Contemplative Outreach Ltd. <www.contemplativeoutreach.org >
Open Mind, Open Heart by Thomas Keating

"Prayer is not primarily saying words or thinking thoughts. It is, rather, a stance. It's a way of living in the Presence."—Richard Rohr

CONTEMPLATIVE PRAYER

DESIRE	to develop an open, restful receptivity to the Trinity that enables me to always be with God just as I am
DEFINITION	Contemplative prayer is a receptive posture of openness toward God. It is a way of waiting with a heart awake to God's presence and his Word. This kind of prayer intentionally trusts and rests in the presence of the Holy Spirit deep in our own spirit.
SCRIPTURE	"Meanwhile, the moment we get tired in the waiting, God's Spirit is right alongside helping us along. If we don't know how or what to pray, it doesn't matter. He does our praying in and for us, making prayer out of our wordless sighs, our aching groans. He knows us far better than we know ourselves, knows our pregnant condition, and keeps us present before God." (Romans 8:26-27 *The Message*) "Now the Lord is the Spirit, and where the Spirit of the Lord is, there is freedom. And we, who with unveiled faces all reflect the Lord's glory, are being transformed into his likeness with ever-increasing glory, which comes from the Lord, who is the Spirit." (2 Corinthians 3:17-18) "This mystery has been kept in the dark for a long time, but now it's out in the open. . . . Christ is in you, therefore you can look forward to sharing in God's glory." (Colossians 1:26-27 *The Message*)
PRACTICE INCLUDES	• practicing the presence of God • allowing a portion of Scripture to sink deep into the heart as a prayer to God • practicing breath prayer, simple prayer, prayer of the heart • practicing centering prayer • resting in God and allowing the Spirit to nudge, fill or speak • wasting time with God
GOD-GIVEN FRUIT	• developing prayer that depends on trust more than giving God information about what he should do • living in the awareness of God's presence within me • move out of "doing" prayer into "being" prayer • learning to let go of distractions in prayer • letting God love me

CONTEMPLATIVE PRAYER

WE OFTEN ASSOCIATE PRAYER WITH THE WORDS WE SAY. Contemplative prayer is a way of being with God that does not depend on giving the holy One information about what we would like done in the world. Just as friends can enjoy one another without conversing, contemplative prayer is a way of being with God without wordiness. In contemplative prayer we rest and wait. Keeping our hearts alert and awake to the presence of God and his Word, we listen. Psalm 131 contains a wonderful image of a weaned child stilled and quieted in its mother's arms. A weaned child isn't looking to nurse. A weaned child comes to the mother for love and communion. The psalmist writes. "I have stilled and quieted my soul; / like a weaned child with its mother, / like a weaned child is my soul within me."

In contemplative prayer we rest in God, depending on him to initiate communion and communication. We don't ask for things, we simply open ourselves to the Trinity, trusting we will be received into restful arms. It can be helpful to use the imagination to put yourself in a receptive frame of mind. Use a Scriptural image. Imagine you are a weaned child sitting in your mother's lap. Lean your head against her and rest. Or imagine that the good Shepherd has led you beside the still waters (Psalm 23). Lie down and rest there with God.

Contemplative prayer requires patience, but it is not the heavy work that intercession can sometimes be. It can even be light, playful, tender and joyful. In a world given to activity and work, contemplative prayer is a way we join God in a place of divine rest and love.

Contemplative prayer is a response to God's invitation to "abide in Christ." In Colossians 1:26-27, Paul writes of (1) the saving gospel to those without Christ, and (2) the "mystery of the gospel" to the saints, which is "Christ in you, the hope of glory." Contemplative prayer puts us in a place to become more receptive to the mystery of the gospel, "Christ in you." Contemplative prayer is a container discipline that includes a number of ways of being with Jesus in prayer: centering prayer, prayer of recollection, breath prayer and labyrinth prayer. Contemplative prayer need not be a mystical experience; it is far more likely to be a restful experience of Christ in me.

Life makes it evident that what we contemplate shapes us. Saints down through the ages have trusted that contemplating the truth, beauty and goodness of the Trinity could ultimately shape and change their souls. The interior transformation that the saints call "divine union" is a fruit of this contemplation.

REFLECTION QUESTIONS

1. Is your prayer mostly a one-sided monologue with God? Do your prayers tend to dictate to God what you would like to see happen? Are your prayers a response to God's initiative in your life? What does this tell you about your understanding of prayer?

2. What does it mean to remain in Christ (John 15:4)?

   How would you describe the "mystery" of "Christ in you" that Paul speaks of in Colossians 1:27?

3. Do you feel that being in the presence of God is not the same thing as prayer? Does it seem like wasting time?

   What does God think of your wasting time with him?

SPIRITUAL EXERCISES

1. Settle into a time of quietness with God (if it is hard for you to sit still in God's presence, go for a walk). Say to God, "Here I am. I am with you." Be with God. Welcome him with open arms. Be in the moment without controlling or influencing it. Give God the gift of your love and presence. Do not strive. There is nothing to achieve. Be with God in loving attentiveness. Leave his presence gently when you sense you must go.

2. One way to quiet our minds is to quiet our bodies. Spend five minutes intentionally relaxing your body and breathing deeply. Afterward, spend five minutes noticing where your mind wants to go. Offer your noticing to God. Then let go and open yourself to God's love. Be receptive to a prayer God may be giving you to say. (Remember, contemplative prayer is more receptive than active.) End your prayer by breathing in God's love. Go with the awareness that your every breath is God's gift.

3. Light a candle and become quiet before the creator of light. Allow the candlelight to center your heart in the Light of the world. Offer yourself and all your darkness to Jesus. Remain in his light. Be comforted; all the darkness in the world cannot put out the light of one match. How much greater is the Light in you.

4. *Sacred word.* Choose a prayer word as the symbol of your desire to let Jesus' action and presence form you. The word could reflect a deep desire of your heart (e.g., love, grace, peace), or the word might be a name or title of God (e.g., Jesus, great Shepherd, Counselor, Healer of my soul, Defender). Become still and offer yourself and your love to God. Let this word or phrase draw you into the presence of Christ. When you are distracted, return gently to your word and to the Lord. At the end of the prayer, remain

still for several minutes. • Throughout your day return to your word and remind the Lord of your love for him.

Resources on Contemplative Prayer

The Interior Castle by Teresa of Ávila
The Awakened Heart by Gerald May

"We tend to think of prayer as something we do in order to produce the results we believe are needed or, rather, to get God to produce the results. . . . As a result, our prayer tends to be a shopping list of things to be accomplished, an attempt to manipulate the symptoms of our lives without really entering into a deep, vital, transforming relationship with God."—M. Robert Mulholland

CONVERSATIONAL PRAYER

DESIRE	to talk naturally and unself-consciously to God in group prayer times with others
DEFINITION	Praying conversationally engages two or more people in a shared dialogue with God. Focusing on one topic at a time each participant takes turns praying a few short sentences.
SCRIPTURE	"With this in mind, we constantly pray for you, that our God may count you worthy of his calling, and that by his power he may fulfill every good purpose of yours and every act prompted by your faith." (2 Thessalonians 1:11) "Don't fret or worry. Instead of worrying, pray. Let petitions and praises shape your worries into prayers, letting God know your concerns." (Philippians 4:6 *The Message*) "He knelt down with all of them and prayed." (Acts 20:36)
PRACTICE INCLUDES	• attending concerts of prayers for global concerns • having short, vocal prayer in planned and unplanned venues • praying spontaneously with others around specific topics as they come to mind
GOD-GIVEN FRUIT	• keeping company with Jesus and others in prayer • growing in verbal prayer with others • being free to pray spontaneously with others • receiving support in prayer for the burdens and cares of your heart and for the world • modeling simple ways of talking to God without pretense or flowery speech

CONVERSATIONAL PRAYER

A NUMBER OF YEARS AGO ROSALIND RINKER popularized group conversational prayer through her book *Prayer: Conversing with God.* In an attempt to stem some of the long monologue prayers that characterized prayer gatherings, she suggested a style of prayer that was more like talking with a friend than making a speech before a dignitary. Conversational prayers are not fancy or rehearsed; they are spontaneous, in-the-moment responses to heartfelt concerns. While we can have a conversation with God on our own, conversational prayer generally refers to a way of praying with others that invites everyone to participate. Children as well as adults are on equal ground when praying this way.

In conversations people listen to one another. In conversational prayer people don't pontificate, expostulate and otherwise hold forth. They don't cover every topic they can think of in one long prayer. Instead, as topics of prayer are brought forward, individuals take turns praying about that one topic. A prayer of a few sentences is all one offers. As others pray, participants listen and add other prayers as the Spirit prompts them. In due course the group will sense when to move on to another topic. Once again, they take turns praying through the next concern.

Conversational prayer is particularly meaningful for those who do a better job praying when they are with others than when they are alone. The simplicity and freedom in this discipline can truly encourage growth in personal prayer as well.

REFLECTION QUESTIONS

1. What is it like for you to be in conversation with others?

2. Do you like to think and then talk, or do you talk in order to think?

3. How might your comfort level in ordinary conversation affect your comfort level when you are invited to pray with others?

4. What is the experience of praying with others like for you?

   Where is it life giving?

   Where is it frustrating?

5. How would you like to be able to pray with others?

6. What benefits might learning to pray conversationally bring to you and your relationship with God?

SPIRITUAL EXERCISES

1. When you find yourself talking to a Christian friend about concerns of your heart, suggest that the two of you pray together conversationally.

2. Invite your children to take turns praying sentence prayers. You suggest the topics, inviting them each to pray one after the other: pray for mommy, daddy, a friend, children who are hurting, teachers, people who need help, etc. • Ask them to talk about what it is like for them to pray this way.

3. When praying in a small group, pray one topic at a time. Allow several people to pray about the same thing. Then move to another topic.

4. When you pray with others, listen to their prayers. What do you see about God through their eyes and prayers? • How might something they pray give you more freedom in prayer? • Don't worry if you are a beginner and want to follow examples of how others pray. Jesus told his disciples to copy his prayers. As you grow in prayer, you will gain greater freedom to speak.

5. If you are uncomfortable praying out loud, ask someone who feels confident in verbal prayer to mentor and encourage you. Break your silence by praying with one other person.

Resources on Conversational Prayer

Too Busy Not to Pray by Bill Hybels
Learning Conversational Prayer by Rosalind Rinker

"Practices are the nuclear reactors of the Christian faith, arenas where the gospel and human life come together in energizing, even explosive ways. Practices create openings in our lives where the grace, mercy and presence of God may be made known to us."—Craig Dykstra

FASTING

DESIRE	to let go of an appetite in order to seek God on matters of deep concern for other, myself and the world
DEFINITION	A fast is the self-denial of normal necessities in order to intentionally attend to God in prayer. Bringing attachments and cravings to the surface opens a place for prayer. This physical awareness of emptiness is the reminder to turn to Jesus who alone can satisfy.

SCRIPTURE	"When you fast, do not look somber as the hypocrites do, for they disfigure their faces to show men they are fasting. . . . But when you fast, put oil on your head and wash your face, so that it will not be obvious to men that you are fasting, but only to your Father, who is unseen; and your Father, who sees what is done in secret, will reward you." (Matthew 6:16-18)
	
	"Is not this the kind of fasting I have chosen:
	to loose the chains of injustice
	    and untie the cords of the yoke,
	to set the oppressed free
	    and break every yoke?
	Is it not to share your food with the hungry,
	    and to provide the poor wanderer with shelter?" (Isaiah 58:6-7)

PRACTICE INCLUDES	• abstaining from food, drink, shopping, desserts, chocolate and so on to intentionally be with God • abstaining from media: TV, radio, music, e-mail, cell phones, and computer games to allow space for listening to the voice of Jesus • abstaining from habits or comforts: elevators, reading and sports in order to give God undivided attention • observing fast days and seasons of the church year • addressing excessive attachments or appetites and the entitlements behind them, and partnering with God for changed habits • repenting and waiting on God • seeking strength to persevere, obey and serve • overcoming addictions, compulsions, whims and cravings
GOD-GIVEN FRUIT	• keeping company with Jesus in relinquishment • praying for needs in the body of Christ • identifying and fellowshiping with Jesus by choosing to follow his sacrificial example • freeing up more time for prayer • repenting of self-indulgent, addictive or compulsive behaviors • letting these small deprivations remind you of Jesus' great sacrifice on your behalf • seeking strength from God for obedient love and service

FASTING

FASTING HAS BEEN PART AND PARCEL OF THE Judeo-Christian tradition for millennia. Scripture is replete with examples of people who fast for a variety of reasons.

Old Testament saints fasted at times of mourning and national repentance. They fasted when they needed strength or mercy to persevere and when they wanted a word from God (see 1 Samuel 7:6; Nehemiah 1:4; Esther 4:16). However, fasting was no magical guarantee that God would answer as the intercessor wanted. King David fasted when he wanted God to spare the life of Bathsheba's child, but the child died (2 Samuel 12:16-20).

Fasting was a normal practice for the Jews of Jesus day. Jesus began his ministry with a forty-day fast. He also practiced fasting before healings and to overcome temptation. But he did not hold his followers to a strict regime of fasting (Matthew 4:2; Mark 2:18-19; Luke 5:33).

The New Testament church sometimes fasted when it sought God's will and needed the grace and strength to remain faithful to God's work. There were also fast times linked to times of worship (Acts 13:2-3).

In many Christian traditions fasting is an important part of preparing to embrace a particular liturgical season. During Lent, fasting reminds the church of how Jesus gave up everything—even his life—for us.

Scripture also gives a variety of warnings about fasting for the wrong reasons or with the wrong attitude: (1) When people do not live as God desires they should be prepared for fasting to accomplish nothing (Isaiah 58:3-7). (2) Fasting is not for appearances. It does not make anyone pious or holy, and it does not earn points with God (Matthew 6:16; Luke 18:9-14).

Fasting is not a magical way to manipulate God into doing our will; it's not a way to get God to be an accomplice to our plans. Neither is fasting a spiritual way to lose weight or control others. Fasting clears us out and opens us up to intentionally seeking God's will and grace in a way that goes beyond normal habits of worship and prayer. While fasting, we are one on one with God, offering him the time and attentiveness we might otherwise be giving to eating, shopping or watching television.

Fasting is an opportunity to lay down an appetite—an appetite for food, for media, for shopping. This act of self-denial may not seem huge—it's just a meal or a trip to the mall—but it brings us face to face with the hunger at the core of our being. Fasting exposes how we try to keep empty hunger at bay and gain a sense of well-being by devouring creature comforts. Through self-denial we begin to recognize what controls us. Our small denials of the self show us just how little taste we actually have for sacrifice or time with God.

This truth is not meant to discourage us. It's simply the first step in realizing that we have to lay down our life in order to find it again in God. Brian Taylor puts it like this in *Becoming Christ:* "Self-denial is profoundly contemplative for it works by the process of human subtraction and divine addition." Deny yourself a meal, and when your stomach growls "I'm hungry," take a moment to turn from your emptiness to the nourishment of "every word that comes from the mouth of God" (Matthew 4:4). Feed on Jesus, the bread of life. Skip the radio or TV for a day and become aware of how fidgety you are when you aren't being amused or diverted. Then dodge the remote, and embrace Jesus and his words "my food . . . is to do the will of him who sent me" (John 4:34). Taste the difference between what truly nourishes the soul—the living bread and the life-giving water—and what is simply junk food.

Fasting reminds us that we care about "soul" things. We care about the church. We care about the world. We care about doing God's will. Thus we willingly set aside a little comfort so we can listen and attend to the voice and nourishment of God alone. For God can give us grace and comfort and nurture we cannot get on our own.

Guidelines for Fasting from Food

- Don't fast when you are sick, traveling, pregnant or nursing. People with diabetes, gout, liver disease, kidney disease, ulcers, hypoglycemia, cancer and blood diseases should not fast.

- Don't fast if you are in a hurry and are fasting for immediate results regarding some decision. Fasting is not magic.

- Listen for a nudging from God to fast.

- Stay hydrated. Always drink plenty of water and fluids.

- If you are new to fasting, begin by fasting for one meal. Spend the time with God that you would normally be eating.

- Work up to longer fasts. Don't attempt prolonged fasts without guidance. Check with your doctor before attempting long periods of fasting.

- If you decide to fast regularly, give your body time to adjust to new rhythms of eating. You may feel more tired on days you fast. Adjust your responsibilities appropriately. (Expect your tongue to feel coated, and expect to have bad breath.)

- Begin a fast after supper. Fast until supper the next day. This way you miss two, rather than three, meals.

- Don't break your fast with a huge meal. Eat small portions of food. The longer the fast, the more you need to break the fast gently.

What to Do in the Time Set Apart for Fasting

- Bring your Bible and a glass of water during your fast.

- Relax and breathe deeply. Place yourself in the presence of God. Offer yourself and your time to God by repeating Samuel's words "Speak Lord, your servant is listening." Or simply say, "Here I am."

- Spend some time worshiping God for his faithfulness. Thank him for where he has come through for you. Psalm 103:1-5 also provides a starting point for praise.

- Bring your desires to God. Ask him if this desire is in line with his will and his word for you and the church. Be still and listen. Offer your desires and prayers to God.

REFLECTION QUESTIONS

1. When you feel empty or restless, what do you do to try to fill the emptiness?

   What does this tell you about your heart?

2. What is your attitude toward fasting or self-denial?

3. In what ways do you currently deny yourself?

4. When has self-denial brought you something good?

5. What has the experience of fasting been like for you?

6. Where do you operate from an entitlement mentality?

   How can you wean yourself from this way of life?

SPIRITUAL EXERCISES

1. To deepen your understanding of how Jesus denied himself and embraced suffering and death for you, practice some sort of fasting during Lent. • When the fasting is difficult, share your thoughts and feelings with Jesus. What does Jesus say to you? • Tell Jesus what it means to you to share and fellowship with him in his sufferings.

2. Fast one meal a week. Spend your mealtime in prayer. When you feel hungry, sit with Jesus in the wilderness and feed on the bread of heaven. • Talk to Jesus about what his self-denial means to you.

3. For a period of one week, fast from media, sports, shopping, reading or use of the computer. Dedicate the time you now have to God. What feelings arise in you? What thoughts interrupt your prayer?

5. During Lent, particularly focus on Jesus and his temptation in the wilderness. Enter the story in your imagination. What do you and Jesus talk about? How are you tempted to indulge yourself? • How does it help you to talk to Jesus about this?

6. Make two lists: one of needs, the other of wants. Ask God to show you where to fast from some of your wants. Offer to God the time you spend hankering after your wants.

7. Abstain from purchasing morning coffee or daily sodas or evening videos. Offer the money or time to God.

8. When facing a trial, decide on a fast that gives you time to seek God's strength in your journey.

Resources on Fasting

Celebration of Discipline, chapter 4, by Richard Foster

Soul Feast, chapter 5, by Marjorie Thompson

"Suggestions for Fasting Prayer for the Church" in appendix 9 of this book

"It is a paradox of human life that in worship, as in human love, it is in the routine and the everyday that we find the possibilities for the greatest transformation."—Kathleen Norris

FIXED-HOUR PRAYER

DESIRE	to stop my work and pray throughout the day
DEFINITION	Fixed-hour prayers call for regular and consistent patterns of attending to God throughout the day.
SCRIPTURE	"One day Peter and John were going up to the temple at the time of prayer—at three in the afternoon." (Acts 3:1) "Seven times a day I praise you." (Psalm 119:164) "About noon the following day, . . . Peter went up on the roof to pray." (Acts 10:9)
PRACTICE INCLUDES	• interrupting work at set times for prayer • following the prayers in the Liturgy of the Hours • following a personal liturgy for prayer at set hours of the day • stopping at the top of every hour for prayer
GOD-GIVEN FRUIT	• keeping company with Jesus throughout the hours of the day • turning the heart and mind to God at specific hours of the day and night • growing detached from the all absorbing compulsiveness of work • integrating being and doing in your daily life • developing the ability to hear a word from God in the midst of daily activities • joining the timeless prayer rhythms of the church throughout the ages

FIXED-HOUR PRAYER

JESUS LEARNED TO PRAY IN THE TRADITIONAL HEBREW WAY. In the morning he prayed the Shema: "Hear O Israel: The LORD our God, the LORD is one" (Deuteronomy 6:4) as well as a series of blessings known as the *tephilla*. In the afternoon the *tephilla* was prayed again. Evening prayer was identical to morning prayer but included private petitions. Like David, who prayed seven times a day (Psalm 119:164), and Daniel, who prayed three times a day (Daniel 6:10), Jesus and the Jews of his day prayed at set hours of the day. It was a devout Jew's habit to go to the temple at the sixth and ninth hour (noon and three o'clock). After Jesus' death, his disciples continued to pray at fixed hours of the day (Acts 3:1; 10:3, 9, 30). This custom of praying at set daily intervals quickly became part of the early church's rhythm of prayer. The *Didache,* an early manual of Christian practices, encouraged believers to pray the Lord's Prayer three times daily (*Didache* 8.3)

Given this history, it is quite understandable how the early church fathers would develop patterns for praying Scripture at fixed hours that integrated rhythms of prayer and work. Since all time belongs to God, why not punctuate the entire cycle of day and night with regular times for prayer, which could potentially shape both laity and clergy. Certainly within monasteries, rhythms of prayer governed community life. And some of these prayer rhythms have been practiced without interruption since the third and fourth century.

Dorothy Bass writes in *Receiving the Day:*

> The Liturgy of the Hours of the Order of Saint Benedict, which has structured the prayers of communities of women and men around the world for nearly fifteen hundred years, consists of up to eight sessions of psalmody during each twenty-four-hour period. The rhythms of Benedictine life embody a steadfast attention to the "sanctification of time," not just for the sake of the monastics but for the sake of the world.

> Benedict believed that both physical labor and prayer were in God's hands. They were both God's work. He is renowned for saying, *"Orare est laborare, laborare est orare"* (To pray is to work, to work is to pray). Benedictines today continue to punctuate their work with prayer rhythms begun over 1,600 years ago.

The prayer times are

- night prayer—*Vigils*
- waking-up prayers—*Lauds*
- prayers for beginning work—*Prime*
- giving-thanks prayers in mid-morning—*Terce*
- noon-day prayer of commitment—*Sext*
- mid-afternoon prayer—*None*
- evening prayer of stillness—*Vespers*
- going-to-sleep prayer of trust—*Compline*

Few of us can look at this list and not be overwhelmed. But this is not where beginners to fixed-hour prayer start. We begin where we are. We may already have one fixed time of prayer in the morning. So we simply add one more time—perhaps in the middle of work—as a reminder that time is a gift made for work and relationship, relationship with God and others. As we regularly honor this one intentional moment with God, we begin to realize how the world and its demands control us, leaving us frantic and overwhelmed. And stopping to pray, even if we have to set the timer, cultivates an awareness of the unseen reality of God's presence in all time and things. Annie Dillard says that fixed times of prayer shape our days: "How we spend our days is, of course, how we spend our lives. What we do with this hour and that one is what we are doing. A schedule defends us from chaos and whim. It is a net for catching days. It is a scaffolding on which a worker can stand and labor with both hands at sections of time."

Prayers offered at fixed hours can be spontaneous or liturgical. We can pray Scripture, the Divine Office, memorized prayers or simply pour out our hearts to God.

REFLECTION QUESTIONS

1. What times of the day do you like to pray?

   What is important to you about that particular time or times?

2. How do you remind yourself throughout the day that there is more to life than work, tasks and transactions?

3. If you have children do you have specific times that you pray with them?

   What do you want these fixed times of prayer to do in their lives?

4. How do you feel about memorized prayers or using the prayers of others?

5. What makes a prayer authentic?

SPIRITUAL EXERCISES

1. In addition to your normal time of prayer, establish one new time of prayer during the day. Set a timer or your computer to remind you to stop for one to fifteen minutes to pray. • After one week, consider what this has been like for you.

2. If you would like to pray the Liturgy of the Hours, try using *The Divine Hours* by Phyllis Tickle. These three volumes are guides to prayer for the entire year.

3. Choose one time in the day to stop for five minutes and pray with a friend. Use a liturgy or pray spontaneously.

4. When you wake in the middle of the night, don't fight with yourself about why you are awake. Enter into *Vigils*. Lean deeply into God and simply pray for the things that come to mind. Don't hurry. Attend to God as David did "in the watches of the night."

Resources on Fixed-Hour Prayer

The Divine Hours by Phyllis Tickle
The Music of Silence by David Steindl-Rast and Sharon Lebell
Network for Grateful Living <www.gratefulness.org>
Receiving the Day by Dorothy C. Bass

"Every traumatic rejection untouched by the vital kind of forgiveness the cross has won for us, whether at a conscious or unconscious level, will be acted out in some negative fashion."—Leanne Payne

INNER-HEALING PRAYER

DESIRE	to assist the emotionally broken and wounded as they seek God for the healing only he can give
DEFINITION	Prayer for inner healing invites those with emotional wounds to enter the safe and healing presence of Jesus. In this safe place those seeking wholeness and freedom open themselves to listen to Jesus and his word to them.
SCRIPTURE	"Dear friend, I pray that you may enjoy good health and that all may go well with you, even as your soul is getting along well." (3 John 2)
	"And the prayer offered in faith will make the sick person well; the Lord will raise him up. If he has sinned, he will be forgiven. Therefore, confess your sins to each other and pray for each other so that you may be healed. The prayer of a righteous man is powerful and effective." (James 5:15)
	"And pray in the Spirit on all occasions with all kinds of prayers and requests. With this in mind, be alert and always keep on praying for all the saints." (Ephesians 6:18)
PRACTICE INCLUDES	• prayer that includes appropriate touch: laying on of hands, anointing with oil or holy water • prayer that invites Jesus into past injuries, memories and wounds • listening for Jesus' prayer for the wounded • attending to the invitation to place one's wounds into the wounds of Christ • prayer that listens for the effect of lies or vows in one's life • prayer that invites people to receive an identity embedded in God's love, forgiveness and grace • prayer that listens to God over a period of time
GOD-GIVEN FRUIT	• keeping company with Jesus and the wounded • entering into Jesus' prayer for the healing of others • praying from the healing presence of Christ • calling forth the true Christ-in-you identity • listening to where the diseased thoughts and words come from: the world, the flesh and the devil; praying for healing • listening with others to discern false and true guilt; seeking God for forgiveness and freedom in Christ • proclaiming God's forgiveness of dark and burdensome sins and bondage • bringing past hurts into the healing light of God • praying consistently over a period of time for healing and renewal of another • identifying areas where one is cut off from God; prayerfully and lovingly opening these places to God

INNER-HEALING PRAYER

IN MY EXPERIENCE IT IS NOT UNUSUAL FOR PEOPLE to feel ambivalent about the New Testament instruction to pray for the sick (James 5:15; 3 John 2). It would be great if everyone we prayed for were healed. But prayers aren't magic. And God isn't obligated by them. Furthermore, he has a much bigger picture in mind than we can see. So since we can't see the whole picture, are we to leave a sort of safety net and pray, "Lord, your will be done?" or is that lack of faith? When our prayers don't "work," is something wrong with us?

Prayer for healing of any kind invites us to stay in the space between desiring healing and demanding it. The space between desire and demand invites us to take a risk on God. Without risk, you can never have trust. Trust is not a concept—it is waiting in the space between desire and demand for what the Lord wants to do. God is the Healer, but he does not always heal in our time frame and follow our agenda. The Holy Spirit sets the pace and the agenda. The healing may happen in a moment or over time. Or we may be asked by God to live, like Paul, with a thorn in our flesh. But even with a thorn in our flesh we can keep company with Jesus and know the gift of his presence—whether in life and health or in sickness and death.

Inner-healing prayer focuses attention on emotional wounds, needs, lies, vows and dysfunctions. Issues like self-hatred, fear, addiction, depression, the inability to give or receive forgiveness, bitterness, the need to perform, defensiveness and obsessive-compulsive traits commonly surface in prayer for inner wounds. Many of our dysfunctional coping mechanisms are ways of addressing our longings to be significant and loved. To handle the pain that comes from not feeling significant and loved moves us into unhealthy coping patterns. Richard Rohr suggests that pain that is not transformed is transmitted. Untransformed pain leaks onto others. We kick the dog, yell at the kids, oversleep, overeat or numb ourselves on TV—but the pain is still there.

Inner wounds can be so painful that we can't name and face them alone. We need the presence and encouragement of a healing-prayer partner who can take the healing journey with us. Jesus often asked people to cooperate in the miracle of their healing: a blind man had to wash mud from his eyes in the pool of Siloam (John 9:11); an invalid by the Sheep Gate had to answer the question, "Do you want to get well?" Then he had to get up and walk even though he hadn't walked in thirty-eight years (John 5:6-9).

Healing prayer assumes that wounded souls will cooperate with Christ in the healing process. It assumes that the wounded have choices to make. They must choose to be honest and humble and surrendered. They must choose to share their thoughts, feelings, experiences and what they do to numb their pain.

A ministry of inner-healing prayer brings the wounded to Jesus in a place of safety and love. Healing-prayer ministers accompany those who honestly want to open their souls and griefs to Jesus. Together they enter Christ's healing presence. Together they listen for the word Jesus has to speak. Together, in the light of Christ, they open the darkness, lies and stresses that damage and bind. Jesus is available. He is ready to be with the wounded in their pain.

When those in pain do not know how to live with or where to put their pain, Jesus invites them to put their wounds in his own bleeding hands. In Jesus, pain has somewhere to go. On the cross Jesus absorbed and died for all the wounding and sin of the world. In him all pain can be transformed into something redemptive. The light of the presence of Jesus is a transforming ray that can radiate cancerous wounds of the soul. Prayer for inner healing rests on this reality. There is hope that even now we can begin to taste the wholeness that awaits us in heaven.

Healing prayer depends entirely on the healing availability, presence and goodness of Jesus. And the presence of Jesus may be experienced in a variety of ways: appropriate touch, anointing with oil or holy water, receiving Communion, tears, words of forgiveness and absolution.

REFLECTION QUESTIONS

1. How has healing prayer intersected with your life?

2. What emotions surface in you when you pray for healing for others?

3. Where might healing prayer address wounds in your own soul?

4. What is it like for you to have someone pray for you?

SPIRITUAL EXERCISES

1. Take a "needs mending" inventory. Set aside time for several days or weeks to be in the presence of Jesus with your wounds. Gather a list of wounded places and tender relationships that need mending. Simply gather the list. Let it grow as other wounds come to mind. Leave it with God. • At another time, come to God in a safe and quiet place where you can attend to the list in the presence of the great Physician. Breathe deeply. Inhale the closeness of Jesus. He is nearer than your own breath. Don't hurry. Wait in his presence. • When you are ready, set the list before the Lord and wait. What *one* item seems to have your attention? (Attend to one wound at a time. Don't move on to another wound until you sense that the time has come to do so.) Ask Jesus what he

wants to tell you about this wound. Listen. What do you sense the Lord is saying to you? • Respond to Jesus. Trust Jesus to do what he needs to do. The fruit of healing may not be a big feeling of release at the time of prayer, but changed internal responses as time goes by. Over time you may notice that your internal responses to people and situations begin to shift. Talk to God about this.

2. Seek out someone who is comfortable with healing prayer. Ask them if they would be willing to pray with and for your healing. • In preparation for this time ask yourself the following questions: (1) What lies or vows have shaped my life? (2) Where am I unable to forgive another? (3) Where do I find it difficult to give and receive love? (4) Where am I unable to forgive myself? Your answers may help reveal the roots to some of your woundedness. • Share your insights with your prayer partner. Open yourself to God and to receiving his healing touch.

3. Read Lamentations 2—3. Allow Jeremiah's painful cry to become your own prayer. Write a lament of your own to God. What do you want to tell him about your pain? Where do you want to find him in your pain?

4. Attend a healing-prayer service or a healing-prayer ministry.

Resources of Inner-Healing Prayer

Healing Light by Agnes Sanford
Healing Care, Healing Prayer by Terry Wardell
Restoring the Christian Soul Through Healing Prayer by Leanne Payne
Dr. Karl Lehman <www.kclehman.com>
Redeemed Lives Ministry <www.redeemedlives.org>

"To intercede for another means that in our prayer we stand between—or next to—them and God."
—Brian C. Taylor

INTERCESSORY PRAYER

DESIRE	to turn my concerns and worries into prayer; to enter God's heart for the world and then pray from there
DEFINITION	Intercessory prayer invites us into God's care and concern for us, our families and friends, and the entire world. No concern is too trivial for God to receive with loving attention. However, intercession is not a means of manipulating heaven into doing our will. Rather it is a way we become aware of God's prayer for a person and join in that intercession.
SCRIPTURE	"And he who searches our hearts knows the mind of the Spirit, because the Spirit intercedes for the saints in accordance with God's will." (Romans 8:27) "Don't fret or worry. Instead of worrying, pray. Let petitions and praises shape your worries into prayers, letting God know your concerns." (Philippians 4:6 *The Message*) "In the same way, prayer is essential in this ongoing warfare. Pray hard and long. Pray for your brothers and sisters. Keep your eyes open. Keep each other's spirits up so that no one falls behind or drops out." (Ephesians 6:18 *The Message*)
PRACTICE INCLUDES	• going to prayer meetings: concerts of prayer, small group prayer • contributing to prayer lists, prayer chains • going on prayer walks • participating in healing prayer • doing spiritual warfare • praying for the world, for peace, for God's kingdom to come • praying for personal concerns, tasks, transactions and relationships
GOD-GIVEN FRUIT	• responding to Jesus' invitation to pray with him and for others • converting all anxieties, fears, sorrows and concerns into dialogue, not monologue, with God • replacing my tendency to control with prayerful trust • partnering with God in his concern for the world • training my heart in expectancy • learning to find God in every answer: yes, no and wait • developing a regular rhythm of turning to God with requests and petitions • gaining discernment in how the Spirit intercedes—and to intercede as the Spirit leads • supporting others in need of healing, care, courage and patience

INTERCESSORY PRAYER

IN *THE DIVINE CONSPIRACY* DALLAS WILLARD WRITES, "Asking is indeed the great law of the spiritual world through which things are accomplished in cooperation with God and yet in harmony with the freedom and worth of every individual." Requests anticipate responses. Willard suggests that even the dog begging at your feet puts you "up against a fundamental force of the universe." Requests have power to moves us. Some of us have a propensity to say yes to requests because we like to please. Others immediately say no because we don't like feeling obligated.

God tells us to ask him for what we need, regardless of our own intuitive responses to requests. He wants us to know that he's invested in us and concerned about our lives and world. The almighty One wants our prayers. In fact, God will change this world through them. But it is important to realize that we don't always know what we or others need most. So listening in our spirit to God's desires for us and this world is an important part of intercession. God's Spirit is always concerned with his glory and his kingdom. And his Spirit can lead us to pray in a different manner than we would pray on our own.

Intercession is one of the ways God invites us into the heart of the Trinity. As we keep company with Jesus through intercession, we begin to see the world and the people in it from his perspective and heart. Increasingly we long for the same things he longs for. The Holy Spirit guides our intercessions so they sound more and more like Jesus' own intercessions for this world. "Your kingdom come; your will be done."

When we intercede, it is important to humbly trust that the King of all creation can bring in the kingdom no matter what our circumstances look like.

Intercession is not always an easy thing to do. It can engage us deeply in the spiritual battle. Prayer warriors know that the point of intercessory prayer is to remain faithful and trusting. Being involved in intercessory prayer does not necessarily mean you'll feel great strength, power or joy. The point is to pray, persist and commit the battle to the Lord.

At times our trust wavers and we don't know how to pray, can't find words to pray and are too distressed to pray. At those moments we have the assurance that God prays. The Holy Spirit, who inhabits our being, personally tutors us in praying and even interprets for us when we are unable to articulate our hearts to God. The Spirit intercedes with "groans that words cannot express" (Romans 8:26). Furthermore, Jesus is seated at the right hand of the Father, interceding for us as well (Romans 8:34). We are never left alone. God is with us and praying for us.

REFLECTION QUESTIONS

1. What do your requests to God reveal about your priorities, goals, desires and heart?

   Talk to God about this.

2. If God asked you to pray for something, what do you think he would ask you to pray for?

3. Has intercession led you into something surprising or new? What?

4. What is it like for you to intercede with others?

   What is it like for you to intercede alone?

5. What helps you remember to pray for others?

SPIRITUAL EXERCISES

1. Use the Lord's Prayer as a pattern for intercession:

   - "Our Father in heaven, hallowed be your name." Spend some time thanking God for his fatherly love and attention. Ponder who he is and adore his majesty, holiness, sovereignty, goodness and beauty.

   - "Your kingdom come, your will be done, on earth as it is in heaven." Turn your intercession to God's purposes in the world. Where are you trying to bring in *your* kingdom rather than putting your efforts toward *God's* kingdom agenda? Confess where God's priorities have been replaced with your own. Consider what God's kingdom agenda might be in your relationships and in the world. Pray for these things. What might partnering with God around his will look like?

   - "Give us this day our daily bread." Pray for your needs and those whose lives are closely linked with your own. Pray for those who are in danger, suffering and in places of decision making or costly love.

   - "Forgive us our debts, as we also have forgiven our debtors." Confess your grudges, bitterness and oversensitivity; dwell at the foot of the cross. Thank God for what it is like to be forgiven.

   - "And lead us not into temptation, but deliver us from the evil one." As you look ahead into your day, notice the tasks and transactions ahead of you. Where might you get off track? Become aware of the ways you may be tempted to spin the truth, manage your image, live out of your false self, lose your patience or envy another. Pray for the Spirit to work in you to change you. Ask for protection and courage for the day.

   - "For yours is the kingdom and the power and the glory forever." End your time of intercession with prayers of trust in God's goodness and his redemptive plan.

2. Pay attention to the moments when people come to mind. Sometimes they come to you out of the blue. As a person comes to mind, offer him or her up to the Lord. • If you have the leisure, turn to God and ask him, "What is your prayer for this person?" Listen and pray.

3. Place yourself in the presence of God, bringing your concern with you. Ask God to show you if there is anything you need to surrender in order to better join him in your concern. If something comes to mind, offer it to God. Ask God if there is anything he wants you to do about this concern or if you are to leave him to do the praying.

4. Intentionally come into the presence of God. Become quiet and attentive. As people or places come to mind, picture bringing them to Jesus. Does Jesus say anything to you about these people? • When you have brought everyone to Jesus, leave them with him. Tell Jesus your intent is to leave these people in his care rather than look after them on your own. • Throughout the day, return in your mind to the comfort that these people are with Jesus.

5. As you begin a task or transaction, commit your efforts to the Lord. Dedicate this time to the Lord. Ask the Lord to use your efforts for his glory and the good of the world.

6. Intercede with a newspaper in hand. As you read, what do you feel called to pray about? Gently bring the fears and concerns of the news to the Lord.

7. Create an intercession journal with pictures of people, places and concerns for which you wish to pray. Record answers to prayer beside the photos in your journal.

8. Create a weekly prayer list. Vary the topics of prayer for each day. • Spend some of the time you would normally speak to God in listening for his guidance as to how to pray. When you don't know how to pray for others, offer them up to the Holy Spirit, who perfectly intercedes for us all.

9. Go in your mind's eye to a place where you felt especially close to God, to a time when the veil between you and the Lord was lifted and you were very aware of his presence. Wait quietly before God. Does he prompt you to pray for something or someone? Attend and pray.

Resources for Intercessory Prayer

Soul Feast by Marjorie Thompson
Prayer: Finding the Heart's True Home by Richard J. Foster
www.projectpray.org/home/prayer_links.html

"A spiritual discipline sets us free to pray or, to say it better, allows the Spirit of God to pray in us."
—Henri Nouwen

LABYRINTH PRAYER

DESIRE	to make a quiet, listening pilgrimage to God
DEFINITION	Labyrinth prayer is a contemplative spiritual discipline on a simple marked path that is based on the ancient practice of pilgrimage. On a pilgrimage, a pilgrim intentionally (1) leaves the world, journeying away from the noise and distractions of life, (2) eventually arrives and rests with Christ, and (3) returns home to live more deliberately and obediently as Christ's own.

SCRIPTURE	"Blessed are those whose strength is in you,
	    who have set their hearts on pilgrimage. . . .
	They go from strength to strength,
	    till each appears before God in Zion." (Psalm 84:5, 7)
	
	"He guides me in paths of righteousness
	    for his name's sake.
	Even though I walk
	    through the valley of the shadow of death,
	I will fear no evil,
	    for you are with me." (Psalm 23:3-4)

PRACTICE INCLUDES	• prayerfully and attentively walking along a circular path or labyrinth toward God • becoming quiet, slowing down and intentionally taking a journey that leaves the world behind, attends to God and returns to the world fortified with the presence of Christ • considering what hinders your journey to God; contemplating the grace given to return to the world
GOD-GIVEN FRUIT	• keeping company with Jesus in a prayer labyrinth • visualizing the convoluted nature of the spiritual journey • slowing down and leaving behind the noise and busyness of life • listening receptively • intentionally seeking God and his guidance by bringing the concerns of your heart to the Lord • returning to the world with a deeper sense of God's power at work in you and your circumstances • gaining perspective on your journey and how God is at work in your comings and goings

LABYRINTH PRAYER

PILGRIMAGES TO HOLY SITES HAVE BEEN PART OF THE Christian tradition for millennia. Many of us still visit the Holy Land today. And Orthodox and Catholic believers are not unfamiliar with pilgrimages to various holy places. However, when a pilgrimage is not affordable or accessible, the discipline of pilgrimage can be honored through the symbolic prayer walk of the labyrinth. Labyrinths seem to have developed around the twelfth century as a substitute for making a pilgrimage to a holy site. Labyrinths are not mazes, nor are they something magical. Walking the labyrinth is not a newfangled technique to jump-start your spiritual life. It is a slow, quiet, meditative practice that has historically attended to the desire to make a journey toward God. The floor of Chartres Cathedral in France has a labyrinth that has been used by pilgrims for centuries.

In walking the labyrinth you leave behind the noise and hurry of life. Just as you would pack simply for a pilgrimage, you offer your load to Jesus as you begin your prayer journey. The prayer-path structure moves you slowly toward the center and toward God. At times you are close to the center, further along the path you may be farther from the center. This represents the reality of the spiritual journey. But as we keep moving, we are always getting closer to the center and to God, no matter how far away it looks in real space. At the center of the walk you can stop and rest in the presence of God, listening for his word to you. With his word in your heart you begin your journey back to the world.

Not all labyrinths have the same shape. Here are two:

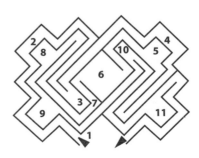

Dave Mahar, a student ministries pastor, writes:

Two of the most treasured books in my library are our prayer path journals. These thick books hold the words of students and adults who have journeyed the multisensory prayer path. What jumps off these journal pages is the challenge for each participant to put their personal experience into words—to translate what has happened in their heart and soul as they walked *alone* on the prayer path, yet *together*, in a mysterious community of fellow journeyers. Here is a peek inside the journals as participants attempt to translate their prayer path experience into words:

Oh my word—that was amazing. Who knew that an hour on a tarp could completely give someone a religious shock-charge? In a world like today's, nothing should make me so mellow and have me just sit still. Everything that was spoken had an impact on me. I may look at some people and think that they are the worst people in the world, but as soon as I get to school tomorrow I'm going to stick my hand out and tell them my name. The Prayer Path was amazing, and now I feel 10x closer to God. (a high school student)

How easy to do everything but spend time with God—to be caught in the craziness of day-to-day "stuff." Taking time to slow down, reflect and experience God is so important but so easy to forget. In the end, he is there, waiting, ready, loving and forgiving. This was a special time. (an adult)

This was a wonderful experience. I couldn't think of a better way to connect. I hope (and wish) to be able to go through this experience again! I feel that I have never been able to focus as well as I did here today. Every station had a different aspect of God and our world. The music and environment is so, so nice because it takes you away from all the hustle and bustle that our lives bring us. These times where we relax and praise our God in a quiet manner are what really brings us closer. This experience is definitely going to further improve my relationship with God. Thank you . . . for such a deep and wonderful experience! (a high school student)

REFLECTION QUESTIONS

1. Where are you in your current spiritual journey?

   Have you traveled a long way?

   Do you feel close to God or far away?

2. If you were to go on a spiritual pilgrimage, what things would you leave behind?

   How might you leave these things behind you here and now?

3. What has been your experience of pilgrimage: a trip to the Holy Land, visiting an old family homestead?

   How did it affect you?

SPIRITUAL EXERCISES

These exercises require a labyrinth.

1. You can make a virtual labyrinth walk by logging on to <web.ukonline.co.uk/para-digm/discoverframe.html>. Christian bookstores also have small circular labyrinths that fit the palm of your hand. You use a pencillike stylus to move through the labyrinth. Using a small labyrinth requires patience and very slow movements.

2. Labyrinths are often found at retreat centers. Call a few retreat centers in your area and ask if they know where you can find a labyrinth. Set aside at least an hour to walk the labyrinth.

3. To walk a labyrinth:

   • Intentionally leave behind all the noise and haste and clamor of your life. Prepare your heart to listen. God may bring a word of Scripture to your mind. Nature may speak of God's love and care. Be patient. Pay attention. How does the journey to the center reflect your current spiritual path?

   • As you walk intentionally toward God and the center of the labyrinth consider what you might need to surrender in order to live more fully in the love and fullness of his presence. Is there bitterness, addiction, expectation, pride, self-orientation, past hurts that you want to leave behind as you walk toward God? When you arrive at the center, offer these things to God. Leave them in the center with him.

   • Once in the center, abide in the presence of Christ. Ask for the grace you are seeking for your return to life in the world. Receive the comfort, inspiration or word the Spirit has for you. When you sense that it is time to leave, slowly and with a quiet mind make your way from the center back into the world, listening and stopping as you are prompted by the Spirit. How can you consciously live out of the word God has given you on your prayer walk?

   • When you receive a word from the Lord for your journey, hold on to it. It has been given specifically for you, specifically for now. Don't move away from this word too quickly. Return to it during the week.

Resources on Labyrinth Prayer

Labyrinth <web.ukonline.co.uk/paradigm/discoverframe.html>

"Prayer therefore is the act of dying to all that we consider to be our own and of being born to a new existence which is not of this world."—Henri Nouwen

LITURGICAL PRAYER

DESIRE	to open myself to God through established patterns or traditions of written prayers and readings
DEFINITION	Liturgical prayer is a written or memorized prayer that serves as a framework for individual or corporate worship and devotion.
SCRIPTURE	"This, then, is how you should pray: 'Our Father . . .'" (Matthew 6:9) "Assemble the people—men, women and children, and the aliens living in your towns—so they can listen and learn to fear the LORD your God and follow carefully all the words of this law. Their children, who do not know the law, must hear it and learn to fear the LORD your God." (Deuteronomy 31:12-13)
PRACTICE INCLUDES	• praying prayers written by others • praying or singing Scripture as part of worship (e.g., the Lord's Prayer, psalms, responsive readings, doxologies, etc.) • praying prayers of the church that have come down to us from the past • praying the Liturgy of the Hours • praying the prayers written for each season of the church year
GOD-GIVEN FRUIT	• keeping company with Jesus through the prayers and writings of others • allowing yourself to be led in prayer rather than leading in prayer • detaching from my own prayer agenda and to-do list for God • entering into God's heart for the world as found in the Liturgy of the Hours • allowing the prayers of others to become your own when your heart feels empty • allowing the repetitive nature of the liturgy to shape your life • joining with believers throughout the world in voicing an account of your sins and failures • staying in dialogue with God when spontaneous prayers run dry

LITURGICAL PRAYER

AS CHILDREN, MANY OF US LEARNED TO PRAY by memorizing prayers. We said "grace" before meals and bedtime prayers with their inevitable lists of thank yous, God blesses and forgive mes. Furthermore, churchgoers eventually memorized the Lord's Prayer, the Gloria Patri, some hymns and probably a creed or two without even trying. These prayers and confessions became ours through countless recitations as a congregation. They represent the liturgies that formed and shaped us. Generally the Roman Catholic, Orthodox, Anglican and Lutheran churches count themselves as "liturgical churches." But no church is without a liturgy. Every community of faith has their own particular pattern and format for prayers, responsive readings, music, offerings, sermons, offering and so forth. (Even spontaneity tends to fit into a particular slot within the pattern.) This pattern is the way they do church.

Liturgy invites us into Scripture, prayers and words of the church in a pattern that is not simply ad hoc. Liturgy is grounded in repetition, not improvisation. Its stable framework shapes community worship from week to week. The order of a service may be adjusted for a special season or reason, but the framework remains largely unchanged. Liturgical patterns call us to let go of our compulsion to lead or plunge ahead in any way we want. Their rhythms draw us into established patterns of attending to God. They give us space to use our voice, find our words, name our sin, hear God's Word and gaze on our Creator.

Though our age tends to value spontaneity and individuality, a growing number of people are searching the depths of liturgical prayer. Alongside the popularity of conversational prayer, with its up-to-the-minute spontaneity, stands the desire to be rooted in something ancient that has survived the centuries. Liturgy can reach back two thousand years to the early church practice of daily prayer, which included the Lord's Prayer and the Psalms.

The prayer rhythms known as the common lectionary guide the church through the Old and New Testament with readings connected to the celebration of church seasons. There are readings and prayers that guide the church through Advent, Epiphany, Lent,

Ash Wednesday, Good Friday, Easter, Pentecost and Ordinary Time. Following the lectionary readings assures that the church continually hears the redemption story year after year, season after season. Even the unpopular or difficult parts of Scripture are included in the lectionary readings. Churches that embrace the lectionary bind their scattered and diverse communities into a unified chorus of worship. (Typically the Orthodox, Roman Catholic, Anglican and Lutheran churches follow some version of the lectionary in their liturgy.)

The liturgical traditions contain vast reservoirs of prayers and collects as well as readings that take a Christian through the entire scope of the church year. By attending to the set readings found in the church lexicon, we read the entire Bible over the course of a few years.

REFLECTION QUESTIONS

1. How do you feel about written and rote prayers?

2. What is the benefit or disadvantage of having said something so often that you know it by heart?

3. What kind of prayer patterns do you use in prayer now?

4. How has your prayer pattern changed over time?

SPIRITUAL EXERCISES

1. Visit a church with a different tradition than your own. What do you see about the use of liturgy in their services? Did their worship open you up to God and his family in some new way? • Where did you sense God's presence most in the worship?

2. Explore the practice of liturgical prayer through using the book *The Divine Hours* by Phyllis Tickle, or *The Daily Office* of the Catholic church.

3. Attend the traditional Good Friday Tennebrae service or the Easter Vigil in an Anglican, Orthodox or Catholic church. How is the liturgy designed to lead you into God's presence? • What is this service like for you?

4. Check out *A Guide to Prayer for Ministers and Other Servants* or *A Guide to Prayer for All God's People* published by The Upper Room. These books provide readings and prayers for daily use.

5. Use *The Book of Common Prayer.* Pray the Psalms in the back of the book or collects for the particular week. • What is this like for you?

6. Ask someone who uses written prayers to talk to you about their prayer life. How do these prayers help them know God and grow in faith?

Resources on Liturgical Prayer

The Book of Common Prayer
The Divine Hours by Phyllis Tickle

"Men and women are at their noblest and best when they are on their knees before God in prayer. . . . To pray is not only to be truly godly; it is also to be truly human."—John Stott.

PRAYER PARTNERS

DESIRE	to share the journey of prayer with a trusted companion
DEFINITION	Prayer partners agree to support one another and pray together for their own concerns as well as world affairs. They engage in regular and consistent times of shared intercession.
SCRIPTURE	"Stay alert, be in prayer, so you don't enter the danger zone without even knowing it. Don't be naive. Part of you is eager, ready for anything in God; but another part is as lazy as an old dog sleeping by the fire." (Mark 14:38 *The Message*) "And pray for us, too, that God may open a door for our message, so that we may proclaim the mystery of Christ." (Colossians 4:3) "Brothers, pray for us." (1 Thessalonians 5:25) "Is any one of you in trouble? He should pray. . . . And the prayer offered in faith will make the sick person well. . . . Therefore confess your sins to each other and pray for each other so that you may be healed. The prayer of a righteous man is powerful and effective." (James 5:13, 15-16)
PRACTICE INCLUDES	• meeting regularly to pray for personal as well as global concerns • confessing sin and praying for strength to face trials • using *Operation World* as part of the prayer practice • giving thanks for answers to prayer • praying for particular events, mission endeavors, schools, churches, etc. • participating in Moms in Touch
GOD-GIVEN FRUIT	• keeping company with Jesus through sharing my prayers with him and others • growing in bringing all aspects of my life to God in prayer • sharing my journey and burdens with another in prayer • developing a rhythm of prayer with others • learning to pray out loud • practicing thankfulness • sharing my joy over answered prayer with another

PRAYER PARTNERS

SOME PEOPLE DO THEIR BEST PRAYING WITH OTHERS. Some do their best praying alone. If praying with others helps you to concentrate and be consistent in prayer, then prayer partnerships can be a wonderful way of encountering God and offering your concerns to him. Prayer partnerships may be established around shared concerns regarding the workplace, school and family issues. But prayer partnerships may also evolve as two people discover they both care about particular missionaries or a particular part of the world. The partnership may form for a short period of time, or it may last over decades.

Prayer partners meet together regularly to share prayer requests and pray. Prayer partnerships are more than chat sessions with a brief prayer tacked on at the end. Prayer and thanksgiving for answered prayer is the essential stuff of the gathering. Some prayer partners agree to pray at certain times of the day even though they are not together. This common discipline becomes a thread they share until their next meeting. Prayer partnerships can also be done over the phone (see also "Intercessory Prayer," "Fasting" and "Prayer Walking")

ACTS is a simple acronym to serve as a framework for your prayers:

A—adoration of God and his character, plans and purposes

C—confession of anything in us that has broken relationships; naming anything in our lives that would hinder serving God in prayer

T—thanksgiving for God's presence, blessings, Word and goodness

S—supplication for the world, ourselves and those whose lives are closely linked with ours

REFLECTION QUESTIONS

1. What is it like for you to pray with others?

2. What are your rhythms of corporate prayer and private prayer?

3. How do you meet God differently in each of these kinds of prayer?

4. How do you pray about personal concerns that bring you constant anxiety?

5. How might sharing prayer concerns with another help you bear your anxieties differently?

SPIRITUAL EXERCISES

1. Pray for a prayer partner. Listen to who God might bring to mind. Approach them
   about becoming a prayer partner for the next six weeks. At the end of six weeks determine if you will continue.

2. Where do you feel a deep desire to pray for a particular need surfacing in your life?
   Consider if there is anyone else who shares your desire. If God brings a name to mind,
   contact that person and see if they would be willing to join you in prayer twice a
   month. • What is this experience like for you?

3. Become a prayer partner with someone in your immediate family. Form a partnership
   with a child or a spouse for a particular situation and season. When the concern is answered, spend time talking about what it was like to share prayer concerns. What sense
   of trust developed?

4. Form a prayer partnership in which you experiment with the various types of prayer disciplines described in this book. Spend several weeks on each prayer discipline. • What
   is it like for you? Is one style of prayer easier for you than another? For your prayer
   partner? • What do you learn about God in these prayer settings?

Resources on Prayer Partners

Moms in Touch International <www.momsintouch.com>

"For Jesus prayer seems to be a matter of waiting in love. Returning to love. Trusting that love is the bottom stream of reality. "—Richard Rohr

PRAYING SCRIPTURE

DESIRE	to allow God to shape my prayer life through the words of Scripture
DEFINITION	Praying Scripture allows God to direct the content of prayer. It opens the heart to praying particular prayers, psalms, teachings and hopes found in the Bible.
SCRIPTURE	"You diligently study the Scriptures because you think that by them you possess eternal life. These are the Scriptures that testify about me, yet you refuse to come to me to have life." (John 5:39-40) "Oh, how I love your law! I meditate on it all day long." (Psalm 119:97) "The unfolding of your words gives light." (Psalm 119:130)
PRACTICE INCLUDES	• meditating on Scripture; interacting with God around the revelation its stories bring • listening to the Lord and lingering at the spaces for reflection that biblical stories allow • listening for the questions Jesus puts to the disciples as if they were questions he is putting to you • placing your name in the place of "you" pronouns • adopting a prayer of David, Daniel, Paul, Mary, Jabez or Jesus
GOD-GIVEN FRUIT	• letting Jesus lead you into prayer through Scripture • growing in your love for God and his Word • receiving guidance in prayer • allowing a biblical story to give voice and action to inner needs, desires and feelings • entering into prayer through the touch, confrontation, healing, invitations and challenges of Scripture • releasing your agenda in prayer and responding to God's agenda as revealed in Scripture • slowing down Scripture reading to a pace that serves listening • personalizing Scripture by substituting your name where it is appropriate to do so

PRAYING SCRIPTURE

IN THE EARLY CENTURIES OF THE CHURCH, believers were taught to pray the Scriptures. Since the Bible is divinely inspired, they believed that praying Scripture deeply connected them to the mind and heart of God. Furthermore, as Scripture was repeatedly prayed, it became memorized. This was a wonderful benefit for those who were illiterate. It also meant that memorized Scripture could lead them to pray at any hour of the day or night.

Praying Scripture is a way of entering deeply into the text with a heart alert to a unique and personal word from God. Words and verses that catch our attention become invitations to be with God in prayer. When our prayers seem to be more about maintaining control and offering God our agenda for his stamp of approval, praying Scripture can return us to a simpler state of openness and attentiveness to God. We lay aside our own agendas and open ourselves to the prayers given to us in the Bible.

The book of Psalms is a wonderfully human prayer book. It doesn't clean up the mess of life before prayer. It brings the totality of life to God. Here we find prayers that voice our needs, fears, joys, sorrows, anger, loneliness, dryness and joy. The Psalms invite us to be authentic and honest and come to God as we are. The Bible also contains wonderful prayers by people like Jesus, Paul, Daniel, Mary, Moses and Hannah. Their prayers can provide a framework for intercession for peoples and nations. When we are at a loss for words and have no prayers in our heart, the prayers of Scripture are ready to guide us to God. They can provide the help and structure that keeps us on the path through a difficult season. (See also "Devotional Reading," "Liturgical Prayer," "Intercessory Prayer.")

REFLECTION QUESTIONS

1. Do you let God set the agenda in your praying? Explain.

2. What prayers of the Bible have helped you in the past?

3. How might praying Scripture for yourself or a loved one lift the burden from your shoulders and place it squarely on God's?

SPIRITUAL EXERCISES

1. Use the Lord's Prayer as a framework for your prayer. (See exercise 1 in "Intercessory Prayer" for a detailed description.)

2. Become quiet and breathe in God's love. Breathe out your self-doubts and self-recriminations. • Turn to Psalm 139. Slowly read the psalm aloud, pausing after each verse. Substitute your own name for the pronouns *me* and *I*. For instance, insert your name in the blanks:

For you created _____'s inmost being;
   you knit _____ together in _____'s mother's womb.
_____ praises you because _____ is fearfully and wonderfully made.
   Your works are wonderful,
   _____ knows that full well. (Psalm 139:13-14)

Do not hurry. There is no need to get through the entire psalm at once. • Respond to God's nurturing knowing.

3. When you are convicted of your own sinfulness, turn to Psalm 51 or Psalm 32. Offer yourself to God in repentance. Read the psalm one verse at a time. Stop after each verse and talk to God about what you have read. For instance: "When I kept silent, /my bones wasted away/through my groaning all day long" (Psalm 32:3). Consider where you are hiding from God and others. What secret are you afraid to face or share with God and perhaps others? How is your denial or rationalization of some sin eating away at your peace of mind? • Talk with God about this verse and move to the next verse. Continue throughout the chapter.

   Let the words of the psalmist comfort and sustain you. David and the other psalm writers struggled like you. They all sinned like you. And yet in God's economy David was a hero of the faith. Tell God what it means to you that the heroes of faith struggled just as you do.

4. When you are filled with concern for the church, place yourself in the presence of God and pray one of Paul's prayers for the church: Ephesians 1:15-21 or Philippians 1:3-6, 9. Or turn to Jesus' prayer for the church in John 17. Slowly read the passage. Listen for the prayer God places in your heart for the church. Take that prayer with you.

5. Sing God's Word. When a song comes into your mind, receive it as a word of God to you. Listen to the song. What is God saying to you? What do you want to say to him?

6. Is there a story in Scripture that reminds you of your life or a situation in your life? Go to that story and begin to meditate on it. What is God saying to you? • How might the life of a biblical character help shape your prayers?

7. Is there a prayer in Scripture you can make your own as a love song to God? Memorize it and say it often to the Lord.

8. If you find it hard to pray for someone you love (or even hate), ask God to give you a

prayer for him or her from his Word. Don't stray from that prayer until you are prompted by the Holy Spirit to do so.

Resources on Praying Scripture

Praying the Parables by Joyce Huggett
A Call to Spiritual Reformation by D. A. Carson

"The point is that we should make a gift of our hearts, emptying them of ourselves that they may be filled with God. Our Almighty Father becomes one with us and transforms us, uniting Creator and creature. How desirable is this union!"—Teresa of Ávila

PRAYER OF RECOLLECTION

DESIRE	to rest in God, allowing him to calm and heal my fragmented and distracted self
DEFINITION	The prayer of recollection represents a specifically "restful attitude" of connecting with the reality that God is in me. As we let go of distractions, this prayer recalls the soul to its true center and identity in Christ.
SCRIPTURE	"But I have stilled and quieted my soul; like a weaned child with its mother, like a weaned child is my soul within me." (Psalm 131:2) "Come to me, all you who are weary and burdened, and I will give you rest." (Matthew 11:28) "Be at rest once more, O my soul, for the LORD has been good to you." (Psalm 116:7) "I pray that out of his glorious riches he may strengthen you with power through his Spirit in your inner being, so that Christ may dwell in your hearts through faith. And I pray that you, being rooted and established in love, may have power, together with all the saints, to grasp how wide and long and high and deep is the love of Christ, and to know this love that surpasses knowledge—that you may be filled to the measure of all the fullness of God." (Ephesians 3:16-19)
PRACTICE INCLUDES	• identifying and confessing the false self with its addictions, sins, idols and pretense so as to move into the restful reality of forgiveness and communion • withdrawing from urgent affairs and the whirlpool of activities to the depths of life in Christ • being receptive rather than active in prayer
GOD-GIVEN FRUIT	• resting in God alone • discovering how scattered and distracted you are • honestly confessing disordered passions and surrendering them to God • living your true identity as the beloved of Christ • accepting your limits • recognizing the motivation for your spiritual practices

PRAYER OF RECOLLECTION

THE PSALMIST RECOLLECTED HIS SOUL WITH THIS PRAYER, "Be at rest once more, O my soul, / for the LORD has been good to you" (Psalm 116:7). A recollected soul is the opposite of a distracted, fragmented soul. It is a soul collected and at rest in God. Because it is natural for the mind to make random associations and wander off in a million directions, we need a prayer that recalls our soul to its center in God. The prayer of recollection reveals where our distracted hearts are going—where they are sidetracked by books on the desk, the sound of the radio in the next room and the new color scheme for the kitchen. Jesus said, "Where your treasure is, there your heart will be also" (Matthew 6:21). Distractions reveal our attachments. Attachments reveal what in our heart needs recollecting back to God once again.

Teresa of Ávila, John of the Cross, François Fénelon, St. Francis de Sales and Dietrich von Hildebrand are a few of the authors (besides the psalmists) who write about recalling or "recollecting" our souls back to their home in God. Though they don't share one formula for this kind of prayer, they all agree that the flood of distracting thoughts in prayer can be received as a gift! When you want to recollect your soul and end up rewriting the agenda for the next meeting in your head or when you begin praying for a colleague and end up imagining where you want to go on vacation, don't push these thoughts aside. Notice them. You cannot recollect what you don't know to be scattered. You cannot abandon what you don't see. The way to a heart at rest in God comes through confessing and abandoning our limited, preoccupied heart.

Thomas Dubay, in his book *Fire Within,* notes that John of the Cross suggests, "The more a pane of glass is free of anything not pure glass the more it can be transformed into a ray of sunlight." In the prayer of recollection we pay attention to our wandering thoughts and attachments so that we can be transformed "into a ray of sunlight." We open ourselves to seeing how secondary things have become idols of our heart—how our agendas, possessions, appearances and comforts matter more than keeping God first in our lives. The attachment to secondary things acts like a cataract on the eye, sapping out strength and spiritual energy and leaving us blind to what drives us. Throughout the ages, the faithful consistently proclaim, as Jesus did, that relinquishment of secondary things is the key to delight in God.

Transformation into Christlikeness requires detachment from whatever keeps us from returning to and resting in God, who is our treasure and our core. In the prayer of recollection we offer our distractible self to Christ. We name our escape tactics and the fantasies designed to shield us from disappointment. Then we offer them to God who alone can save us from a divided heart and reunite us with the undivided heart of God. In the book *Spiritual Letters to Women* we find a letter François Fénelon wrote to a busy lady living in 1692: "Recollection is the only cure for your haughtiness, the sharpness of your contemptuous criticism, the sallies of your imagination, your impatience with inferiors, your love pleasures, and all your other faults."

Confessing our attachments before the holy One, we return to our true root identity in God. We abandon the false self to embrace the true one. Remember, the self caught up in worry, power plays and image management is not the true self; it's a self that creates its identity through attachment to secondary things. But God has given you an identity. Receive it. Recollect your Christ-in-me identity. Over time, the prayer of recollection is meant to shape your soul so you rest in the bosom of Christ, in the arms of God, in the love of the Spirit.

REFLECTION QUESTIONS

1. What makes it difficult for you to concentrate while praying?

2. How do you tend to react to distractions in prayer?

3. What do distractions in prayer reveal about your core identity and concerns?

4. When do you tend to be most secure in your identity?

5. What is it like to not have a clear role that defines how you are to interact with others?

SPIRITUAL EXERCISES

1. Find a quiet place where you can sit comfortably before the Lord. Take some deep breaths, relaxing your body and quieting your mind. Offer yourself to God. Ask him to gather up the fragments of your scattered life and recollect your soul. Rest before him. When distracting thoughts come up, write down one word that expresses your distraction. Let the thought go and return to your rest in God. • After ten minutes look at the words you have jotted down. What stands out to you? What anxieties do you see? Where is your identity centered? • Confess that you are not called to control all that disrupts your life. Return these concerns to the Lord. Let him hold the concerns of your heart as you rest in him.

2. Intentionally come into the presence of God. Spend several moments thanking Jesus that he is present with you. Then quietly settle into resting with and in him. • When you become distracted, invite Jesus to look at the distraction with you. What does Jesus

want to say to you about the distraction? Give the distraction to him again and settle into rest. Continue the process of handing distractions to Jesus as you settle more and more deeply into your restful identity in him.

Resources on the Prayer of Recollection

The Interior Castle by Teresa of Ávila
Transformation in Christ by Hans Urs von Balthasar

"When we pray 'through Christ' more is involved than merely asking God in heaven to make some kind of intervention. The community too, and we ourselves, must be involved not just in the petition but also in trying to bring about what the petition pleads for."—Ronald Rolheiser

PRAYER WALKING

DESIRE	to align myself, while walking in particular places, with Christ and his intercession for the kingdom to come
DEFINITION	Prayer walking is a way of physically walking with Jesus through places (hospitals, homes, businesses, churches, schools, playgrounds, housing projects, service agencies, counties, countries, etc.) that you are concerned about. From the vantage point of proximity, prayers for the kingdom to come are offered to God.
SCRIPTURE	"Everything in the world is about to be wrapped up, so take nothing for granted. Stay wide-awake in prayer." (1 Peter 4:7 *The Message*) "I urge, then, first of all, that requests, prayers, intercession and thanksgiving be made for everyone—for kings and all those in authority, that we may live peaceful and quiet lives in all godliness and holiness. This is good, and pleases God our Savior." (1 Timothy 2:1-3)
PRACTICE INCLUDES	• slowly and deliberately walking through places for the purpose of intentional and listening prayer • walking through your church, school grounds or job site, giving to God the people and activities that go on there • walking through housing projects and government facilities, in places of need, fear, conflict, and decision making, blessing the rooms and praying for the activities and people that gather there • walking through neighborhoods and bringing each household to God one by one • taking a group of children or adults on a prayer walk; talking to them about what it is like for them
GOD-GIVEN FRUIT	• seeing places through Jesus' eyes • becoming quiet and listening to God's prayer for a particular place • allowing the visual nature of this journey to prompt prayers • gaining a perspective on the larger activity of God • holding a place or person before the Lord when you don't know how to pray for them; growing in awareness that the Spirit is praying for him or her—and you are with the Spirit in his prayer • becoming aware of people and places that you ignore, don't care about or have hard feelings toward; repenting • praying with others in environments of shared concern • exploring God's vision for places and people who gather there

PRAYER WALKING

SOME PEOPLE DO THEIR BEST PRAYING WHILE THEY ARE MOVING. Prayer walking can be a wonderful gift for those who like to get up and move around. This type of intercession intentionally invites people to go to the site of their concern: the office, the conference room, the dining room, the kitchen, the school, the hospital, the government buildings. The immediacy of context can fuel prayer and offer a way for listening more deeply to God, to what his concerns for this place might be.

Prayer walking is a way of saturating a particular place and people with prayer. This discipline draws us out of prayers that are limited to our immediate concerns and into a larger circle of God's loving attention. Sometimes prayer walking precedes a particular mission endeavor. A team of people go beforehand to walk through the neighborhood, country or project in order to pray. The actual mission team follows. Often this type of prayer is intentionally organized rather than happening spontaneously. It can be a one-time event or part of an ongoing prayer ministry.

REFLECTION QUESTIONS

1. What does it mean to you that God is in every place?

   How does this affect how you pray?

2. How does moving or being still affect the way you pray?

3. What most helps you concentrate on God?

   Is what helps you concentrate on God part of your regular prayer practice?

4. What is it like for you to pray, listening for what God's heart for a particular request might be?

SPIRITUAL EXERCISES

1. Walk through your home or church in the company of Jesus. Pray for each room and what happens there. • How would recognizing Jesus' presence there reorient your interaction?

2. Spend some time walking with other believers through your workplace. Pray for your colleagues, the custodial help, the customers, the delivery people, the kitchen staff. Offer yourself to be Jesus' hands and heart in this place.

3. Visit the playground and school near you. Walk through it in the company of Jesus. Pray for those who work, play and study there. • How do you see the heart of God for this place?

4. When you are on vacation or in a natural setting, allow God to draw you into prayer for this particular place. Let your interaction with the created world lead you into prayer. Pray that the exquisite beauty of the world will not be snuffed out.

6. Before a neighborhood picnic or school event, join other believers who will prayer walk for the crowds and people they know who will attend. Ask the Lord to give you his heart for them. Pray for the Holy Spirit to work even in this event.

Resources on Prayer Walking

WayMakers <www.waymakers.org>

APPENDIX 1

Spiritual Growth Planner

"Search me, O God, and know my heart;
test me and know my anxious thoughts.
See if there is any offensive way in me,
and lead me in the way everlasting."
PSALM 139:23-24

THE SPIRITUAL GROWTH PLANNER INVITES YOU to allow God to search your thoughts and explore the orientation of your soul. While a tool like this can never assess the interiority of a soul, it can give a glimpse of where you are at a particular moment in time. The spiritual growth planner acts like the marks we put on the door frame to show the kids how much they have grown. The marks reveal the progress of an organic, invisible process we call growth. These measurements don't force growth to happen; they reveal where you are and where you hope to be next time you get measured.

The planner is a way to mark your inertia, your desire and your growth. It is rather like taking your blood pressure as a measure of your health. If you take the inventory in another six months, you may be able to see where the invisible process of growth is producing fruit or not. This is no one-size-fits-all program—just the invitation to recognize where God is at work and calling you deeper into himself.

This spiritual growth planner will not measure behavior or chart standards of excellence. It can't assess your qualification for leadership, your gifting or your ministry skills. It won't account for the fruit of the Spirit in your life, nor will it fix your soul. This planner can, however, put you in touch with a longing or desire for God that translates into intentional motivation for the spiritual journey. Disciplines don't work by fiat. Spiritual disciplines must be engaged in freely and out of desire for God, not outward appearance. Desires can keep you open to God even when nothing seems to be happening. Attend to the desires rummaging around in your soul. Notice where the Holy Spirit is nudging you toward love of God, neighbor and self. The goal of the Christian life is not so much a set of behaviors as it is an orientation of the soul toward God and his kingdom.

Each section of the planner asks questions that attend not simply to outward behavior but to the roots of behavior. Don't blitz through the inventory section. Take time to notice your desires and inclinations as well as your resistances.

HINTS FOR

Linear thinkers: The inventory provides some structure and "next steps." It allows you to form your own spiritual health plan and set goals if you so desire.

Intuitive people: You may find the question grid frustrating because it seems boxy and incomplete. The open-ended questions at the beginning of each section, along with the box marked "desire," may be most helpful for you. If you are not someone who likes structure, name your reticence as you take an intentional look at your soul. If you begin to feel you should desire all of the disciplines or that you should do something about everything that is missing in your life at once, stop. Ask God to help you discern your most important desire at the moment. Stay with that.

New disciples: You may feel both overwhelmed and excited by all the disciplines. Remember that your goal is not to master all of these disciplines. You are simply to make a beginning. Attend to the desire of your heart and the prompting of the Holy Spirit in this particular moment.

For the sake of brevity, this inventory is designed around the acronym WORSHIP. Each letter of the word *worship* represents a way we can open ourselves to God. Within each of these headings are a series of practices and relationships that can help you grow more deeply in your worship of God.

Begin by asking yourself, *Which one of these seven expressions of desire for God resonates most deeply within me?* Underline the word that connects with you. What would you like to see happen in your life of worship? Name your longings, desperations and needs that surface for you in each area. (Briefly write your response to each category in the box.)

Where are you today in your desire to

Worship the Trinity	
Open yourself to God	
Relinquish the false self and idols of your heart	
Share your life	
Hear God's Word	
Incarnate the love of Christ	
Pray your life	

Choose your strongest desire and go through the following assessment.

WORSHIP THE TRINITY

Am I celebrating the love and glory of God with reverence and joy (Psalm 95:1-7)? Explain.

Where am I longing to move into deeper celebration of God?

Fill out the chart below using the following guide: 1 = not true, 2 = needs improvement, 3 = most of the time, 4 = consistently true. Choose one or two categories for which you feel a deep or passionate desire. Put a check in the "Desire" column.

	1	2	3	4	Desire
I am aware of God's presence in my life, confident of his love for me and intentionally celebrate our connection.					
Worshiping with fellow believers gives me a deep sense of joy and God's presence.					
I take time to celebrate God and acknowledge my limits by deeply entering into a weekly sabbath day that is different from every other day.					
I am aware of where I place people, experiences and images before God.					
I am a joyful, thankful person who expresses gratitude to God and others easily and often.					

Total Score: _____

Note which desire most resonates with you and touches a longing to go deeper with God in this place.

OPEN MYSELF TO GOD

How am I opening myself up to God in deeper ways?

Where am I longing to let go of defenses and busyness so I can become more open to God's activity in my life?

Fill out the chart below using the following guide: 1 = not true, 2 = needs improvement, 3 = most of the time, 4 = consistently true. Choose one or two categories for which you feel a deep or passionate desire. Put a check in the "Desire" column.

	1	2	3	4	Desire
I regularly and intentionally make space in my life for prayerfully listening to God at home, at work and with others.					
I can admit my mistakes, weaknesses and growing edges to God as well as others.					
I enjoy time spent alone with God in quiet reflection.					

	1	2	3	4	Desire
I recognize and live freely within my limits. I pay attention to my feelings, my body, my losses and my needs.					
I don't need to be doing something for God or others in order to feel good about myself.					

Total Score: _____

Note which desire most resonates with you and touches a longing to go deeper with God in this place.

RELINQUISH THE FALSE SELF AND IDOLS OF YOUR HEART

How am I growing in self-awareness and becoming more authentic in my relationships?

Where am I longing to let go of secondary things so I can give myself more authentically to God and others?

Fill out the chart below using the following guide: 1 = not true, 2 = needs improvement, 3 = most of the time, 4 = consistently true. Choose one or two categories for which you feel a deep or passionate desire. Put a check in the "Desire" column.

	1	2	3	4	Desire
I am aware of my sin and blind spots and how they hurt others. I easily apologize to others and seek to live out of my true self in Christ.					
I am able to leave the crowded, noisy world of acclaim and doing behind, retreating into silence and solitude with God and letting him restore me.					
I recognize the voice and activity of the Holy Spirit in my life.					
I recognize my addictions and compulsions, and am committed to living free of them.					

Total Score: _____

Note which desire most resonates with you and touches a longing to go deeper with God in this place.

SHARE MY LIFE

Am I connecting with God and others in a caring community? Explain.

How am I longing to be with others in spiritual community?

Fill out the chart below using the following guide: 1 = not true, 2 = needs improvement, 3 = most of the time, 4 = consistently true. Choose one or two categories for which you feel a deep or passionate desire. Put a check in the "Desire" column.

	1	2	3	4	Desire
I have a relationship with someone who helps me grow in my spiritual walk.					
I feel comfortable opening my home, my heart, my faith and my life to people not in my family.					
I am not judgmental toward others. I know how to make peace and deal with anger in constructive ways. I am not argumentative and contentious.					
Others describe me as honest, vulnerable, open and approachable.					
I am not hypersensitive and easily offended. I give and receive love freely and easily.					

Total Score: ____

Note which desire most resonates with you and touches a longing to go deeper with God in this place.

HEAR GOD'S WORD

Am I cultivating the knowledge of God, the character of Christ and the presence of the Spirit in my life (John 16:5-15)? Explain.

Do I want to connect more deeply with God and his Word? If so, how?

Fill out the chart below using the following guide: 1 = not true, 2 = needs improvement, 3 = most of the time, 4 = consistently true. Choose one or two categories for which you feel a deep or passionate desire. Put a check in the "Desire" column.

	1	2	3	4	Desire
I am growing in biblical literacy and know how scriptural truth intersects with my life.					

	1	2	3	4	Desire
On a regular basis I am nourished by spending time with God and his Word.					
The Bible is alive and interesting to me.					
I have a plan for reading Scripture.					

Total Score: _____

Note which desire most resonates with you and touches a longing to go deeper with God in this place.

INCARNATE CHRIST'S LOVE

Am I contributing myself and my God-given gifts for the growth of Christ's kingdom? Explain.

How am I giving myself and my resources away to God and others?

Fill out the chart below using the following guide: 1 = not true, 2 = needs improvement, 3 = most of the time, 4 = consistently true. Choose one or two categories for which you feel a deep or passionate desire. Put a check in the "Desire" column.

	1	2	3	4	Desire
I work for justice and have a heart for the dispossessed and needy that is visible to others.					
I am just and fair in dealing with others. I honor my contracts and commitments, even if they inconvenience me.					
I know my gifts and contribute them to the kingdom of God. I am more concerned about building God's kingdom than my own.					
I willingly set aside my agenda in order to share my possessions, skills and time with others.					
The fruit of the Spirit is more and more evident in my life.					
People with problems, needs, sorrows and losses seek me out. They know I care.					

Total Score: _____

Note which desire most resonates with you and touches a longing to go deeper with God in this place.

PRAY MY LIFE

Am I attending to God's activity in my life and listening to him on a regular basis? Explain.

Where am I longing to connect more deeply with God? What do I want this to look like?

Fill out the chart below using the following guide: 1 = not true, 2 = needs improvement, 3 = most of the time, 4 = consistently true. Choose one or two categories for which you feel a deep or passionate desire. Put a check in the "Desire" column.

	1	2	3	4	Desire
It's easy for me to get around to prayer.					
My prayer life is not mostly about myself and my needs.					
I am able to authentically pray my emotions, losses, anger, doubts and desires. I feel comfortable telling God all the 'good, bad and ugly" in me.					
I am comfortable praying out loud with others.					
I am aware of how God speaks to me, and I know how to listen to God and recognize his voice.					

Total Score: _____

Note which desire most resonates with you and touches a longing to go deeper with God in this place.

Look back over the personal growth planner and your life as a worshiper. Write your score totals below. They reveal areas of desire, neglect and need. Consider who you want to become. For each category, pick one growing edge that engages your desire to become more like Christ. Write it in the box below.

	Score	Desire
Worship the Trinity		
Open to God		
Relinquish the false self and idols of the heart		
Share my life		

	Score	Desire
Hear God's Word		
Incarnate the love of Christ		
Pray my life		

Number the desires in order of importance to you. Attending to the category of your deepest desire, turn to the table of contents where the disciplines are listed under their corresponding heading for WORSHIP, found on pages 7-8. Which discipline peaks your interest? Notice the desire listed immediately beside the name of that spiritual discipline. Which desire resonates with your own desire? When you find a desire that resonates with your own, you have found a practice, relationship or experience that provides you with a way to make space for the God you worship. This spiritual discipline can be a gift to you on your journey.

Appendix 2

A Series on Spiritual Disciplines for the Congregation

The word *worship* easily lends itself to an eight-week series on what it means to offer our bodies to God as a spiritual act of worship (Romans 12:1).

Set aside eight weeks.

Week 1.   Designed to Worship—exploring the purpose of spiritual disciplines

Week 2.   "**W**orship": Valuing the Right Stuff—practices that address the most important thing in life

Week 3.   "**O**penness" to a God You Can't Control—practices that let the light in

Week 4.   "**R**elinquishment": Letting Go in a World Dedicated to Accumulation—practices that lead to authenticity and surrender

Week 5.   "**S**haring" Your Life in a Culture Designed for Privacy—practices that lead us to interdependence and community

Week 6.   "**H**earing" from God—practices that form the mind of Christ in us

Week 7.   "**I**ncarnating" Jesus—practices that let us be Jesus to the world

Week 8.   "**P**raying" My life—practices that lead me to pray without ceasing

In between each week, invite the congregation into the practice of *one* of the disciplines found in the handbook under the current letter for WORSHIP. Encourage small groups and Sunday school classes to discuss people's experiences with the practice, using the reflection questions found in the handbook.

Follow the suggestions for small groups found in the "Using the *Spiritual Disciplines Handbook* with Small Groups," appendix 4.

Each year set aside eight weeks on worship, introducing a new discipline each time.

APPENDIX 3

Suggestions for Spiritual Mentors

One of my favorite words for pastor is *curate*. The term is unfamiliar to many of us. But the word *curate* signifies a person who partners with God for the "cure of the soul" or, in Dallas Willard's words, the "renovation of the heart." Mentors, spiritual directors, spiritual friends, parents, teachers, pastors and disciplers are called to take a risk on God as they accompany people in the Spirit's soul-curing work.

The *Spiritual Disciplines Handbook* provides a variety of ways for soul shepherds to partner with God and others in the cure of the soul. However, this book can never substitute for a shepherd's personal journey with the Holy Spirit. Shepherds wanting to partner with the Holy Spirit for long-term change in others will find they have to address their own wounds, distortions and desperations. Shepherds cannot lead others where they have not traveled. Don't just use this book for others; follow your own soul's desires into disciplines that grow your own communion with God.

Shepherds can help fellow pilgrims recognize and name a desire, hunger, need, conviction, sin or thirst for God. We can offer questions like these:

- What are you longing for in your relationship to God?
- Where do you experience the Trinity in your life right now?
- What lies at the root of your most persistent longings?
- Where does your mind go when it is not focused on work?
- Where are you wounded and longing for healing?
- Who are you longing to be?
- Where are you not living out of your true identity in Christ?

For instance, someone who feels life rushing down on them like a stampede of horses may confess, "I'm trying to do everything and it's killing me. I need mercy and help to change." Tucked away in all the frustration and busyness is a desire to live in an unforced, peaceful rhythm of grace. Practices such as slowing, unplugging, retreat, contemplation and solitude are fueled by the desire to live in a saner rhythm. As the hard-packed soil of desire is exposed to God, the Spirit of truth settles into his transforming work. There are disciplines for those learning to love God through holding their tongue and disciplines for those learning to cherish God by speaking up in truth. There are practices for people who are burned out and depleted, and practices for those revved up and ready to roll. No matter where desperation and desire begin, there are spiritual disciplines that are fueled by just those desires and desperations.

Not everyone is connected to their God-given desires. People who are cut off from their desperations and longings are severed from an artery of connection with God and themselves. So shepherds must listen to where desire has been derailed or grown compulsive. They are present to help others connect more authentically with God.

"Pleasers" need shepherds who can help them identify their heart's lost desperations and desires for God. Those who spend years substituting other's longings and desires for their own can lose track of how they want to be with God. The needs and wants of kids, boss, spouse, church, school, community and parents can derail a pleaser's own journey toward God. In fact, pleasers may be practicing spiritual disciplines suited to others rather than doing the hard work of naming their own desires before God. Shepherds help reveal the desire for God at the root of people's souls.

Shepherds can also provide direction for those who feel they shouldn't have wants and desires. When questions about legitimate wants and needs are ignored or punished, people learn to shut down emotionally. They ask for nothing. A soul shepherd can ask the questions that lead to practices which promote healing, hope and transformation.

When a person grows up learning that asking for something was never a safe thing to do, there is much to unlearn. People who have experienced deep disappointment around unmet longings also need soul shepherds that can point them to trust God's goodness. They may also need guidance in how to live in the open space between desire and demand.

Entitled people also need shepherds who can help them reach beyond personal preferences to the God-given desires buried under the numbing weight of accumulating secondary things. They need to address what they really worship and where true life can be found.

The practices, relationships and experiences found in this handbook provide ways for spiritual directors, spiritual friends, mentors, parents, teachers, pastors and disciplers to tend to their own journey as well as the journey of others. The following suggestions are simple ways of attending to the soul of another in his or her spiritual journey. The questions open doors for discussion as well as deep prayer.

- Familiarize yourself with the spiritual disciplines found in this book. Consider how these practices have affected your own life.
- Help people name the desire they have for growth. Familiarity with the disciplines will enable you to help them match a discipline to their desire.
- Use the "Spiritual Growth Planner" if the person struggles with self-awareness. Discuss the responses and desires that surface.
- Once a discipline is chosen, discuss any new self-awareness that comes through the reflection questions. Where is God trying to get his or her attention? What responses are forming in the heart?
- Allow time for exploration of the spiritual exercises in each discipline. Invite responses and talk about what is happening in the soul through the practice of the discipline.
- Together notice where God is at work.
- Are there wounds that surface? Dysfunctional behavior that he or she longs to see change?
- What resistances to obedience surface?
- Where is there self-deceit, spiritual blindness or belief in lies?
- How is the person experiencing God in his or her life right now? What is that like for the person? What does he or she want to say to God about this?
- What next step would be a step of surrender and trust?
- Let what you see continue to deepen the conversation with God.

APPENDIX 4

Using the Spiritual Disciplines Handbook *with Small Groups*

The *Handbook* provides a user-friendly way of helping a group of two or more people attend to their spiritual journey. The study can be led by one facilitator, or leadership can rotate from meeting to meeting. Decide which way you will proceed.

Take your time with each discipline. Pay attention to God-given desires and desperations. The desire that fuels the discipline is always listed first. The "Reflection Questions" section is designed to bring up authentic dialogue with God in prayer. The "Spiritual Exercises" section offers a variety of ways of entering into the discipline. The disciplines offer you a way of making space in your overwhelmed and preoccupied life for God to show up and master you. Let your practice be a humble invitation for God to make his home in your daily life. Loving God through spiritual practices will never make you glow in the dark, but over time they will root you in the deep, rich soil of God who loves you.

"MAKING SPACE IN YOUR LIFE FOR GOD": A SMALL GROUP STUDY

Meeting 1

Invite each participant to share why they feel drawn to "making space in their lives for God." Consider asking:

- Are you stuck or frustrated in your spiritual journey? If so, how?
- What desires are stirring in your soul?
- What would you like to receive from God through this study?

Assignment: Read the introduction. Use the "Spiritual Growth Planner" appendix if it is helpful to you.

Meeting 2

1. Begin with a few minutes of silence followed by a slow reading of Matthew 11:28-30. Invite each person to share their response to this Scripture.

2. Ask each person to form a one-sentence prayer of desire in response to this Scripture. Pray your response.

3. Discuss the introduction. What stood out for you?

4. Share which letter of the acronym WORSHIP most captured the place of desire.

   Which desires are shared by the group?

5. Decide on the worship category you want to focus on as a group. (You may also want to explore a particular discipline on your own.)

6. Read the brief introduction to this category.

7. Scan the practices, relationships and experiences offered in your disciplines category. You can begin with the first discipline or choose a discipline the group prefers.

8. Look at the reflection questions and spiritual exercises for your discipline. Decide if you will answer all the reflections questions for next week's meeting. (Leaders can also make the call on this.) Some reflection questions take more time than others. It may be appropriate to answer only one or two questions. The point is to reflect, not just get answers on paper.

9. Choose one or two spiritual exercises for the week.

Assignment: Answer the reflection questions. Practice one or two of the spiritual exercises for the week.

Meeting 3 and Later

1. Begin each meeting with a few minutes of silence and a short reading from Scripture (see the "Devotional Reading" discipline for ideas about this). The leader can choose the passage, or a different person can take responsibility for this each week.

2. Check in with one another. You might ask, "Where did God show up for you this week?"

3. Share your answers to one or two of the reflection questions.

4. Pray together in pairs or as a small group over what you noticed about yourself this past week.

5. Share your experiences around the spiritual exercises. What temptations or circumstances derailed you from your practice? What happened for you in your exercises? Some weeks it will feel like nothing happened. That is not unusual. Heartfelt desires can lead us into places of tension and waiting. When God trusts you with his silence don't give up on him. He hasn't given up on you.

6. Decide if you will move to other exercises or continue the same exercise until you meet again. (If an individual feels called to practice an additional exercise on their own, that should not be discouraged.)

7. When the group is ready, move on to another discipline listed in your category. There is no need to do every discipline in one category before you move to another category. You might wish to do two disciplines for each letter of the acronym *worship*. Then consider whether you want to begin again. Remember, the goal of the disciplines is not to master them all. The disciplines are ways we love and surrender to God. Through our partnership with the Holy Spirit in these disciplines, God masters us and leads us deeper into his own heart of love.

APPENDIX 5

Names for Worshiping God

- Alpha, Almighty, Awesome, Adored, Arm, Advocate, Ancient of Days, Abounding, All, Answer, Answerer, Adequate, Author, Authority, Anchor, Amen, Adonai, Abba

- Bread, Breath, Brother, Bridegroom, Blessed, Blesser, Beloved, Burden-Bearer, Barrier-Breaker, Boundless, Bountiful, Branch, Bruised, Beautiful, Beloved

- Christ, Creator, Counselor, Carpenter, Captain, Conqueror, Crowned, Companion, Center, Cornerstone, Compassionate, Comforter, Crucified, Captor

- Dwelling, Destination, Deliverer, Defender, Delight, Divider, Desire, Dew, Door, Day-Spring, Divine

- Emmanuel, El Shaddai, Enlightener, Everlasting, Expectation, Eternal, Expert, Expectant, Encourager, Example, Exalted, Examiner, Elohim, Enduring, End, Enthroned, Exalted, Exhorter

- Father, Friend, Fellow, Fountain, Fire, Forgiving, Faithful, Forsaken, Fairest, Finisher, Fullness, Foundation

- Guide, Guardian, Good, Great, Gatherer, Glorious, Gracious, Gift, Giver, Gardener, Goal, Griever, Gate

- Holy, Highest, Hallowed, Humble, Habitation, Hiding Place, Hidden, Heart-Broken, Husbandman, Head, Hope, Healer, Helper, Hand, Home, Holy Spirit

- I AM, Incarnate Word, Instructor, Immortal, Incomprehensible, Incomparable, Infinite, Invisible, Infallible, Invincible, Ineffable, Indwelling, Intercessor, Inspirer

- Jehovah, Judge, Just, Justifier, Jealous, Joy, Jesus

- King, Kinsman, Keeper, Kind, Key

- Lamb of God, Lord, Light, Life, Love, Leader, Long-Suffering, Lowly, Listener

- Messiah, Maker, Most High, Master, Mighty, Meek, Merciful, Measureless, Majesty, Mindful, Manna, Mysterious, Morning Star

- Nigh, New, Needed, Nearest, Nourisher, Nurturer

- Omniscient, Omnipresent, Omnipotent, Only-Begotten, Owner, Overcomer, Omega

- Prophet, Priest, Paraclete, Prince of Peace, Physician, Patient, Peace, Purest Pleasure, Protector, Provider, Preserver, Possessor, Precious, Pastor, Perfect, Priceless, Praiseworthy, Pioneer, Prize, Pardoning, Persistent, Pearl, Pure, Prayer-Hearer, Potter
- Quickener, Queller-of-Storms, Quietness
- Redeemer, Resurrection, Refiner, Refuge, Righteous, Righteousness, Rule, Radiant, Reprover, Reformer, Renewer, Ransom, Refresher, Rescuer, Receiver, Road, Rewarder, Ruler, Restorer, Rock, Rest, Rod, Rich
- Son, Son of Man, Servant, Savior, Shepherd, Sacrifice, Salvation, Splendor, Spirit, Satisfaction, Satisfier, Source, Spring, Sanctification, Sanctifier, Stronghold, Strength, Strengthener, Sun, Shield, Steadfast, Sufficient, Skillful, Strong, Succorer, Supreme, Shade, Silent, Star, Song, Seeker, Sovereign, Slow-to-Anger, Sanctuary, Sower, Seed of the Woman
- Triumphant, Transcendent, Transformer, Teacher, Treasure, Treasury, Truth, True, Tender, Tower, Trustworthy, Trinity, Three in One
- Uncreated Light, Unchangeable, Understanding, Undefeated, Unhurried, Unforgetting, Unfailing, Unhindered, Unwearied, Unlimited, Uniter, Uplifter, Upholder
- Vine, Vindicator, Vision, Visible, Veil, Vanquisher, Verity, Victory, Voice
- Way, Water of Life, Word, Wine, Wisdom, Wonderful, Well-Spring, Worthy, Wise, Watcher, Wounded
- Yahweh, Yours, Yearning, Yearned-for, Yokefellow
- Zeal, Zealous

God took the initiative in revealing himself to humankind. God showed himself to Moses in a burning bush and then told Moses his name—Yahweh—I AM WHO I AM. God's name revealed the transcendent immediacy of a God who was present. Flippant or magical uses of God's name was forbidden by the third commandment. The holiness of God's name was not lost on Israel; they would not speak it or write it out in full. In fact, to use his name was to stand at the doorway to the presence of the divine.

God revealed himself to Israel in a variety of names. In the Bible, names carry particular significance. They are sources of revelation and a glimpse into the mystery of the bearer's identity. Names and titles for God express something of the character, presence, authority and nature of the divine being. It should not surprise us that images for and names of God can be more mysterious than comprehensible. They invite us into contemplation of the holy One. They compel us toward *worship* rather than explanations. Behold. Look. See. Meditate. Open wide to the God who is beyond and above, yet at the same moment God in and with us.

The following are a few of the many ways God identified himself to Israel (from the *International Standard Bible Encyclopedia*).

- Adonai, the Lord (Isaiah 61:1)
- Elohim, "God" (Exodus 20:3; Joshua 24:16)
- El Shaddai, "God Almighty" (Genesis 17:1)
- El Olam, "the everlasting God" (Genesis 21:33)
- E Roi, "the God who sees me" (Genesis 16:13-14)

The ad hoc list presented above is neither exhaustive or precise. But it offers a way of attending to the mystery of the

Immortal, invisible, God only wise,

in light inexpressible hid from our eyes.

Most blessed, most glorious, the Ancient of Days.

Almighty, victorious, thy great Name we praise.

SUGGESTIONS FOR MEDITATION ON THE NAMES OF GOD

Take time to become still. Let the noise go. Do not follow the stray thoughts and distractions. Let them go as best you can. Prepare to be in the presence of God. Imagine yourself coming to one of the persons of the Trinity: Father, Son or Holy Spirit. What image comes to mind? Are you walking hand in hand with Jesus? Are you laying your head on the Father's shoulder? Are you sensing the wind of the Spirit that blows where it wills? Stay with God. Be open to listen. Allow God's name to draw you in to the company of the holy Three in One.

- Is there a name of God that is particularly meaningful to you at this moment? For instance, "Healer," "Good Shepherd" or "Creator." Breathing deeply, quietly repeat the name. Let God's name move from the crown of your head to your feet. Rest in the name. Tell God what you sense about him through this name. Thank and honor the God who comes.

- Slowly and quietly run your eyes over the names of God listed above. Does any particular word catch your attention? Stay with the word that touches you and draws you into contemplation of God. Don't hurry to another word. Listen and wait. Contemplate the beauty of God represented in the name. Sing a song that uses the name. Write your own psalm of praise to the God who is named here. Knowing a name for God can be quite different than resting in the *presence* of the One whose name you honor.

- Form a breath prayer using the name for God that touches you (see "Breath Prayer").

- Timothy Botts has some wonderful books that attempt to capture the meaning of God's names and character in calligraphy. Look through one of these books and allow the calligraphy to reveal something of who God is.

- If you desire a deeper connection with some part of God's character and person at particular times of stress, temptation or responsibility, write the name of God that touches you with its sufficiency. Place this name where you can see and remember it: by your computer, on a mirror, in your gym bag. When you can, enter into the name with your attention and intention. Rest in God. Continually thank God for his presence using your chosen name.

- Sing some hymns or choruses that lead you into reflecting on the names and revelations of who God is.

- Slowly, over days and weeks, wend your way through the names of God written above. Let these names lead you into prayers of gratitude for the immensity and presence of God in your life. And when God is silent, remember that he somehow made himself known to Elijah in a whisper (1 Kings 19:12).

Appendix 6

One Anothers

"Because there is one loaf, we, who are many,
are one body, for we all partake of the one loaf."
1 Corinthians 10:17

Just as the Trinity is one, so followers of Jesus are one. No matter how many schisms divide us, the supreme reality we are to incarnate is oneness. We belong to one another. We cannot apprentice ourselves to Jesus and live without regard for others.

What does Christian oneness and community look like? Scripture is replete with examples and directives that can shape healthy relationships and engender safe, thriving body life.

LOVE ONE ANOTHER

"A new command I give you: Love one another. As I have loved you, so you must love one another. By this all men will know that you are my disciples, if you love one another." (John 13:34-35)

"Let no debt remain outstanding, except the continuing debt to love one another, for he who loves his fellowman has fulfilled the law." (Romans 13:8)

"Now that you have purified yourselves by obeying the truth so that you have sincere love for your brothers, love one another deeply, from the heart." (1 Peter 1:22)

"This is the message you heard from the beginning: We should love one another." (1 John 3:11)

"And this is his command: to believe in the name of his Son, Jesus Christ, and to love one another as he commanded us." (1 John 3:23)

"Dear friends, let us love one another, for love comes from God. Everyone who loves has been born of God and knows God." (1 John 4:7)

"Dear friends, since God so loved us, we also ought to love one another. No one has ever seen God; but if we love one another, God lives in us and his love is made complete in us." (1 John 4:11-12)

"And now, dear lady, I am not writing you a new command but one we have had from the beginning. I ask that we love one another." (2 John 1:5)

ENCOURAGE ONE ANOTHER

"Therefore encourage each other with these words." (1 Thessalonians 4:18)

"Therefore encourage one another and build each other up, just as in fact you are doing." (1 Thessalonians 5:11)

"But encourage one another daily, as long as it is called Today, so that none of you may be hardened by sin's deceitfulness." (Hebrews 3:13)

BEAR ONE ANOTHER'S BURDENS

"Each helps the other / and says to his brother, 'Be strong!' " (Isaiah 41:6)

CARE FOR ONE ANOTHER

"God has so arranged the body, giving the greater honor to the inferior member, that there may be no dissension within the body, but the members may have the same care for one another." (1 Corinthians 12:24-25 NRSV)

ACCEPT ONE ANOTHER

"Accept one another, then, just as Christ accepted you, in order to bring praise to God."(Romans 15:7)

"Accept him whose faith is weak, without passing judgment on disputable matters. One man's faith allows him to eat everything, but another man, whose faith is weak, eats only vegetables. The man who eats everything must not look down on him who does not, and the man who does not eat everything must not condemn the man who does, for God has accepted him. Who are you to judge someone else's servant? To his own master he stands or falls. And he will stand, for the Lord is able to make him stand." (Romans 14:1-4)

BE KIND TO ONE ANOTHER

"Get rid of all bitterness, rage and anger, brawling and slander, along with every form of malice. Be kind and compassionate to one another, forgiving each other, just as in Christ God forgave you." (Ephesians 4:31-32)

"The fruit of the spirit is . . . kindness." (Galatians 5:22)

LIVE IN HARMONY WITH ONE ANOTHER

"Finally, all of you, live in harmony with one another; be sympathetic, love as brothers, be compassionate and humble." (1 Peter 3:8)

FORGIVE ONE ANOTHER

"Be kind and compassionate to one another, forgiving each other, just as in Christ God forgave you." (Ephesians 4:32)

BE HOSPITABLE TO ONE ANOTHER

"Offer hospitality to one another without grumbling." (1 Peter 4:9)

"Be hospitable to one another without complaining." (1 Peter 4:9 NRSV)

HONOR ONE ANOTHER

"Honor one another above yourselves." (Romans 12:10)

BELONG TO ONE ANOTHER

"In Christ we who are many form one body, and each member belongs to all the others."(Romans 12:5)

"We are members of one another." (Ephesians 4:25 NRSV)

"Finally, brothers, good-by. Aim for perfection, listen to my appeal, be of one mind, live in peace. And the God of love and peace will be with you." (2 Corinthians 13:11)

"Let us not give up meeting together, as some are in the habit of doing." (Hebrews 10:25)

"God has so arranged the body, giving the greater honor to the inferior member, that there may be no dissension within the body, but the members may have the same care for one another." (1 Corinthians 12:24-25 NRSV)

BE DEVOTED TO ONE ANOTHER

"Be devoted to one another in brotherly love [mutual affection]." (Romans 12:10)

SPEAK TRUTHFULLY TO ONE ANOTHER

"Do not lie to one another, seeing that you have stripped off the old self with its practices." (Colossians 3:9 NRSV)

"So then, putting away falsehood, let all of us speak the truth to our neighbors, for we are members of one another." (Ephesians 4:25 NRSV)

TEACH ONE ANOTHER

"Let the word of Christ dwell in you richly as you teach and admonish one another with all wisdom, and as you sing psalms, hymns and spiritual songs with gratitude in your hearts to God." (Colossians 3:16)

AGREE WITH ONE ANOTHER

"I appeal to you, brothers, in the name of our Lord Jesus Christ, that all of you agree with one another so that there may be no divisions among you and that you may be perfectly united in mind and thought." (1 Corinthians 1:10)

LOOK OUT FOR ONE ANOTHER

"Each of you should look not only to your own interests, but also to the interests of others." (Philippians 2:4)

WORSHIP WITH ONE ANOTHER

"Speak to one another with psalms, hymns and spiritual songs. Sing and make music in your heart to the Lord, always giving thanks to God the Father for everything, in the name of our Lord Jesus Christ." (Ephesians 5:19-20)

LAY DOWN YOUR LIVES FOR ONE ANOTHER

"We know love by this, that [Jesus] laid down his life for us—and we ought to lay down our lives for one another." (1 John 3:16 NRSV)

DO NOT PROVOKE ONE ANOTHER

"If we live by the Spirit, let us also be guided by the Spirit. Let us not become conceited, competing against one another, envying one another." (Galatians 5:25-26 NRSV)

DO NOT GRUMBLE AGAINST ONE ANOTHER

"Do not grumble against one another, so that you may not be judged. See, the Judge is standing at the doors!" (James 5:9 NRSV)

DO NOT ENVY ONE ANOTHER

"If we live by the Spirit, let us also be guided by the Spirit. Let us not become conceited, competing against one another, envying one another." (Galatians 5:25-26 NRSV)

SUGGESTIONS FOR PUTTING THE SCRIPTURAL "ONE ANOTHERS" INTO PRACTICE

Any of the suggestions found below can be done with a prayer partner, accountability partner, mentor or spiritual director. They are also suitable for small group interaction and follow-up.

1. Choose a "one another" that you want to become a hallmark of your life. Consider why this "one another" is important to you. Picture what practicing the "one another" will cost you. It could cost you time, money and a variety of self-indulgent moods and behaviors. Commit yourself to practicing the "one another" every day for two weeks. At the end of each day, notice where you lived your "one another." Where did you not live your "one another"? Seek grace to continue to incarnate Christ's self-donating love. At the end of two weeks, consider whether or not you should dedicate two more weeks to intentionally living your "one another." Do you feel called to move on to a different one?

2. When and how have you received the "one another" love and encouragement found in Scripture? Which "one anothers" did or didn't you receive growing up? How have these affected your attitude to "one another" directives? Talk to Jesus about your experiences. Offer him your desire around "one another" living.

3. On a monthly basis focus on a particular "one another." If you are in a small group, you might call a month "Encourage One Another Month." During that month, each participant opens his or her heart to encourage others in the group. At the end of the month meet to discuss what this was like for all of you. What touched you most deeply? What was most difficult? How did you find God in the "one anothers?"

4. Consider the people in your world that have little experience of the biblical "one anothers." How could you intentionally bring a "one another" experience to these people? Plan a time to do so.

APPENDIX 7

Postures for Prayer

Explore some of these biblical postures for prayer.

STAND

Standing is a way of honoring the presence of another and giving him or her your full attention. Stand before the majesty of God.

"The LORD said, 'Go out and stand on the mountain in the presence of the LORD, for the LORD is about to pass by.' " (1 Kings 19:11)

"And when you stand praying, if you hold anything against anyone, forgive him." (Mark 11:25)

"Abraham remained standing before the LORD." (Genesis 18:22)

OUTSTRETCHED ARMS

Lifting up our arms or hands pulls our awareness toward heaven. It is a posture that opens the core of our body toward God.

"May the lifting up of my hands be like the evening sacrifice." (Psalm 141:2)

"In your name I will lift up my hands." (Psalm 63:4)

"At night I stretched out untiring hands." (Psalm 77:2)

"I want men everywhere to lift up holy hands in prayer, without anger or disputing." (1 Timothy 2:8)

UPLIFTED EYES

Looking up to heaven with open eyes draws our attention above earthly realities to eternal verities. We are not alone. God is watching us.

"I lift up my eyes to you,

   to you whose throne is in heaven.

As the eyes of slaves look to the hand of their master,

as the eyes of a maid look to the hand of her mistress,

so our eyes look to the LORD our God." (Psalm 123:1-2)

"He looked up to heaven and with a deep sigh said to him '*Ephphatha!*'" (Mark 7:34)

"Taking the five loaves and two fish and looking up to heaven, he gave thanks and broke the loaves." (Mark 6:41)

"After Jesus said this, he looked toward heaven and prayed." (John 17:1)

KNEELING

Kneeling is a way we express humility and reverence.

"When Solomon had finished all these prayers and supplications to the LORD, he rose from before the altar of the LORD, where he had been kneeling with hands spread out toward heaven." (1 Kings 8:54)

"He got down on his knees and prayed." (Acts 9:40)

"Three times a day he got down on his knees and prayed, giving thanks to his God, just as he had done before." (Daniel 6:10)

"A man with leprosy came to him and begged him on his knees." (Mark 1:40)

PROSTRATE

Lying face down or bowing low to the earth reminds us that we were created from dust and to dust we will return. It is a posture of submission and obedient worship.

"Abram fell facedown, and God said to him . . . " (Genesis 17:3)

"They bowed down and worshiped." (Exodus 4:31)

"They bowed down and worshiped the LORD with their faces to the ground." (Nehemiah 8:6)

"Jehoshaphat bowed with his face to the ground, and all the people of Judah and Jerusalem fell down in worship before the LORD." (2 Chronicles 20:18)

"When he saw Jesus, he fell with his face to the ground." (Luke 5:12)

"Then the woman, seeing that she could not go unnoticed, came trembling and fell at his feet." (Luke 8:47)

"All kings will bow down to him." (Psalm 72:11)

"All the earth bows down to you." (Psalm 66:4)

Spending Time with God

When my children were young, I was very conscious of bonding with them. I would look into their eyes, whisper their names and caress their heads. (Someone had told me that head stroking gave babies a sense of well-being.) In any case I was eager to log in the hours needed to create trust and relationship.

Bonding is real. It happens as we spend time with others. Bonding is something that requires presence, not simply information about someone. Magazines are full of information about famous people. Biographies give us a glimpse into the lives of others. But it is only in the presence of another that we bond to them.

Bonding with God is not an all-or-nothing endeavor. Some of us feel that if we can't give God a good uninterrupted half hour, we aren't giving him anything. Intentional time set aside for bonding is one of the best gifts we give anyone. But even small moments spent with God (or others) matter and eventually add up. If you spent fifteen minutes with God every day for a year, at the end of the year you would have logged over eleven eight-hours days. If you spent a half hour with God every day for a year, at the end of the year you would have logged over a month of eight-hour days. Fifteen minutes, a half hour—it doesn't seem like much, but over time they become days logged with God! It counts as bonding time. If spending an hour, not to mention a day, with Jesus seems daunting to you, let me suggest it may not be as out of your reach as you think.

BEGIN WHERE YOU ARE

If fifteen minutes is what you have, give yourself to God as deeply as you know how for fifteen minutes. Trust God to receive and work with what you give him.

If you can give more time one day a week, add this appointment with God to your regular rhythm.

If you want to intentionally bond with God for an hour or more, choose a place away from your home or work: a park, the sanctuary of a church, a garden, a retreat house. Get away from the distractions that keep you preoccupied and distracted.

SUGGESTIONS FOR BONDING HOURS WITH GOD

Allow 5-10 minutes between each exercise. Don't hurry. There are enough suggestions below to fill many hours. Begin with one hour and add a second and a third as you can.

Hour 1

1. Spend 5-10 minutes in silence. Let the internal noise die down. Breathe in the presence of Jesus. He is the oxygen that sustains your soul. Open yourself to God in prayer:

   - Practice "palms down, palms up." (A full description of this exercise is found under "Centering Prayer.") Place your palms down on your lap as a symbolic indication of your desire to release the concerns you name to God. Turn your palms up to demonstrate your openness to receive what the Trinity brings. Wait before God.
   - What do you desire from God during this time of bonding?
   - Express your feelings and expectations to God about this time.
   - Dialogue with God about where you have sensed his presence in the last week or month.

   Ask God what he wants for you to receive during this time. Listen. Respond to any nudgings you receive from the Holy Spirit.

2. Choose one or two of the following suggestions. Follow your desire.

   - Go for a walk and *be with God*. Notice signs of God's love. Read nature as a revelation of God. If possible, gather a symbol of your time with God—a rock, a branch, a flower. Thank God for how he reveals himself in his creation.
   - Slowly read a psalm out loud. Psalm 16, 19, 23, 42 and 51 are great places to begin. Let the psalm echo through your heart and mind. What do you hear God saying to you? Pray your response to God.
   - Worship God through song. Listen to some hymns or praise music on your headphones.

3. Take a posture that reflects your attitude and desire toward God (kneel, lie prostrate, stand with arms lifted or look up to heaven). Remain in the posture and let your heart seek God.

   Write a psalm to God. It can be anything from a lament to a song of praise.

Hour 2

1. Eat a snack in the presence of God. Let the process of eating remind you of what it means to be nourished through God and his Word.

2. Use the framework found in "Devotional Reading" to listen to one of the following Scriptures: Mark 10:13-16; Luke 7:36-50; Luke 4:1-13 or a Scripture of your own choosing. Put yourself in the story. What is God saying to you?

3. If you are sleepy, take a rest or a catnap.

4. Listen to your desires through the examen questions:

   - What is life-giving to you? What is life-thwarting?
   - Where do you find love, joy and peace in your life? Where does it seem absent?
   - Where are you sad? Where are you glad?

   Pray about what you see.

Hour 3

1. Consider the Scriptural names and metaphors that reveal God's nature and character: Good Shepherd, Comforter, Healer, Lord, Father, Mighty God and so on (see "Names for Worshiping

God," appendix 5). Let the names of God to draw you into worship.

2. Confess the truth about yourself and your relationships to God. Invite God to look intimately at you. Intimacy can mean "into me see." Confess your sins using the Ten Commandments as a guide. Or confess using the following questions:

   - What occupies most of your time and attention?
   - Where is your first love these days?
   - What relationships need attention?
   - What temptations knock you for a loop?
   - Where do you rationalize, deny and blame?

3. Pray David's prayers of confession in Psalm 51 or Psalm 32. Read 1 John 1:9 and receive God's forgiveness. Say aloud: "Because of Jesus, before a holy and righteous God you stand completely in the clear."

Hour 4

1. Thank God for making you and living within you. Read Psalm 139, replacing the appropriate pronouns with your own name.

2. Pray for the anxieties and sufferings that weigh you down. Name these before the Lord.

3. Imagine Jesus on the cross. Pour your sufferings and worries into his wounds. Put all your pain and worry into his nail-pierced hands. Use Psalm 56 to express your own troubles.

4. Pray for the people you love and for the world and its needs. Take your time and listen for the prayer Jesus may be praying for these people and situations. Enter into his prayer. Leave these concerns with Jesus.

Hour 5

1. Take a walk. Choose a symbol from nature to express your experience of God in this day.

2. Explore drawing a picture, photographing an image or writing a poem that captures something significant about your time with God. Let this creative act remind you of your time with God.

3. Ponder how this time with God has been different than what you anticipated.

4. As you return, what do you want to leave behind with God? What do you want to take back with you?

There is no right way to spend a day with God. Receive the day that has been given. Don't fret if you feel that nothing happened. Trust that a moment will come when the seeds planted today will sprout. Perhaps days from now you will have an insight that comes from a deep insight you didn't have before. Or perhaps in stressful times ahead you will notice an inner shift toward patience and kindness. Bonding with God will bring forth fruit in due season.

APPENDIX 9

Suggestions for Fasting Prayer for the Church

Throughout history the people of God have been called together to fast and pray. The fast may call for

- a time of corporate repentance
- attention to the time it takes to attend to the Holy Spirit in times of choice
- attention to the world with its needs and hurts
- attention to what the church needs to *be* in order to *do* the will of God in the world

GUIDELINES FOR THOSE WHO LONG TO PRAY FOR THE CHURCH

"Unless the LORD builds the house,
  its builders labor in vain." (Psalm 127:1)

- Pray that the Lord will pour his Holy Spirit out on the church in full measure.
- Pray that the Lord will build the church into a place where people are free to worship, grow and serve.
- Pray that the work of the congregation will be for God's glory and not its own.
- Pray to recognize where the Lord is at work and building his church at this moment.
- Go through the various rooms of the church in your mind's eye: children's classrooms, student center, narthex, sanctuary, pastoral offices. Pray for God to build his kingdom in each of these locale.

"And the Lord added to their number daily those who were being saved." (Acts 2:47)

- Pray that the church will provide a safe and winsome place for people to share their stories and connect with God.
- Pray for the church to be a light in your community.
- Pray for the courage and opportunity to reach out to friends, colleagues and neighbors with the love of Christ.

"There are different kinds of gifts, but the same Spirit. There are different kinds of service, but the same Lord. There are different kinds of working, but the same God works all of them in all men.

Now to each one the manifestation of the Spirit is given for the common good." (1 Corinthians 12:4-7)

- Pray for the pastors and teachers to encounter and connect with God. Pray that they will have wisdom to guide, lead and nurture.
- Pray for God to give his people vision to worship, grow and serve.
- Pray for God's hospitable Spirit to shape individuals and teams with hearts to reach out to others with the love of God.
- Pray for the stewardship of the time, money and resources God has given his church.
- Pray for perseverance to grow and serve in global and local ministries.
- What do you think Christ's desire for your church is? Pray out of this desire.

"In this you greatly rejoice, though now for a little while you may have had to suffer grief in all kinds of trials." (1 Peter 1:6)

- Pray for fellow believers who are suffering persecution because of their trust in Jesus.
- Pray for God to thwart the power of the enemy to harass the church.
- Pray that those suffering for Jesus would experience the presence of Christ among them.
- Pray for the church to grow in the face of suffering.

"Because there is one loaf, we, who are many, are one body, for we all partake of the one loaf." (1 Corinthians 10:17)

- Pray for the unity of the church. Enter into Jesus' prayer in John 17.
- Pray for all those who have been wounded through schisms and strife within the church.
- Pray for churches wounded by splits and riddled with factions.

PRAYERS FOR YOURSELF OR THOSE CLOSE TO YOU

1. Turn to Psalm 62:1-2. Where is your soul shaken? What is God's desire for your soul? Pray God's desire along with your own.

2. If you are praying for others, turn to Philippians 1:3-6. What work is God doing in the life of those you pray for? Join his pray for them to your own desires for them.

3. Close with prayers of thanksgiving for the God who is at work in you and his world.

Stretch. Wash your face. Drink some water. Place yourself in God's hands for the remainder of your day.

APPENDIX 10

Seasons, Stages and Ages of Transformation

There is a time for everything,
and a season for every activity under heaven.
ECCLESIASTES 3:1

The spiritual journey is a marathon of seasons. Sometimes you can hold your own. Sometimes your side aches, you're hot and you can't get your breath. Spiritual disciplines are intentional ways to keep moving through the seasons. They aren't magical means to an effortless race. The disciplines simply provide us with exercises that keep us open to God and aware of the limits of our endurance.

As the seasons run, we can find that spiritual practices that once gave us joy become frustrating and empty. Dark nights, temptations, frustrations and struggles dog our heels, seemingly sabotaging our endurance and our times with God. The reality of a "long obedience in the same direction" hits home. Practices that keep our souls in shape don't have to make us feel good. Spiritual exercises can stretch our capacities to depend and trust. Discomfort in a practice is not unusual. Desire for God can lead us into tension between faith and doubt, hope and effort, love and pain. Discomfort with a particular discipline does not automatically mean we should jettison it. God may be calling us to develop new soul reflexes of trust and patience.

Coaches always tailor exercise regimens to each individual athlete. They take into account age, weaknesses, injuries and circumstances. The Holy Spirit inhabits you as your personal growth coach. This divine Coach is present to help you recognize spiritual exercises appropriate to your current stage and season. The Spirit helps you notice when longings shift and when endurance runs short. The Spirit of God coaches you into disciplines that uniquely suit your (1) spiritual season, (2) age and stage, and (3) life circumstances.

SPIRITUAL SEASONS

Like every other living thing, humans have seasons. Winter, summer, autumn and spring are real places on the spiritual journey. These seasons cycle through our lives bringing times of fruit-bearing, root-deepening, drought and deep waiting. No matter how old or young we are, seasons come and go and return to come and go again. Some disciplines can be more suited to one season than another. When choosing a spiritual discipline, pay attention to your spiritual season.

Spring

Spring is the season of new life, new beginnings, new growth. Enthusiasm for the things of God accompanies spiritual springtimes. Desire for more of God breaks forth in a beautiful way. Disciplines of *worship* and *hearing God's Word* seem to come naturally in this season of love for God. Often the desire to *share* our lives with others takes root in the spring.

Summer

In summer seasons of abundance the capacity and desire to give overflows. Serving others, working for justice, volunteering and engaging in outreach all bring us life. During this season, the fruit of the Spirit of God seems tangible to us. We sense God's love, joy and peace in deeply satisfying ways. In the summer season disciplines that *share* our lives with others and *incarnate* God's love keep us partnering with the Holy Spirit for transformation.

Autumn

Autumn is the season of transition standing between the bounty of summer and the barrenness of winter. This season is a mixed bag of harvest and loss. Sometimes even as we reap the fruit of *sharing* our lives with others, we sense a weariness of soul and a desire to hibernate for a time. *Praying* the authentic realities of our lives at this moment can be an important part of noticing God's desire to move us more deeply into relationship with him. Seasons remind us that we are not always in summer. It is natural to move into times of transition. It is natural to wait and wonder what is next.

Winter

Winter is the season when the well runs dry and we feel we are running on empty. Psalm 42 and Psalm 63 express this season and its dark longing.

> O God, you are my God,
>   earnestly I seek you;
> my soul thirst for you,
>   my body longs for you,
> in a dry and weary land
>   where there is no water. (Psalm 63:1)

I moved from Boston to Chicago in deep winter. My soul followed suit. Leaving friends, neighbors, work, a son, a home and a life I loved took me directly into the wilderness. In the unfamiliar barrenness of a new place, I sensed Jesus calling me to sit and wait with him in the winter wilderness. I pictured myself with Jesus during his own wilderness temptation (Luke 4). I saw how he was tempted by the devil to *do* something to prove who he was. And I felt the same temptation rise in me. I wanted to do just about anything rather than wait and trust God's timing. But Jesus made it clear that I was to do nothing to prove who I was. I was simply to keep company with him. I was to grieve my losses, cry my tears, face down my temptations to doubt God and wait with Jesus. In that long, cold Chicago winter I found that God had not forgotten me. He was trusting me with his silence in the wilderness of a new place and season.

Winter seasons often call us to *relinquish* our agendas and *open* new spaces in our lives for God to show up. These *R* and *O* spiritual practices offer us ways of becoming more authentic with God. These disciplines address wounds, sins and weaknesses that keep us from being completely open with God. They give us ways to wait in hope when hope seems gone. Effort alone can never change our winter to spring. But winter is not the last word or only season of the spiritual journey. The presence of God within us is loaded with thawing power. We need to offer up the dark places of our soul to God. Ask the Spirit of God who hovered over the darkest deep on creation morn to hover over our darkness: "Now the earth was formless and empty, darkness was over the surface of the deep, and the Spirit of God was hovering over the waters" (Genesis 1:2). From the beginning it has been God's nature to bring light to darkness and order to the chaos within and without. Keep company with Jesus. Dry times can orient our souls in the direction of God's patience. Winter seasons can yield rich growth that flowers in other seasons.

STAGES OF GROWTH

Besides seasons that cycle through the journey, the life of faith can be characterized by a series of stages that lead friends of Jesus progressively on toward spiritual maturity. The apostles made distinctions between beginners on the Christian journey and those who were farther along the road. In 1 Peter 2:2 the apostle Peter writes: "Now, like infants at the breast, drink deep of God's pure kindness. Then you'll grow up mature and whole in God" *(The Message)*. The author of Hebrews writes: "By this time you ought to be teachers yourselves, yet here I find you need someone to sit down with you and go over the basics on God again, starting from square one—baby's milk, when you should have been on solid food long ago. Milk is for beginners, inexperienced in God's ways; solid food is for the mature, who have some practice in telling right from wrong" (Hebrews 5:12-14 *The Message*).

Stages of growth happen incrementally through the initiative of the Holy Spirit and our cooperation with him. Throughout the history of the church the journey of transformation has often been characterized by the following stages:

Awakening

Awakening is the stage in which we encounter God and ourselves. This stage can be gradual or radical, a moment of conversion or a long journey to trusting God. The awakening stage gives us the comfort of belonging to God.

Purgation

Purgation is the stage of growing awareness of sins, blindness and the life of the false self. In this stage, desire to bring behavior and attitudes into line with Christ's behavior and attitudes calls forth confession. Patterns of willful disobedience, rationalization, denial, blame, addiction, compulsion and weakness are renounced. Disciples intentionally partner with the Holy Spirit in willing trust and obedience.

Illumination

Illumination is the stage where being in love with God gives rise to the desire to live totally in and for God's glory. Prayer becomes a way of life. It is the lived and regular rhythm of attending to the presence of the Holy Spirit within. Illumination finds evidence of God in pain and sorrow as well as joy and peace. Social concern and contemplation both become ways of adoring God.

Union

Union is the stage characterized by receiving God's gift of union and oneness. "Spiritual marriage," "transforming union," "ecstasy," "the unitive way" and "contemplation" are all terms that attempt to capture the soul's relationship to God in this stage. The union stage is a receptive, quiet place where God's agenda, presence and will are embraced. And prayer is a way of entering into wordless communion with the divine. All need for human approval, reinforcement or success is lost in surrender to Christ and an abandonment to grace.

SEASONS OF THE SOUL (A Diagnostic)

	Spring	Summer	Autumn	Winter	Seasoned Saint
KEY QUESTION	What is life about? Who am I?	How can I grow as a disciple and share my faith?	How do I shoulder responsibility for my gifts and bear fruit?	What happens when the well runs dry? Who is God when the darkness comes?	How do I remain open and in communion with Jesus? How do I graciously let go and prepare for my last letting go?
PRIMARY LONGINGS	• To know and belong to God	• To love and be loved • To grow in grace and truth	• To live an authentic life of meaningful contribution	• To find God in the darkness • To experience the God who is beyond me	• To abide in God • To love God above all else in life, keeping him first
SIGNS OF THE SEASON	• Thirst for meaning • Awareness of longing or need or awe • Spiritual awakening but may not yet embrace Jesus	• Passion to belong and grow • Discovery of and rightness about my new identity and call • Feeling of homecoming and security (*This is the leader, church, cause or group for me.*)	• Bear fruit, and use my gifts • Take initiative and responsibility • Spiritual industry and aspirations • In touch with my strengths	• Feel stuck, angry or distant from God • Doubts and crises of faith • Longing for new directions, and encounter with God • Face personal limits and identify inner brokenness • Find God in my weakness • Begin to realize the link between weakness and fruitfulness, between being and doing	• Calling and vocation flow from experiential sense of being God's beloved • Live out God's love for others, investing in their growth • Let go—receive everything as part of God's goodness • Habitual openness and thankfulness to God • Communion with God
TEMPTATIONS	• Thinking a decision for Christ means missing out on life • Avoiding implications of the gospel	• We-they mentality, "I know"; judgment of those who don't believe like me • Head and heart begin to separate	• Overidentification with titles, praise, influence, giftedness, etc. • Anxiety, materialism, control • Burn out, too much *doing*, too little *being* the beloved	• Depression, fear of being found out, naval gazing • Rationalization, denial, blame • Pretense • Bitterness, isolation	• Side-tracked in personal agendas and second things • Refuse to let go, thus becoming rigid, overly opinionated, demanding • Critical and complaining

SIGNS OF STUCKNESS AND FAILURE TO THRIVE	• Too busy to be connected • Remain anonymous • Take no intentional steps toward growth	• Diminished sense of longing for God • Myself and my family come first; Christ and his kingdom come second	• Responsibility without joy • Defensive when challenged to change • Denial of doubts and out of touch with my weaknesses • Lack of awareness of where God is at work in me	• Lack of hope that anything can change • Christian fellowship seems contrived and superficial • Can't find God in my life • Anger at simple answers • Lagging desire to pray	• Bitterness and resentment about life • Feeling that I have nothing more to give • Inability to let go
DISCIPLINES	• Confession • Bible Study • Conversational Prayer • Worship • Spiritual Friendship • Teachability • Discipling	• Small Group • Service • Community • Simplicity • Unity • Truth Telling • Intercession • Stewardship	• Examen • Mentoring • Rule for Life • Rest • Self-Care • Walking Prayer • Hospitality • Meditation • Slowing	• Journaling • Devotional Reading • Detachment • Solitude • Labyrinth • Fixed-Hour Prayer • Spiritual Direction • Healing Prayer • Unplugging • Discernment	• Contemplative Prayer • Detachment • Humility • Practicing the Presence • Breath Prayer • Submission • Gratitude

QUESTIONS

1. Do you identify with one of the key questions?
2. Are you in touch with your longings? Do any of the primary longings above ring true for you today?
3. Which temptations express where you are?
4. Are there any signs of being spiritually stuck in your journey?
5. Which stage reflects your heart at this moment in time?

The language of these stages may be unfamiliar to many who have no trouble distinguishing between baby Christians, disciplined followers, responsible shepherds and seasoned saints. For a visual of the seasons and stages of spiritual growth, read through the chart on pages 288-89. The divisions integrate the cyclical seasons with the trajectory toward spiritual maturity of a seasoned saint. The seasons and stages found here roughly correspond to stages developed in *The Critical Journey* by Janet Hagberg and Robert Guelich.

There is no ironclad rule about what disciplines work best and when. Still, every age and stage is characterized by something to know, be and do.

Every age can grow in *knowing* about the faith they confess. The gospel is a deep river of life, and the depths can't be sounded. But you can dive more deeply into its depths and learn.

No matter how old or young you are, there are things you can learn to *do* as a disciple of Jesus. Apprenticing yourself to Jesus will lead you into offering your body to God in worship, obedience and love. It is something we do.

Doing comes out of being. And at any age we can grow into what it means to *be* personally related to Jesus in vital, life-altering ways.

A simple age breakdown might look like this:

To Know

- Children know the stories.
- Adolescents know the truths.
- Seasoned saints know God, themselves and what they don't know.

To Do

- Children obey their parents (do what you are told).
- Adolescents internalize obedience (obey because you want to please God—character formation).
- For seasoned saints, love and obedience become one; they are able to give and let go.

To Be

- Children learn who they are through being loved.
- Adolescents explore who they are meant to be.
- Seasoned saints live out of being God's beloved.

Spiritual disciplines weave their way throughout all of life. New Christians often profit from spiritual disciplines that provide information about God and the Christian faith. Disciplines like Bible study, small groups and conversational prayer invite them to make space in their lives to *hear* God's word, *share* their stories and *pray*. When the new Christians are children, spiritual practices focus on their love of stories, music, celebration, teachability and the ease with which they learn and memorize. Bible stories readily shape their moral imagination. Music and celebration lead them into experiencing God in *worship*. Disciplines of *relinquishment* usually are not appropriate for young people because they have not yet discovered the self they have to give away.

It's important to provide young people with disciplines that link self-discovery with discovery of God. Since they often take cues about who they are from others, it is important to link them with a community that authentically *shares* their journey together. Typically, adolescents don't want to miss out on anything in life—and often their temptations revolve around a fear of missing out on something. Disciplines that lead them into experiences of presenting their bodies to God as their spiritual act of worship (Romans 12:1) are particularly appropriate.

As responsibilities for both older and younger generations bear down on disciples in midlife, practices that address the temptation to be materialistic, anxious and controlling promote growing authenticity, wholeness, healing and discernment. Disciplines like the examen, devotional reading and slowing intentionally *open* the heart to *hearing* a fresh word from God.

Spiritual practices like detachment, contemplation and unplugging address the busyness, compulsions and scatteredness of life.

Seasoned saints might find that disciplines like mentoring, discipling and intercession intentionally provide opportunities to *share* their lives and come close to God in *prayer.* Mature disciples leave a legacy and an example of what it is to keep company with Jesus. They also model well the disciplines of *relinquishment.* They practice detachment because they know it will prepare them for the end of life and the final letting go.

Remember that each letter of the acronym WORSHIP contains spiritual practices suitable for every age and stage of growth. Choosing disciplines from more than one grouping keeps us developing in wholeness and holiness. In some seasons of the journey we don't look entirely balanced. We shouldn't worry much about this. Instead, we trust that the spiritual disciplines we practice will root us in the soil of God's love. In the Trinity's good timing, we may well find ourselves attracted to disciplines that never appealed to us before.

A WORD ABOUT CIRCUMSTANCES

Besides ages, stages and seasons of growth affecting the spiritual marathon, life circumstances play their own part. Illness, job changes, moving, weddings, vacations, work, caring for children or elderly parents, divorce, accidents, deaths—these are just a few of the many life circumstances that affect our ability to meaningfully engage and practice spiritual disciplines. It is important to consider the limitations as well as the opportunities that life circumstances bring.

Spiritual disciplines must be adapted to fit the reality of the life we are living. A person with a houseful of noisy children may long for solitude! But the realities of such a life takes him or her more deeply into disciplines of *incarnating* God's love for others. Disciplines he or she can share with the children—care of the earth, hospitality, walking prayer or service—can be especially meaningful at this time. We must attend to what's on our plate and not put emotional energy into wishing for a solitude that will definitely come. If the longing for solitude persists, we should ask God how to find time each week when someone else is in charge of the homefront while we spend time alone with him. Maybe it's just an hour alone in the bathtub.

As I encourage people in the practice of spiritual disciplines, I find it intriguing to see how people with different life circumstances respond. Circumstances matter when it comes to disciplines. The grandmother living alone doesn't really warm to the discipline of solitude; she has all she needs. But the busy CEO finds solitude a breath of fresh air. A mother of young children finds breath prayer suits her busy day, while a doctor seeking discernment on a new responsibility embraces the examen. I have found that my disciplines shift when I am on vacation, sick or traveling for work and when I have guests that stay for extended lengths of time. The more I attend to what God wants of me in these circumstances, the clearer I am on the practices that suit the situation. Disciplines are fluid; they flow in and out of our circumstances.

Ages, stages, seasons and circumstances always affect our relationship with God. So we should expect the journey to take us into new ways of noticing and attending to the divine romance.

GLOSSARY

Christ-in-me identity. The indwelling presence of Christ given as gift to each true follower of Jesus. This identity is pure gift; it cannot be earned.

collect. A short, written prayer inviting God's presence, followed by a petition and blessing. Collects are part of liturgical prayer and are arranged to accompany the church year and its calendar.

Divine Office. The historically established liturgy of the hours found in Breviaries of the Catholic Church and the Anglican/Episcopal *Book of Common Prayer*.

false self. An identity rooted in secondary things like accomplishments, productivity, people pleasing, fame or success. The false self is always an identity that can be lost because it is a "self" we develop.

lectio divina. Approaching a text for the sake of a transforming encounter with God. Listening to Scripture to develop a friendship with Christ.

lectionary. Regular patterns of reading and praying Scriptures that correspond to the church calendar. Lectionary readings can be found in the *Book of Common Prayer* or in *The Divine Office*.

Liturgy of the Hours. An offering of prayers of praise and thanksgiving before God at fixed hours of the day. Manuals of prayer can offer a framework for these prayers.

BIBLIOGRAPHY

Barton, Ruth Haley. *Invitation to Solitude and Silence.* Downers Grove, Ill.: InterVarsity Press, 2004.

Bass, Dorothy. *Receiving the Day.* San Francisco: Jossey-Bass, 2000.

Benner, David G. *The Gift of Being Yourself.* Downers Grove, Ill.: InterVarsity Press, 2004.

———. *Sacred Companions.* Downers Grove, Ill.: InterVarsity Press, 2002.

Carson, D. A. *A Call to Spiritual Reformation.* Grand Rapids: Baker, 1992.

Crabb, Larry. *Soultalk.* Nashville: Integrity, 2003.

De Waal, Esther. *Living with Contradiction: An Introduction to Benedictine Spirituality.* Harrisburg, Penn.: Morehouse, 1989.

DuBay, Thomas. *Fire Within.* San Francisco: Ignatius, 1989.

Edwards, Tilden. *Living in the Presence: Disciplines for the Spiritual Heart.* San Francisco: Harper & Row, 1987.

Fénelon, François. *Spiritual Letters to Women.* Grand Rapids: Zondervan, 1984.

Foster, Richard J. *Celebration of Discipline: The Path to Spiritual Growth.* San Francisco: HarperCollins, 1988.

———. *Streams of Living Water: Celebrating the Great Traditions of Christian Faith.* San Francisco: HaperCollins, 1998.

Foster, Richard J., and James Bryan Smith. *Devotional Classics.* San Francisco: HaperCollins, 1993.

Fryling, Alice. *The Art of Spiritual Listening.* Colorado Springs: WaterBrook, 2003.

Hart, Archibald D. *The Hidden Link Between Adrenalin and Stress.* Dallas: Word, 1991.

Huggett, Joyce. *Praying the Parables.* Downers Grove, Ill.: InterVarsity Press, 1996.

Hybels, Bill. *Too Busy Not to Pray.* Downers Grove, Ill.: InterVarsity Press, 1988.

Jones, Timothy. *Finding a Spiritual Friend.* Nashville: Upper Room, 1998.

Keating, Thomas. *Open Mind, Open Heart.* New York: Continuum, 1998.

Lawrenz, Mel. *The Dynamics of Spiritual Formation.* Grand Rapids: Baker, 2000.

———. *Patterns: Ways to Develop a God-Filled Life.* Grand Rapids: Zondervan, 2003.

Lewis, C. S. *The Joyful Christian.* New York: Macmillan, 1977.

Mains, Karen. *The God Hunt: The Delightful Chase and the Wonder of Being Found.* Downers Grove, Ill.: InterVarsity Press, 2003.

May, Gerald G. *The Awakened Heart: Opening Yourself to the Love You Need.* San Francisco: HarperCollins, 1993.

Miller, Wendy. *Invitation to Presence.* Nashville: Upper Room, 1995.

Mulholland, M. Robert, Jr. *Invitation to a Journey.* Downers Grove, Ill.: InterVarsity Press, 1993.

———. *Shaped by the Word.* Nashville: Upper Room, 2000.

Muller, Wayne. *Sabbath: Finding Rest, Renewal, and Delight in Our Busy Lives.* New York: Bantam, 2000.

Norris, Kathleen. *Amazing Grace.* New York: Riverhead, 1998.

Nouwen, Henri J. M. *Reaching Out: The Three Movements of the Spiritual Life.* New York: Image Books, 1995.

———. *The Way of the Heart.* New York: Ballantine, 1981.

Pennington, M. Basil. *Centering Prayer.* New York: Image, 1979.

Peterson, Eugene H. *The Contemplative Pastor.* Grand Rapids: Eerdmans, 1989.

Pippert, Rebecca Manley. *Out of the Saltshaker and into the World.* Rev. ed. Downers Grove, Ill.: InterVarsity Press, 1999.

Pohl, Christine D. *Making Room: Recovering Hospitality as a Christian Tradition.* Grand Rapids: Eerdmans, 1999.

Rohr, Richard. *Everything Belongs.* New York: Crossroad, 1999.

Rolheiser, Ronald. *Holy Longing: The Search for a Christian Spirituality.* New York: Doubleday, 1999.

———. *The Shattered Lantern.* New York: Crossroad, 2004.

Rubietta, Jane. *Quiet Places.* Minneapolis: Bethany House, 1998.

———. *Still Waters.* Minneapolis: Bethany House, 1999.

Smith, Gordon T. *Listening to God in Times of Choice.* Downers Grove, Ill.: InterVarsity Press, 1997.

———. *The Voice of Jesus.* Downers Grove, Ill.: InterVarsity Press, 2003.

Steindl-Rast, David, and Sharon Labell. *Music of Silence.* Berkeley, Calif.: Seastone, 2002.

Taylor, Brian C. *Becoming Christ: Transformation Through Contemplation.* Cambridge: Cowley, 2002.

Thompson, Marjorie J. *Soul Feast.* Louisville: Westminster John Knox Press, 1995.

Tickle, Phyllis. *The Divine Hours.* New York: Doubleday, 2000.

Vest, Norvene. *Gathered in the Work.* Nashville: Upper Room, 1996.

Whitney, Donald S. *Spiritual Disciplines for the Christian Life.* Colorado Springs: NavPress, 1992.

Index of Spiritual Disciplines

Also available from the Transforming Center

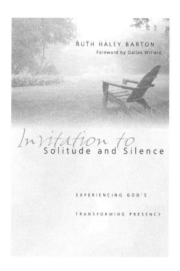

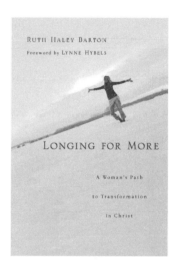

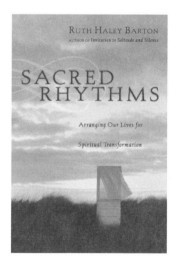

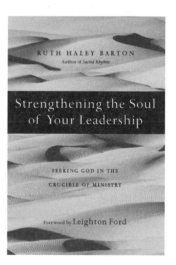

TRANSF✹RMING CENTER
Strengthening the Soul of Your Leadership

The Transforming Center is dedicated to caring for the souls of pastors and ministry leaders through retreats, community experiences and spiritual direction. We offer guidance for individuals and groups in the areas of spiritual formation, community and discernment at the leadership level. For more information about The Transforming Center please visit <www.thetransformingcenter.org>.